UNEQUAL PROTECTION

America was promises—to whom?

— ARCHIBALD MACLEISH

LOIS G. FORER

UNEQUAL PROTECTION

Women, Children, and the Elderly in Court

W · W · NORTON & COMPANY · *NEW YORK* · *LONDON*

The text of this book *is composed in Times Roman, with the display set in Syntax and Garamand Oldstyle. Composition and manufacturing by the Haddon Craftsmen. Book design by Marjorie J. Flock.*

Library of Congress Cataloging in Publication Data
Forer, Lois G., 1914-
     Unequal protection: women, children, and the elderly in court /
Lois G. Forer.
     p.   cm.
     Includes bibliographical references.
     1. Women—Legal status, laws, etc.—United States.   2. Children—
-Legal status, laws, etc.—United States.   3. Aged—Legal status,
laws, etc.—United States.   4. Equality before the law—United
States.   I. Title.
KF475.F67   1991
346.7301'3—dc20
[347.30613]   90-34876

ISBN 0-393-02949-2

W. W. Norton & Company, Inc., 500 Fifth Avenue, New York, N.Y. 10110
W.W. Norton & Company, Ltd., 10 Coptic Street, London WC1A 1PU

2 3 4 5 6 7 8 9 0

For Hope, who has given me
happiness, love, and understanding

Contents

Preface

THE LIFE OF A TRIAL JUDGE is solitary. No one shares the duties of presiding over the trial. No one participates in the judge's deliberations. And no one else bears the burden of responsibility for the decisions. In the midst of the multitudes of a large city and a trial bench consisting of eighty judges, I found the judiciary a lonely occupation. The pressure of a heavy trial schedule allowed little opportunity for discussions with colleagues and scholars.

Lacking the opportunity for such interchange, I have had to rely upon published works for inspiration, ideas, and countervailing arguments. I am greatly indebted to many seminal thinkers. Carol Gilligan's *In a Different Voice* provided confirmation of my experiences indicating that women's perceptions of morality and obligations to other persons and to society are different from those of men. The pioneering work of the late Dr. R. D. Laing awakened my interest in the effect that families exert on troubled children. I then realized that all too often the legal system accepts the evaluation of the child's behavior when evidence would be required with respect to adults. I have learned much about the problems of the elderly from the studies of Elaine Brody.

The law has many detractors. I am not one. In my fifty years of practice and service on the bench, I found that the American legal system did provide substantial justice in the vast majority of cases. My criticism of the law is limited and sharply focused on those categories of cases in which serious miscarriages of justice occurred, unlike the critical legal studies movement, which paints with a broad brush.[1] This school of jurisprudence offers a radical rethinking of the law by means of the techniques of deconstruction. It views the litigational process as a power struggle rather than a means of fairly resolving conflicts. Although this perspective does not accord with my observations, it offers a helpful corrective to traditional mystiques of the law. Other legal scholars who view rights and obligations through the narrow lens of economics[2] provide a useful tool for analyzing purely fiscal problems. But this affords an inadequate guide to interpreting statutes, doctrines, and constitutional provisions that deal with other significant aspects of life. Maximizing profits and minimizing costs are, I believe, an inappropriate standard by which to judge interpersonal conflicts, environmental protection, nuclear power, products liability, and other problems in which economic interests are pitted against human values.

Nor do I agree with those who consider law a science that is "incompetent to answer either the question of whether a given law is just or not or the more fundamental question of what constitutes justice."[3] Supreme Court Justice Abe Fortas, expressing this view, declared: "[Once a person has been] arrested, charged, and convicted, he should be punished by fine or imprisonment, or both, in accordance with the provisions of law, unless the law is invalid in general or as applied. . . . He may, indeed, be right in the eyes of history or morality or philosophy. These are not controlling."[4] I maintain, on the contrary, that law and the litigational process must serve the ends of justice.

With insights gained from authors who have studied women, children, and the elderly I have reexamined cases in which such individuals were treated unfairly and the legal doctrines and procedures under which they were tried, judged, punished, and abandoned.

I am heartened in this undertaking by Justice William J. Brennan, who explained in a lecture at the Harvard Law School that he would discuss how he, a sitting judge, engaged in the process of adjudication:

> . . . let me be clear. I am not going to attempt a revised historical account of the eighth amendment; I will leave that task to the professional historians. Nor will I offer a new theoretical approach to the jurisprudence of the cruel and unusual clause. . . . What I will do is discuss how I, a sitting judge who must decide cases, have engaged in the process of answering the lawyers' contention that the Constitution prohibits the government from killing men and women for the crimes they commit. You will hear the story as I see it, from the Court.[5]

I, too, do not attempt to offer a historical study or philosophical overview, but an account of how the cases* over which I presided were

---

*All the names in this book are fictitious. The facts are true but have been altered in minor details to protect the privacy of the litigants, their families, their lawyers, and the witnesses.

tried and how I see them. The reader who follows me through the account of cases that have troubled me over the years will, I believe, agree that these decisions were wrong.

I am also greatly indebted to many lawyers and scholars whose analyses of landmark cases involving these categories of persons and whose studies of their problems have been most helpful. To mention only a few, Dr. Robert Coles, Judge Patricia Wald, Professor Martha Minow, and Lois Weithorn.

As always, I am grateful to my publisher, Donald S. Lamm, for his faith in this undertaking and to my husband, Morris L. Forer, for his unfailing support.

This book, like my entire experience on the bench, is exclusively mine, and I alone am responsible for its shortcomings.

UNEQUAL PROTECTION

Introduction

The law is the law.

—W. H. AUDEN

I THINK OF HIM as Oedipus. The court personnel called him Lousy Sherman. In this book I call him LeMoyne Sherman. When I saw him, he was an average-looking twenty-three-year-old tall, husky man. He is the embodiment of the fears and fantasies of humankind, a man who raped his mother. I convicted him and sentenced him to ten to twenty years, the maximum penalty the law allowed. Eight years later he was released from prison for "good behavior," which was legally permissible and routine procedure. Prisons are overcrowded. Old offenders are released to make room for new ones. Within three days he had raped an elderly woman. He was convicted by another judge and again sentenced to ten to twenty years. At that time he was thirty-one. He will undoubtedly be released again when he will be in his early forties, still physically and sexually powerful and most probably still afflicted with the same psychiatric problems.

All of us involved in the case—police, prosecutor, defense counsel, expert witnesses, and I, the judge—did exactly what we were supposed to do. We faithfully followed the substantive and procedural mandates of the law. LeMoyne's future conduct was clearly foreseeable. But none of us could have acted other than we did even though we were painfully aware of what was likely to occur after his release.

Emily's problems were so usual that she could be considered a

stereotype. When I saw her, she was in her mid-thirties, a college graduate, a divorcée, the mother of one child. She was no longer a member of
the middle class but one of the new poor. She lost custody of her child
and most of her property as a consequence of decisions made by judges
who faithfully followed the law.

Robert is a statistic, one of more than two million children arrested
and brought to court in the United States each year. At the age of
sixteen he was tried before me in adult criminal court. From the age of
seven until I saw him, Robert had been under the jurisdiction of the
juvenile court. Despite the fact that he had never received the help and
guidance he needed, this child was transferred to criminal court to be
tried as an adult and subjected to adult penalties because he had failed
to benefit from the ministrations of juvenile court. Under the law, I had
no authority to treat Robert like the child he was but was required to
subject him to adult legal procedures, adult law, and adult criminal
penalties.

These are but three of several scores of cases I presided over during
my sixteen years on the trial bench that continue to haunt me. I cannot
dismiss them as anomalies. Nor can I make the usual excuses that in
any human enterprise there is bound to be error, that an imperfect
world peopled by imperfect individuals cannot be expected to function
perfectly at all times.

In these cases there were no legal errors. The lawyers were competent. The juries conscientiously evaluated the testimony and followed
the court's instructions. I, as the presiding judge, followed the law. And
yet the decisions were tragically wrong. When strict adherence to the
law and established procedures bring about clearly wrong results, a
logical mind seeks reasons. This book is the story of my search for the
causes of these wrong decisions and my conclusions.

Tolstoy observed that all happy families resemble one another and
that every unhappy family is unhappy in its own fashion. Before undertaking this study, I believed that all legal cases in which the outcome is
just resemble one another and that every unjust case is unjust in its own
fashion. After carefully examining these cases, I have discovered that is
not true. The unjust cases do resemble one another. There is a pattern,
and there is a reason for these wrong results. The reason is the law itself.

All laws, whether oral traditions and customs of primitive tribes or
sophisticated acts of Congress, reflect norms of behavior and establish
rules of conduct consonant with those norms. American law provides
both criminal penalties and civil obligations for those who deviate from
these standards. Over more than a millennium the entire structure of

Anglo-American common law has been predicated on what a reasonable man would or would not do in the various circumstances of life. The rules of procedure and evidence that regulate litigation in American courts are based on the responses and reactions of this hypothetical reasonable man.[1]

The cases tried before me in which the results were wrong did not involve reasonable, adult males. The persons wronged by the legal system are those I call the others.* The principal groups are women, children, the elderly, and those the common law called lunatics and persons of unsound mind. Today such people are called mentally handicapped.† This common phrase has no legal or medical significance but is widely used to mean individuals who are retarded, mentally ill, or emotionally disturbed or whose behavior is bizarre or unreasonable. This book does not discuss the legal treatment of the mentally handicapped because their problems are qualitatively different from those of women, children, and the elderly, and the solutions are also different. The number of such persons who are adversely affected by the legal system is enormous. There are no national statistics on the mentally handicapped in the courts. When I extrapolate from my own experience, it is evident that this issue requires careful study. At least one-third of all defendants who appeared before me were mentally handicapped.[2] Many civil litigants were also mentally handicapped. All were prejudiced by the legal system that refused to recognize that they were not reasonable men. If LeMoyne's second rape victim had died (she was seriously injured), he would undoubtedly have been sentenced to death.‡

It was not until I retired from the bench and had the leisure to reflect, to review, and to reconsider the multitude of cases over which I had presided that I reached the conclusion that the law and the legal system are endemically biased against these others. During the many years I was practicing law and the sixteen years I served as a trial judge, I was so occupied with each day's work that I did not have the luxury simply to think. In my court, before one trial was concluded, the lawyers and litigants in the next three cases were in the courtroom, waiting to begin. This kind of pressured schedule, typical of courts in large urban areas, is not conducive to critical analysis.

---

*Throughout this book I use the term "others" to refer to women, children, and the elderly.

†Physically handicapped persons are also subject to discrimination. Legislation has banned some of the most egregious legal barriers to equal rights for both the physically and mentally handicapped. But judicial decisions have nullified many of these gains. See, e.g., *Pennhurst School v. Halderman*, 451 U.S. 1 (1989).

‡The Supreme Court held that it is not unconstitutional to execute a mentally retarded person. Penry v Lynaugh, 109 S.Ct. 2934 (1989)

Few lawyers, legislators, judges, or scholars have the time or re-sources to reflect on the legal system as a whole, to appraise its fairness and its impact on different segments of society. Sociologists analyze statistics: the numbers of cases tried, appealed, and reversed. They pro-vide valuable information about the operations of the judicial bureauc-racy but do not tell us anything about the fairness of the process. Legal scholars rarely write about trials or decisions rendered by juries and trial judges. Many of these cases are decided without opinion. Few of the written opinions are published. Although the transcripts of most trials are available, reading these thousands of pages is tedious and time-consuming. Instead, scholars analyze appellate court decisions and concentrate on the fewer than 160 cases decided with opinions by the United States Supreme Court each year.*

Cases decided at the trial level constitute the overwhelming major-ity of litigation in the United States. They represent the justice that most Americans get. But none of us, in or out of the legal system, knows how fair it is. These cases cannot be dismissed as small matters, al-though the amounts in issue (from twenty thousand dollars to several hundred millions)† may seem trivial in an age of billion-dollar debts and bailouts. Often in cases for civil damages of only a hundred thousand dollars the result may mean the difference between essential medical care or a lifetime of illness and a crippled body. In noncapital criminal cases, the defendant loses not simply the years spent in prison but often his or her family and the ability ever to earn a livelihood. When a guilty person is acquitted, the victims of crime are violated a second time and a possibly dangerous person is released to the community. In all miscar-riages of justice there is a loss of faith in government and in one's fellow human beings.

Fewer than 5 percent of the cases that went to verdict before me were appealed. I should like to think that was because the parties and their attorneys recognized that the decisions were right and fair. It is more likely that the litigants could not afford the money to appeal and the long wait for a higher court to reach a decision. None of the cases that were appealed reached the United States Supreme Court. Al-though my cases constitute only a minute fraction of the approximately eighty-five million civil suits and criminal prosecutions filed in state and federal courts each year, they exemplify the legal and human problems of these millions of Americans.

*In 1989 and 1990 the Supreme Court drastically reduced to fewer than one hundred the number of cases in which it granted review.
†I did not preside over cases involving claims for very small amounts of money. These cases are heard in special small claims courts. They are usually tried without lawyers and rarely involve issues of personal or constitutional rights.

Most Supreme Court decisions involve issues of great importance to the public as a whole. Many are concerned with clarifying, expanding, or revising prior decisions involving the same issue. For example, in the twenty-five years following the Supreme Court landmark libel decision *New York Times v. Sullivan,*[3] the Court has written multiple opinions in more than eighty cases involving libel. During the same period the Court has considered very few cases involving the rights of children and the elderly and only a dozen or so involving discrimination against women.

Most of the cases over which I presided were run-of-the-mill litigation although important questions of constitutional rights of these "others" to equal protection of the laws were implicit. These cases aroused no concern on the part of scholars, public-interest legal organizations, or associations to protect children, the handicapped, the elderly, and the rights of women. Only one case tried before me excited the interest of any of the organizations that routinely file friend of the court briefs in the United States Supreme Court. That was the case in which Mattie, a child victim of sexual abuse, was permitted to testify on closed-circuit television. The local branch of the American Civil Liberties Union appeared on behalf of the defendant.*

Reviewing these cases of injustice was not a pleasant experience. Judges and lawyers, like all human beings, do not care to dwell on mistakes, few though they may be. We prefer to recall the glories of the law, those cases in which despite all odds, justice triumphed. Most popular books by members of the legal profession recount such splendid glorious tales. They make good reading, and they confirm our faith in the legal system. We recall these happy moments and comfort ourselves with the thought that despite its faults, the American system of justice is the best and fairest that has as yet been devised. This is true. A number of Constitutions, including that of the Soviet Union, provide admirable declarations of rights. The Canadian Bill of Rights is closely modeled after the United States Bill of Rights. But no other legal system actually ensures either civil litigants or criminal defendants the safeguards that the American legal system affords.

Nonetheless, appalling miscarriages of justice do occur. Most can be attributed to ordinary, common human failings not peculiar to the legal system: stupidity, ineptitude, and overreaching. All judges should be wise and learned. All lawyers should be competent and diligent. Prosecutors should not bend the rules to obtain convictions. And every-

---

*By contrast, fifty-five friend of the court briefs were filed in *University of California Regents v. Bakke,* 438 U.S. 265 (1978), a case involving affirmative action in the admission of racial minorities to medical school.

one should be honest. It is distressing when one finds a lawyer or judge who is less than adequate. But a few incompetent, lazy, or corrupt individuals do not undermine one's faith in the legal system.

The most common reason for wrong verdicts is the inadequacy of the case presented. While sometimes that is due to incompetence of counsel, more often it is because the litigant could not afford to pay for investigations, expert witnesses, and all the expensive pretrial preparation required to mount an effective prosecution or defense of a civil claim or the defense of a criminal prosecution. When a client lacks the necessary funds, the lawyer must do the best he or she can with limited resources. When the money runs out, the lawyer must attempt to make a deal: plead the client guilty to a lesser criminal charge or get a promise by the prosecutor to recommend a lenient sentence. In a civil case the lawyer for a financially strapped client must reach the best settlement under the circumstances regardless of the extent of the client's losses or the validity of the client's claim. The point when economic necessity prevails over the demand for justice or vindication may come after the expenditure of $3,500,000 by General William Westmoreland and his backers in the libel suit against CBS or it may be when a divorcée seeking custody of her children has spent her last $500 and exhausted her borrowing capacity. There is little, if anything, a judge can do to prolong the trial to verdict and a just conclusion when the litigant gives up the struggle.

In what one hopes is a very small number of cases, a judge has been bought or the case fixed. There is no way even to estimate the amount of judicial corruption. Such complaints are easy to make but difficult to prove. Disgruntled persons sometimes make false charges. However, the impeachments of federal Judges Alcee Hastings of Florida and Harry Claiborne of Nevada as well as the convictions of many state judges, notably those involved in Operation Greylord in Chicago, and William C. Brennan in Queens, New York, indicate that there are times when justice is for sale.

The incompetence of judges who repeatedly make wrong legal decisions is also difficult to prove and to quantify. The annual survey of the ten worst judges by the *National Law Journal* gives a dismaying picture of a very tiny fraction of the judiciary. These ills of the legal system are well known. The need to provide equal justice for the poor* is an en-

---

*Because women, children, and the elderly are disproportionately poor and except when accused of crime are not usually entitled to free legal counsel, they are frequently unable to claim the rights that are recognized by the courts. For a discussion of this problem, see Lois G. Forer, *Money and Justice: Who Owns the Courts?* (New York: W. W. Norton & Co., 1984).

demic problem often discussed by the bench, the bar, and the public. Similarly, the need for better judges is a matter of widespread and continuing concern.

Legal scholars who do not espouse a rigid philosophy seldom discuss or analyze systemic defects of the law. Law reform tends to be a matter of specifics. Statutes are drafted and enacted to correct defined and limited problems—for example, ERISA, providing security for pensions; OSHA, protecting safety of the workplace; and a panoply of laws to protect the environment. Drafting such complicated statutes is difficult and time-consuming. It takes the skills and energies of lawyers who are specialists. It also requires the efforts of legislators, lobbyists, and concerned citizens to get such laws enacted. Most important of all, there must be public awareness of the problem and sufficient concern to demand remedial action.

Although there are countless agencies and individuals working for equal rights for women and many organizations dedicated to helping and protecting children and lobbies for the elderly, to date their primary focus has been on specific substantive issues. They have rarely turned their attention to the routine, daily operations of the courts.

During my sixteen years on the trial bench in a busy city, I was assigned approximately forty-five hundred matters. They included civil cases involving more than twenty thousand dollars, major felonies and homicides, child custody disputes,* and equity matters. Many of the civil cases were disposed of on motions without trial. Many more were settled after conferences with the court. In more than half the criminal cases the defendants pled guilty. Approximately one-fourth of the cases that went to trial were tried before a jury; the others were tried before me without a jury. The problems involved almost every legal issue from arson to zoning. The litigants ranged from the super rich to the destitute. They were white, black, Hispanic, and Asian. The age span was from claims involving fetuses to very elderly, senile persons.

The problems were as old as the Bible and as new as computer fraud. Oscar Wilde remarked that nature imitates art. In my courtroom I have seen not only Oedipus but also Cain and Abel, King Lear, hundreds of little Oliver Twists, and many like Lady Caroline Norton, the Englishwoman whose property and children were awarded to her wastrel husband by the courts.

There were only a few instances in which I felt justified in refusing to follow precedent. They involved claims of denial of constitutional

---

*I did not preside over cases of juvenile delinquency. As a practicing lawyer I represented more than three thousand children accused of delinquency in juvenile court.

rights. One was a routine prosecution for rape. It was settled law that the testimony of a rape victim had to be received with great caution because of her emotional involvement. The judge was required to instruct the jury that unlike the testimony of the defendant and the witnesses, which was to be evaluated fairly on the basis of their credibility and the inherent plausibility and sense of their statements, their consistency, and all the circumstances, the testimony of a rape victim was to be evaluated by a different standard and given lesser weight. I refused to give the charge. Shortly thereafter the law was changed by statute.

After I reviewed all the troubling cases I encountered in which a manifestly wrong result occurred and I considered all the possible reasons, there remained several scores of cases that were tragically and absolutely wrong for which there was no apparent explanation. By a "wrong result" I mean an outcome that the average nonlawyer would consider outrageous. Obvious examples are the conviction of the innocent and acquittal of the guilty. There are also less dramatic instances in which persons are deprived of their property or family relationships, subjected to unduly harsh penalties, and denied opportunities to assert claims and defenses.

For generations the law has recognized that some verdicts "shock the conscience of the court." If a jury verdict is so excessive that it does shock the conscience of the court, the presiding judge has authority to reduce the verdict. If the jury verdict is so inadequate that it shocks the conscience of the court, the judge may grant a new trial. In culling out those cases that I considered wrong, I selected only those that could truly be found to shock the conscience.

This book is not a discussion of justice in the abstract. It deals with particulars, actual flesh-and-blood human beings. Philosophers around the globe and throughout recorded history have been attempting to define justice and fairness in terms of universal application. A judge cannot create an ideal system of perfect justice but is limited to resolving competing claims of rights arising out of specific disputes or allegations of illegal acts. Judicial authority extends only to the deciding of each case in accordance with the evidence presented and the law. The power of a trial judge is properly limited. One must follow precedent in deciding the rights and obligations of the litigants. In the imposition of sentence on convicted offenders, the penalties are specified by statute and may not be exceeded. No matter what the needs of the litigants, their problems and disabilities, my jurisdiction was limited. I could not redistribute wealth, order the provision of nonexistent services and facilities for those who needed them, or transform brutal, greedy individuals into compassionate, caring good citizens. As the cases described in the following chapters reveal, I was compelled by law to enter unjust verdicts.

Today countless legal scholars, philosophers, psychiatrists, and sociologists devote incredible amounts of time and learning to telling judges how to decide cases.[4] We judges are admonished to act with "principled neutrality." Objectivity, not interpretation of age-old principles to contemporary conditions, is often posited as the desideratum. We are also advised to take rights seriously, as if this were a novel command.[5] Lawyers and judges are engaged on a day-to-day basis in doing precisely that.

I believe that most judges, whether or not they consciously articulate their goals, attempt to follow the mandates of the law, including the Constitution, statutes, rules, and judicial precedent, in such a way that the litigants whose disputes they must decide are treated fairly and consonantly with morality and decency. These terms are as difficult to define as "justice" and "fairness." Contrary to a common misconception, a trial judge does not see many "easy cases."[6] If neither the facts nor the law are in dispute, most people settle their differences and do not litigate. In criminal cases when the facts and the law are absolutely clear usually either the prosecution is withdrawn or the defendant pleads guilty. Not only in landmark constitutional cases but in the day-to-day, unnoted, unreported, uncelebrated cases courts are faced with the tension between law and justice.

When I began to review the cases over which I had presided and, in particular, those in which the results were plainly wrong, I had no idea what, if any, conclusions I would reach. Some may think that only approximately sixty cases out of a total forty-five hundred is a good success rate. Statisticians may find an error of 7.5 percent satisfactory. But a judge cannot view even this small degree of miscarriage of justice with equanimity. Each case represents not only the litigant who was wronged but a whole congeries of friends and relatives whose lives were seriously affected by the decision.

I reviewed these cases many times before reaching any conclusions. Law schools claim to teach students how to think like a lawyer. They may sometimes fail in teaching students how to practice law, how to behave ethically, or even how to write comprehensible English. But they do succeed in inculcating a way of looking at problems. Lawyers look at abstract issues, not people. A typical example of legal thinking is in the teaching of the law of sales. The student is given this problem:

Seller agrees to deliver goods to buyer on a date certain for a fixed payment. Seller fails to make timely delivery. What are buyer's rights?

The identities of buyer and seller are irrelevant. So are the nature of the goods and the reasons for failure to make delivery. One is taught to examine legal principles divorced from the vagaries of human behavior.

Having been programmed for decades to think like a lawyer, I carefully examined the facts and the law in each of those cases. Was there a common doctrine? No. Some involved criminal prosecutions; others, civil claims. They covered a multitude of legal issues involved in other cases in which just results were reached. There was no common procedural flaw. Often a litigant with a just claim or defense loses because the essential evidence is in the possession of the other party and cannot be obtained. This problem did not occur in any of the cases that troubled me. Nor did any of these cases involve a guilty defendant who went free because the state's illegally obtained evidence was excluded. I could not attribute the wrong results in these cases to any of the usual complaints against the law.

When thinking like a lawyer failed to provide any answers, I decided to look at these cases from the viewpoint of a writer. A writer would want to know a great deal more than the bare facts given in the case on sales. Who are the buyer and seller? What are their businesses? Was the price fair? The writer would be concerned with the motivations of the parties. Was it a case of greed, misfortune, or business rivalry? What would Chekhov say about the minds and hearts of buyer and seller?

With the eye of a writer I reexamined these cases. Once I looked at the persons involved rather than the legal issues, the reason for the miscarriages of justice was immediately apparent. The individuals were women, children, and the elderly. No case involved rational adult males, corporations, or associations. To my astonishment race was an irrelevant factor. These people were white, black, Hispanic, and Asian.

It may be, as some believe, that the entire criminal justice system is racially biased.* Although black males are disproportionately accused and convicted of crimes, on an individual case-by-case basis I found no evidence that in the ordinary routine criminal and civil matters heard in my court litigants were prejudiced in the outcomes of the trials by reason of race.[7]

Prejudice against women by both males and females is difficult to detect, but it is pervasive. In a routine accident case the plaintiff was severely injured and became a paraplegic. He was a young man with a life expectancy of almost forty years. The undisputed evidence disclosed

*See "A Survey of Crime in America" reporting that 80 percent of those polled believe there is racism in the criminal justice system (National Law Journal [August 7, 1989]).

that his condition was permanent, that he was unable to dress himself or perform any of his bodily functions unaided. His wife catheterized him several times a day. She also had to assist him in moving his bowels. He could not be left alone more than two or three hours. For the rest of his life her life would consist of caring for him. The jury awarded the injured man an adequate sum. The wife, who was also a plaintiff, sued for loss of consortium. The jury awarded her ten thousand dollars, a sum that the defendant and his insurance carrier admitted was woefully inadequate. The real issue in the case was liability, not damages. After the verdict was entered, one of the jurors asked to speak to us (judge and both counsel). He explained that eleven of the jurors wanted to give the wife several hundred thousand dollars but one juror would not agree. She insisted that marriage was "for better or for worse" and that the wife was not entitled to anything. After a day of wrangling with her, the jury compromised on ten thousand dollars. The other jurors, six women and five men, thought the verdict was inadequate but were not sufficiently outraged to deliberate further. The case was settled for a fairer amount without the necessity of appeals or a new trial.

There were a number of cases in which nonwhites were found guilty by racially mixed juries when I had a reasonable doubt as to guilt. In other instances some defendants were found not guilty by jurors of the same ethnic background in cases in which I was convinced of their guilt. But there was evidence on which the juries reached their conclusions.

These are not the kinds of decisions I consider outrageously unfair. In the civil case of the paraplegic the jury did award him adequate damages.

Instances of bias such as these are probably inevitable in any system that requires the exercise of judgment. Jurors reflect the values and beliefs of the community. That is a great strength of the jury system. From my observation, it works as well as any other social institution.

Economic status was a significant factor in the cases that I believe were shockingly wrong. Many of the people involved were poor. But similar injustices also befell women, children, and the elderly who were not poor.

This analysis of wrong decisions is not a scientific study.* It cannot

*Anthropologist T. M. Luhrmann believes that what is needed are "ethnographies that describe the cognitive impact of cultural experience in its natural setting, rich detailed accounts that are sensitive to psychological theories and philosophical problems but which are neither experimentally based nor speculatively abstract" (*Persuasions of the Witch's Craft: Ritual Magic in Contemporary England* [Cambridge: Harvard University Press, 1989]). The material on which this book is based is derived from actual trials and describes their impact on the litigants and witnesses. This be done with a computer. There are too many variables in the determination of what is a just result or a gross miscarriage of justice. Human responses cannot be quantified. It may be charged that my material is anecdotal, but the lives of all persons are stories, brief anecdotes or long sagas. Psychiatrist Robert Coles[8] teaches the importance to a psychiatrist of listening to the life stories of the patients. As a practicing lawyer and a judge I learned the most important lessons from listening to the life stories of my clients and the litigants over whose cases I presided.

My basic data, some forty-five hundred cases, have the indicia of reliability. They probably represent as random and typical a selection of American litigation as one could find using elaborate computerized information if such were available. With few exceptions* these cases were assigned to me by court administration automatically by date of the filings and the availability of judges. They involved the problems of American men, women, children, nonprofit associations and corporations (including churches and universities), and business corporations as well as labor unions and public bodies, such as school districts, redevelopment authorities, municipalities, and the state. The pool of litigants from which the cases were drawn and the population from which the juries were selected were the same throughout my tenure on the bench.† During this period there were no startling changes in the law. Instead of a variety of judges with varying perceptions of justice, different trial practices, and different thresholds of reasonable doubt and different senses of outrage, only one judge, myself, presided over all the cases. The time period, sixteen years, is far longer than that of most studies. Forty-five hundred cases are an exceptionally large data base.[9]

The methodology of my study is admittedly unusual. I was a participant as well as an observer in all the cases. Few researchers in problems of law in action have firsthand experience with the data that form the basis of their work. They must rely on questionnaires and hope that those who respond did so accurately. Nobel Prize winner in physiology or medicine Baruch Blumberg notes the importance of the researcher's personally gathering data rather than relying on others. Although I had much information that is not usually available to researchers, it is im-

---

book illustrates the difference between anecdotal reality and statistical reality. My conclusion that 92.5 percent of the cases did not violate the equal protection rights of the witnesses or parties is statistical reality. The accounts of the 7.5 percent who were denied their rights presents another significant form of reality.

*A number of complex commercial matters were specially assigned to me at the request of counsel. None of those cases involved a gross miscarriage of justice.

†I do not know whether the legal problems of rural people are materially different. The applicable laws are the same. And human beings have similar needs and responses regardless of where they live or the occupations they pursue.

portant to bear in mind the limitations on information legally and, in fact, available to me as the presiding judge. In some criminal cases, the presentence investigating staff provides the judge with a fairly complete life history of the defendant. I know the educational and employment background, of each defendant, his or her health problems, and often the family situation. In some cases I know more about the defendants than I do about by best friends. More often I wished that I could step down, sit beside them, and talk to them without the barriers of the bench, the robe, and the inequality of our roles.

All criminal defendants have a right of allocution, the right to address the judge before sentence is imposed. Some persons take this opportunity to explain their problems and motivations and their hopes for the future. Although these are obviously self-serving statements, they frequently provide the judge with deepened understanding.

Many defendants do not testify at trial and refuse to address the court before sentencing. The only time LeMoyne spoke in court was when he was asked the usual questions as to his understanding of his right to a jury trial. His replies were the minimum laconic "yes." Others, like Tyrone, a young man accused of armed robbery, asserted themselves from the beginning of the proceeding until the case was closed. When Tyrone was asked the routine question "Can you read and write the English language?" he replied, "Fluently." He demonstrated that he was in control of himself and his defense.

In civil cases a trial judge must try to find clues to the character and problems of each litigant from the testimony and the appearance and body language of the witnesses. There is little opportunity to ask questions or to probe the life histories of the persons whose disputes one must decide.

In setting forth these cases, I have not attempted to enhance the portraits presented in court. I have not added shadows or highlights or airbrushed away warts and wrinkles. Nor have I taken the liberty of transforming ordinary litigants into mythic figures endowed with yearnings, dreams, and character flaws that illuminate the human condition. There are no Raskolnikovs or Emma Bovarys* in this book because I can relate only what was revealed to me in the course of litigation. Some of the persons whose legal troubles are encountered here could easily be the prototypes of moving, tragic and dramatic novels because they are human beings who were caught in situations

---

*Unlike Truman Capote in *In Cold Blood* and Norman Mailer in *The Executioner's Song,* I have limited myself to the facts disclosed in the course of litigation and reliable information furnished to me after the trial.

that demanded heroic action and endurance. Many litigants and witnesses displayed nobility of character and depth of emotions; others, weakness, selfishness, and greed. In most instances I do not know what happened to these people after they were no longer under my jurisdiction. As countless dramatists have demonstrated, a trial provides an extraordinary setting in which to explore the human psyche. People are brought into court because they find themselves in a situation of extreme conflict over which they have lost control. Either they call upon the agencies of the law to resolve the problem or society demands a resolution.

The judge is the public official to whom this task is confided. Over more than a millennium procedures and rules have been developed to aid in the search for the truth of the facts from which the dispute arose and the principles by which the conflict must be resolved. Truth, like justice, is a noble concept, a goal to seek. But neither truth nor justice can be verified with certainty or measured scientifically.

A new judge who was interviewed in the *New York Times* happily declared, "In this position I can always do what I believe is right. There's nothing to compare with the satisfaction of doing justice, even in the smallest case. That's why this is the best job in the world."[10] When a judge can do justice, it is the greatest job in the world. And most of the time I felt that satisfaction. But when I was compelled to preside over injustice, the office was bitter and painful.

1

The Myth of Equal Protection

Law was the point where life and logic met.

— FREDERIC WILLIAM MAITLAND

AMERICANS NURTURED on the Declaration of Independence and the Bill of Rights believe that all persons should be equal before the law. They also believe that courts are the forum where those rights will be protected and enforced. All too often the claims of the others are denied by judicial decisions predicated on common law precedents that do not recognize the concept of the equality of all persons. This body of judicial decisions created over many centuries by English judges forms the basis of contemporary American law. The Constitution and the Bill of Rights as well as the complex multitude of federal and state statutes and regulations and municipal ordinances are all interpreted in accordance with common law tenets.

Justice Oliver W. Holmes, Jr., in his classic work *The Common Law*[1] declared: "The life of the law has not been logic but experience." It is enlightening to examine whose experiences the common law embodies. The entire legal system in Great Britain and in the United States until the twentieth century was confided exclusively to propertied adult males of sound mind. These men sat in the legislatures and enacted the laws; they staffed the governments that administered the laws; they had a monopoly of the legal profession that litigated important issues; and most significantly, they were the judges who interpreted the laws and created the great body of jurisprudence known as the common law.

Consequently, all other human beings, who, of course, constituted the vast majority of the population, were largely excluded from legal rights and protections. The American judiciary is still dominated by men of property.*

Although the personal beliefs of individual appellate judges and particularly judges of the Supreme Court do make a difference in many cases, the precedents of the common law strongly influence and, indeed, control decisions adversely affecting those whose needs, beliefs, and attitudes did not shape the common law—namely, women, children, and the elderly.

The term "women" needs no definition. I use it to include all females, regardless of sexual preference. "Child," as used herein, means every person from the moment of birth to the age of eighteen. The term "elderly" as used here, means older persons who are sane and legally competent but are handicapped by slower physical and mental responses and beset by fears and concerns peculiar to older people.

Unlike civil law systems prevalent in continental Europe and in Latin America that are based primarily on statutes and codes, the common law that governs most of the English-speaking world relies on precedent, the accretion of doctrines through judicial decisions. Reliance on precedent has many positive values. The common law provides continuity and stability. Basic principles are maintained despite fluctuating views and passing fancies embodied in statutes. But the common law has also left a bitter legacy for those who were excluded from the rights and privileges accorded to men of property.

In the past many men were numbered among the others, who did not have full political and civil rights. Slaves had no rights. Persons who were not technically slaves were denied liberty under the widespread practice of indenturing adults and children.

In both Britain and the American colonies religious dissidents were denied political liberty and many civil rights. Until 1858 in Britain only members of the Church of England had the right to hold political office.† Thus Catholics, Jews, Quakers, members of other Protestant sects, and nonbelievers were denied full citizenship. In the American

---

*The appointment to the United States Supreme Court of one black man, Justice Thurgood Marshall, and one woman, Sandra Day O'Connor, has not appreciably altered the views of the Court. In 1989 fewer than 8 percent of the American judiciary was female, and approximately 12 percent nonwhite. The British press, noting that the law lords, who are roughly the equivalent of the United States Supreme Court, are white men, average age sixty-six, all but two of whom are graduates of Cambridge or Oxford, commented that they render justice in their own image.
†Under the protectorate of Oliver Cromwell, papists, Anabaptists, and other dissenters were prosecuted and severly punished. Quakers, like William Penn, were routinely denied the right to testify in court unless they removed their hats, a practice violative of their religious principles.

colonies discrimination and exclusion from full rights on the basis of religion prevailed. Several colonies had an established church and discriminated against all other sects. Some colonies discriminated against Catholics and Jews. Others required belief in trinitarianism. All required a belief in God as a prerequisite to public office. Even the First Amendment's guaranteeing free exercise of religion did not remove all religious barriers. Members of many denominations and atheists are still litigating to enforce the right to exercise their religious beliefs and practices and to determine the parameters of the prohibition against an establishment of religion.

As Joseph Alsop pointed out, when Franklin D. Roosevelt was elected president in 1932, "Close to 50 percent of all Americans were in some degree excluded from the full rights enjoyed by all WASP Americans. . . ."[2] Even Alsop, a perceptive journalist, did not note the exclusion of women, children, and the elderly.

For centuries poor people were also denied important rights. In many American states they were barred from political participation. The poll tax was not abolished until the Twenty-fourth Amendment was ratified in 1964. Although indigents accused of crime are now entitled to free legal counsel, that right is restricted at the appellate level.[3] In most civil litigation there is no right to free counsel. Filing fees are also required when someone institutes a civil suit.[4] In effect, those who cannot pay are denied access to the courts that are public and supported by tax revenues.

Although the poor were and still are denied many rights, poor white males were recognized as persons who could sue, testify, and hold property and who had many other significant rights under the common law. Women, children, and the mentally handicapped,* however, were bracketed together under the common law as a group that had no personal or legal rights. Since at least the fourteenth century in the reign of Edward III the status of married women, children, and those lacking mental capacity was the same.[5] They were subject to guardianship or wardship, which was a valuable economic asset of the guardian and warden but denied the ward control of his or her life and property. They lacked testimonial and testamentary capacity. They had no right to own chattels in their own names. These disabilities continued for centuries. Significantly, the Act of 1830 (II George IV) in one statute consolidated and amended the law as to the property of married women, infants, and lunatics.

During the course of the nineteenth century many acts of Parlia-

*The common law used the term "unsound mind."

ment mitigated the harshness of the common law with respect to these three categories but did not grant them the legal status of adult males of sound mind. This difference in legal status was based upon the presumption of their incapacity to understand and obey as full-grown men. Married women had no separate legal identity. A married couple was one person, and that was the husband.[6]

Sir William Blackstone, whose *Commentaries on the Laws of England,* published in the 1760s, was the text for American lawyers during the colonial period and well into the twentieth century, stated that the three great relationships were husband and wife, father and child, and master and servant. In all three the first party exercised power and dominion over the second. With respect to the inferior status of women, Blackstone benignly observed that "even the disabilities, which the wife lies under are for the most part intended for her protection and benefit. So great a favourite is the female sex of the laws of England."[7] According to Blackstone, the power of a father over his child included the power of correction, consent to marriage, and management of the child's estate. It is against this background that the claims of these others for the constitutional right of equal protection of the laws must be examined.

Many common law legal disabilities have been mitigated or eliminated by legislation. With respect to the relations of master and servant the entire panoply of statutes giving protections to workers, including the right to strike, the right to organize, minimum wages and maximum hours laws, and safety in the workplace laws, were necessitated by judicial decisions based on common law principles that denied employees these rights and protections.

Legislation was also required to abrogate judicial decisions based on the common law and give women control of their own property, the right to work in many occupations and to receive equal pay for equal work, custody of their children, the right to practice professions and serve on juries and hold public office. A constitutional amendment was necessary in order for women to overcome the common law and obtain the right to vote.

The subjugation of children and the virtually unlimited control over them by parents and custodians has been sustained by the Supreme Court.[8]

Although legislation has provided some economic benefits for older persons, courts have not recognized the difficulties many elderly experience when attempting to claim their rights.

The concept of equality of all persons is of very recent origin. It is not found in Scripture[9] or in classical literature.[10] Throughout the centuries of recorded history, it was assumed without the necessity of discussion or justification that there was a natural hierarchy among human beings and even among deities. In *Gilgamesh,* the earliest written cosmological epic, gods and goddesses as well as human being are given gradations of rank. Egyptian, Greek, and Roman mythologies mirror the human order of life in which kings rule over subjects, freemen over slaves, and those who prevail in battle subjugate their defeated enemies. Even in monotheistic Judaism, the deity is referred to as "our father, our King," the two categories of persons entitled to exact obedience.

Although fashions in anthropology fluctuate, most reliable accounts of primitive tribal life portray these various groups as being dominated or ruled by a leader and/or a priestly class.* Such societal structures have been found in the frozen polar regions, the South Seas, and all the continents of both hemispheres.

Whether such seemingly universal arrangements are the inevitable result of domination by the physically more powerful over the weaker or the cleverer gaining ascendancy over the less able raises many interesting and unanswered questions. What appears to be undisputed is the dominance by one or a few over the many as a fact of life as to which until recently there were few philosophical arguments such as rightness, fairness, or morality.

Equality of human beings did not emerge as an ideal and a principle of political philosophy until the eighteenth century. The battle cry of the French Revolution—"Liberty, equality, fraternity"—sounded in a world where slavery was common and accepted, where women had no political rights, where monarchy was the prevailing mode of government, and where class distinctions were part of the natural order.

In the American colonies the writings of John Locke, James Mill, and Baron Montesquieu found a popular response. The Declaration of Independence proclaimed it was a self-evident truth that all men are created equal. Significantly, the word "equal" is used without definition or exegesis as was appropriate to a declaration of principle that was not law or intended to form the basis of juridical rights.

Neither the Constitution nor the Bill of Rights contains the words "equal" and "equality." In drafting the Constitution, the Founding Fathers (there were no founding mothers at the Constitutional Convention) and the male framers of the Bill of Rights addressed the inequities

*Some societies such as the early Sumerians and the Dobuan tribe in Melanesia were matrilinear, but the vast majority of communities and most of the great world religions have been patriarchal.

of British law that had particularly troubled them. They wanted to abolish monarchy, ensure religious liberty and freedom of the press, protect against arbitrary abuses in the criminal law, limit the powers of government, and reserve powers to the individual. To a remarkable extent they succeeded.* Although a number of the colonial charters had specifically granted rights to women and children, such provisions were not included in the Bill of Rights.[11]

The equal protection clause did not become a part of the Constitution until 1868, when in the aftermath of the Civil War the Fourteenth Amendment was ratified. It provides in pertinent part: ". . . nor shall any state . . . deny to any person within its jurisdiction the equal protection of the laws." In that same amendment, however, voting rights were limited to males and representation in the Congress was based on the number of males, not the entire population.

For more than a century American courts have been struggling to define the equal protection clause and to chart its limits. Many legal terms are easily understood by laypersons. "Malice" is a word that bedevils judges but causes the public little difficulty. "Negligence" is also a word that the public understands but courts often have difficulty in applying. "Equality" is not such a word. Neither lawyers nor laypersons have a clear idea of what is meant by "equality" or "equal protection of the laws."

Webster's defines "equal" as "of the same measure, quantity, amount, or number as another . . . identical." This concept of equality like an equation requires two parts, one measured by the other. In algebra both sides of an equation may fluctuate in value so long as they balance exactly. "Equality" when used in a legal or political sense assumes that one side of the equation is fixed as the standard or norm to which the other must be made equivalent or identical. These words— "equivalent" and "identical"—plague legal definitions of "equality."

The legal approach to establishing new rights is essentially one of pouring new wine into old bottles. Common law judges are trained to follow precedent rather than to analyze novel claims in the light of physical facts, social conditions, and fundamental principles of human rights and to enunciate new doctrines. Lawyers seek an old doctrine and a series of cases that provide analogous rights to which the new claims may be assimilated. Thus lawyers representing the others have turned to the seminal cases interpreting the equal protection clause that arose out of the civil rights movement. This course has been fraught with difficulties.

*The compromise over the peculiar institution of slavery was redressed only by war. As in the case of women, a constitutional amendment was necessary to grant suffrage to black males.

The landmark cases involving racial discrimination beginning in mid-twentieth century preceded the institution of litigation involving the rights of women, children, and the elderly. This was a natural development because the civil rights movement was well organized, well financed, and the invidious treatment of blacks was obvious. Most white men in northern and western states could easily recognize that denial of suffrage, employment, and educational opportunities to blacks was unfair, whereas the inferior legal status of the women, children, and elderly persons in their own families was so customary as to be almost invisible.

Idealistic students, clergymen, and ordinary citizens, both men and women, marched in civil rights demonstrations. They demanded changes in law and in practice. White lawyers went into the federal courts in southern states, where for the most part there were few black lawyers, to represent black Americans. They prosecuted numerous cases raising issues of discrimination in the political process, the job market, and the entire field of education.

The goals of the civil rights movement were clear. Blacks wanted the same rights as whites. Morality and common sense supported these claims. They were recognized by the Supreme Court and the lower courts in a long series of forthright decisions.

When the complainant is a black man, the aim of the courts has been and should be, I believe, to place him in a position comparable with or identical to that of the white man. Although some groups in our heterogeneous society are peculiarly susceptible to certain diseases such as sickle-cell anemia and Tay-Sachs, these differences do not affect their legal rights. Blacks and Hispanics are disproportionately poor, but there are in the United States more poor white people in absolute numbers than poor nonwhites. The average educational and literacy levels of blacks and Hispanics are undeniably lower than those of whites. But a large percentage of white males are also functional illiterates and high school dropouts. The mortality and morbidity rates of blacks and Hispanics as a whole are higher than those of the average white. However, nonwhite males who have had adequate educations, money, cultural advantages, and social opportunities have attained as high economic, intellectual, artistic, scientific, political, and other levels of achievement as have similarly advantaged white males. There are no proven inherent biological, emotional, or intellectual differences between adult white males and adult nonwhite males that militate against a legal definition of equality for the nonwhite adult male as legal rights and entitlements identical to those of a white adult male. Likewise, there are no reasons that militate against granting to atheists and members of small religious denominations and sects the same legal rights and entitlements that are accorded to members of established Christian denominations.

The reasonable man is the paradigm of the common law in both civil and criminal litigation. The rights and obligations of all litigants as measured by the reactions and responses of this hypothetical reasonable man are embodied in centuries of judicial decisions. When a litigant is a nonwhite male or a religious dissident, the use of the reasonable man standard is not discriminatory or prejudicial. But the application of the reasonable man standard to women, children, and the elderly is often grossly prejudicial. This issue has not been raised in the landmark cases decided by the United States Supreme Court involving the rights of these others.

In all cases in which a litigant asserts a denial of equal protection of the laws, the threshold question is the standard of review. The Court in the civil rights cases developed novel doctrines. When the claim is asserted by a member of a "suspect class" or involves a "fundamental right," a test of strict scrutiny is applied. To date race, but not gender,[12] youth, or age has been held to be a suspect class. Fundamental rights as defined by the Supreme Court include suffrage, the right to procreate but not the right to refuse to procreate, the right to counsel for those accused of crime at the trial level but not the right to counsel in civil cases to obtain custody of one's children.[13] Nor have the courts recognized the right of a child not to be physically abused or maimed as a fundamental right.[14]

When identical treatment of white and nonwhite males fails to yield equality of results, courts engage in devising ingenious tests and remedies. No useful purpose would be served by recapitulating the arguments with respect to various forms of affirmative action. The question with respect to the others who are the subject of this book is not the remedies but the standard by which their rights are to be measured and the legal procedures to which they are subject.

These fundamental questions have been largely ignored because both lawyers for the litigants and the courts have relied on the civil rights cases as the precedents by which to decide the claims of these others. It is an approach fraught with difficulties. Admittedly the Fourteenth Amendment was adopted to address the problems of the newly freed slaves. There is nothing in the legal history of that amendment that indicates that women, children, and the elderly were to be included within its ambit. This fact gives rise to the recently promulgated theory of original intent, a doctrine that justifies denial of rights that were not recognized or contemplated centuries ago.

A much older and more widely respected rule of judicial construction of legislative enactments (including constitutional provisions) requires courts to give words their common and ordinary meaning. When there is no ambiguity in the language, a court is not free to interpret the plain meaning of a legislative provision. Because the equal protection clause refers to "any person," it requires a strained construction to exclude from the word "person" more than half the population.*

When dealing with claims of discriminatory treatment asserted by women, children, and the elderly, courts have adopted a curious means of avoiding the issue of equal protection of the laws. Either they conclude that the others are outside the legal system or they treat the others precisely as they would treat a reasonable white adult male. Neither solution is satisfactory. Obviously every human being is a person. To remove any segment of the population from the ambit of the Constitution requires a legal fiction. The assumption that the same treatment accorded to biologically, chronologically, mentally, or emotionally different individuals will result at all times in legal equality is preposterously illogical. All too often it yields manifestly unjust decisions. To acknowledge human differences in order to accord equal protection does not imply inferiority.

There is no reason other than custom to take the male model of life as the standard by which females are judged and found wanting.† Childhood has special gifts and charms that should not be denigrated because they are different from the perspectives and attitudes common to adulthood. Elderly persons also have gifts and perspectives different from average men in the prime of life, but so do many who are not denied rights because of those differences.

In the nineteenth and early twentieth centuries, when women sued to claim the right to vote, to practice professions, to serve on juries, and to assert countless other rights that white males have exercised since the establishment of the American colonies, their claims were denied by the Supreme Court, relying upon the precedents of the common law.‡ Legislation rectified many of these decisions. Others were reversed only after decades of litigation.

A similar pattern of judicial denial of rights occurred in the latter

*The Declaration of Independence states that "all men are created equal." The word "men" can be read generically as meaning mankind, the totality of human beings. Even today the masculine is commonly used to include the feminine. The word is not age-limited or restricted by mental capacity. There is no textual reason to restrict either provision to adult males.
†It is customary for biological and social scientists to compile data based solely on males and apply the conclusions to females. See, e.g., studies on cholesterol based solely on men (*New York Times*, September 26, 1989, p. Cl), and Lawrence Kohlberg's study of developmental modes of thinking and choices in the year ten to sixteen based on a study of eighty-four boys (no girls were included) ("The Congitive-Development Approach," in *Morality, Moral Behavior, and Moral Development*, ed. William M. Kurtines and Jacob L. Gweirtz [New York: John Wiley & Sons, 1984]).
‡See Chapter 5, "Gender and Equal Protection of the Laws."

half of the twentieth century. In these cases the Court has relied not only on the common law but also on a "gender-neutral" concept based on the assumption that if women are treated the same as men, then equality is achieved. Under such mechanical and precedential analysis, the Supreme Court has held that pregnancy is not a gender-related disability.[15] Common sense tells us that only females can and do become pregnant. Again legislation was necessary to correct this glaring inequity and irrationality.

The claims of children to constitutional rights and protections of the law guaranteed to all persons have been treated in similarly unfair and absurd fashion. Children have obviously been members of American society since time immemorial. Native Americans had children. Children arrived in the Western Hemisphere with the first settlers. But it was not until 1966, almost two centuries after the founding of the nation, that the Supreme Court took jurisdiction of a case involving the legal rights of children.[16] More than two decades later the courts are still tergiversating between denying children rights and by means of a legal fiction treating them the same as adults.

This either/or approach denies two obvious facts: (1) Children are persons, not animals or some subhuman species of life, and (2) children are not adults. They lack the physical, mental, emotional, and often the intellectual maturity of the average adult. Their life experiences are much more limited. In most instances they are unable to cope with problems of day-to-day living and certainly of the law on an equal footing with adults. Thus children have been denied the right to an education, the right not to be beaten, the right to a jury trial, and many other rights accorded to all adults.* But children have been prosecuted for crimes in adult court and subjected to the same penalties as adults, including the death penalty.

When children are not treated as adults, they are denied claims to liberty, freedom from sexual and physical abuse, use of their property, education, freedom of expression, and familial life on the ground that it is assumed that their interests are adequately protected by the very adults who are depriving them of these rights. Again legal fiction prevails over obvious fact.

Elderly persons who are not adjudicated incompetent are treated under the same substantive laws and rules of procedure as all other persons. If they are found to be incompetent, they are denied the right to control their property and often their persons. Between the robust vigor and mental acuity of the prime of life and the ravages of senility there is a continuum in which older persons gradually become infirm in

*See Chapter 10, "Children and Equal Protection of the Laws."

body and their mental processes become slower. Memory is often less clear. All too often elderly persons who are intelligent and competent find the testimonial requirements of the courtroom frustrating. They are unable to recall details with precision. They want to tell their stories in their own way. When interrupted by counsel, they lose their trains of thought.

Witnesses whose command of English is inadequate are entitled to have interpreters in court. But no provisions are made to assist either elderly witnesses or children who frequently have great difficulty in finding the right word or in responding to hostile cross-examination. In despair they give up the effort to assert their positions.

Courts and juries do not recognize that elderly persons and children have the same feelings of shame, humiliation, and anger as adults in the prime of life and also that they have the capacity to enjoy pleasures and independence. The loss of such attributes through accident, medical malpractice, and other legally compensable wrongs are frequently inadequately compensated.

There is no reason other than history and intellectual inertia for applying the norm of the reasonable adult male in the prime of life as the standard by which constitutional rights of these others are tested and by which equality is measured. Every day in the courts of this nation such persons are being treated unfairly not because judges act willfully or maliciously but because the legal system applies to them the old norms and procedures developed to protect the rights of the reasonable male adult. At the same time under the rubric of equality, women, children, and the elderly are being denied the special legal benefits developed over the centuries to protect them from inappropriate legal doctrines and life situations.

The most alarming trend in the decade of the 1980s has been the tendency of the courts to give the interests of society and the family precedence over the rights of women, children, the elderly. This is a regressive movement. In the Middle Ages the rights and obligations of the individual were subsumed in those of the family. Families were bound in a tight web of mutual obligations of parents to children, children to parents and spouses to each other. Through the succeeding centuries the common law dissolved family dependency and replaced it under the contract theory with the concept of the primacy of the individual who had rights and obligations.[17] Old family obligations have long been shattered, but the individual rights of the others are now devalued and those of the family exalted without any corresponding duties.

Under the benign theory of protecting the family, courts have intervened in a series of unprecedented decisions involving the medical decisions of women. Court-ordered caesarean operations have been performed on women over their opposition.[18] These extraordinary measures were justified on the grounds of the state's interest in the fetus, to which the woman's rights were subordinated.

All too often children are left in homes where they have been abused in order to keep the family together. Physical violence perpetrated on children by their parents under the rubric of discipline is condoned by judges who exhibit a curious reluctance to interfere with the so-called rights of the family to the prejudice of the rights of individual children.[19]

Elderly persons are deprived of their liberty and institutionalized for the convenience of their families without proof that the individuals violated any law or were dangerous.

These decisions preferring familial interests over individual rights have little precedent or statutory authority. "Family" is an ill-defined term. Under some statutes it includes homosexual partners, unmarried persons living together, and a wide variety of households. The family is not a legal entity with constitutional rights. Nowhere in the Constitution or the Bill of Rights is family mentioned. Rights are assured to individuals.

Neither the common law nor the neutral application of laws designed for reasonable adult males in the prime of life provides legal procedures or doctrines that meet the biological, developmental, and emotional needs of the others, who constitute the majority of the American population.

Both legal scholars and judges have failed to grasp the nettle of difference in the quest for equality.* Courts have unthinkingly assumed that there is one standard, by which all persons are to be judged, and that the norm is the reasonable adult male. Perhaps someday scientific discoveries will enable people to reorder the duality of biological life. Babies can now be conceived in a dish in a laboratory. It may be that in the future a human fetus could be grown in an incubator. This is the macabre world envisioned more than a half century ago in Aldous Huxley's *Brave New World.* The richness of human experience, the yin and yang, as denominated in Eastern philosophy, would be lost in a world in which females become imitation males. At least for the immediate future women will continue to bear children and probably con-

---

*Feminist author Shana Alexander belatedly acknowledged the problem of difference, stating, "We opened some kind of Pandora's box with the women's movement, because it has something to do with the fact that we wanted to be equal, but we forgot that we're different" (Marilyn Lois Polak, interview, *Philadelphia Inquirer Magazine* [May 27, 1990], p. 8).

tinue to be primarily responsible for nurturing and rearing them. It is to be hoped that men will participate more fully in the care of their offspring. To date the law has done little to further these ends or to equalize the physical and economic burdens of household and child care.

The maturation of human children probably cannot be accelerated. I have watched a bird painfully lay her eggs and sit on the nest for weeks. I have seen the fledgling birds hatch and watched while they were fed for several days. Then suddenly one small bird made a first tentative flight of a few feet. After several practice ventures the bird left the nest never to return.

Few, if any, children are able to fend for themselves—find food, clothing, shelter, and protection from human predators and the forces of nature although children as young as three may be used as forced labor. It is most unlikely that human beings can be programmed before birth or in infancy to walk, talk, and care for themselves. Could they be programmed to understand calculus, to appreciate art, music, poetry, and philosophy? I hope that human beings will always need a long period of nurturance and development so that their minds and spirits can grow and that children reared in loving homes and wisely educated will become humane, caring, peaceful, and self-governing adults.

As the numbers of the very old increase in the American population and their claims to live independently, to control their own property and their own medical care become more prevalent, courts will be confronted with many such persons in court as litigants and witnesses. While progress in medicine may arrest the deterioration of physical and mental conditions of the elderly in the distant future, there is an urgent need now to adapt the legal process to conform to their condition.

Therefore, if this nation is to be a truly democratic society in which the rights of every person are assured and the vulnerable protected, the law will have to recognize and accommodate the needs of all segments of the population. This cannot be achieved by reliance on anachronistic dogmas of the common law or legal fictions such as gender neutrality, the reasonable man standard, and the denial of differences between children and adults. The law must recognize these intractable differences and create appropriate procedures that provide meaningful access to the courts and actual equal protection in the trial of cases in which these others are witnesses or litigants. Substantive law must also recognize these others as "suspect classes" that are denied "fundamental rights" under existing law.

Such an approach is diametrically opposed to the trend of the law as it has developed during the past half century. The thrust of civil liberties lawyers, of whom I was one, has been to demand identical treatment for those who have been excluded from the full benefits of citizenship, rights, and equal protection of the laws. Such a disregard of differences is not required by precedent. In other contexts the Supreme Court has required that "all persons similarly circumstanced shall be treated alike."[20] Conversely, the Court has also held: "The Constitution does not require things which are different in fact or opinion to be treated in law as though they were the same."[21]

The American legal system and the Constitution have been sufficiently expansive and flexible to survive the enormous changes transforming this country from a small collection of eastern seaboard colonies to a vast and powerful continental nation. It has adjusted to technological innovations undreamed of two centuries ago in communications, power, and medicine.

Grudgingly the law has recognized the rights of men of every race, religion, and national origin.* The rights of women, children, and the elderly can also be recognized and enforced within the framework of the Constitution.

*Native Americans were granted citizenship by an act of Congress in 1924, those of Chinese birth in 1943, those of Filipino birth in 1946, and of Japanese birth in 1952.

2

Divorce and Custody

> *Every woman should marry—and no man.*
>
> — BENJAMIN DISRAELI

WHEN A BATTLING COUPLE decides to end their marriage, they must divide their property and their children. This is the most common and devastating contact with the law that nonindigent American women experience. In the case of *Williams v. Williams,* it was my duty to make an equitable distribution of their property. A family court judge awarded custody of their little daughter on the basis of the legal doctrine known as the best interests of the child. In both issues the law is ostensibly gender-neutral. In this instance, as in most cases, both doctrines favored the husband and harmed the wife.

This case, like most divorce proceedings, involved the equal treatment of two persons whose situations were drastically different. Tom Williams had an eighty-thousand-dollar-a-year job, robust health, and a new wife. Emily Stonington Williams earned two hundred dollars a week, was in fragile health, and was alone. Both claimed their three-year-old daughter, Jessica, as well as a substantial amount of property.

Both legal rules sound fair. Equitable distribution implies fairness. But equity, like equality, is difficult to define. Is 50 percent for each ex-spouse equitable? And 50 percent of what? As for custody, a rule that appears to be concerned with the well-being of the child sounds appropriate. The criteria by which the child's interests are to be measured are difficult and amorphous. To date no judge, psychiatrist, or psychologist has been able to achieve the wisdom of Solomon in dividing the child between the parents.

When I first saw Emily, she was sitting alone at plaintiff's table. At the defense table were three well-dressed men, legal papers spread out before them. As I entered, the men rose automatically. The court officer motioned to the woman to stand. Court was opened in the time-honored way. The crier intoned, "Oyez, oyez, all having to do before the honorable court of common please draw near and you shall be heard. Be seated. . . . The case of Williams against Williams, Your Honor."

"Where is plaintiff's counsel?" I asked, assuming that the attorney had been delayed.

"Plaintiff is appearing *pro se* [for herself]," the court officer replied.

I looked at the court papers. They were very professionally drawn. But the name of the attorney and his firm, a large and prosperous one, had been crossed out. The complaint alleged that Emily Stonington Williams was suing for the return of her household goods, including a long list of antique furniture, dishes, silverware, jewelry, and other property that she claimed were wrongfully retained by her former husband, Thomas, and his present wife, Charmaine. Attached was an appraisal of the goods valued at more than a hundred thousand dollars. The appraiser noted that he had been refused permission to make an examination of the items and had based his appraisal on descriptions given by the plaintiff.

Tom alleged that these items were marital property and that he was entitled to half the value of all the property. His appraiser estimated the goods at less than $50,000. In a counterclaim, Tom was suing Emily for $120,000 that he stated he had spent on medical care for her after they had agreed to divorce.

The complaint and counterclaim were practically boiler plate, the routine allegations made in cases involving disposition of marital assets. This case was slightly different because it was not heard in family court as part of the divorce proceeding.

My initial problem was the fact that Emily did not have a lawyer. It is very difficult for a judge to be the neutral fulcrum on the scales of justice when one party is represented by able counsel and the other has no lawyer. Tom Williams was represented by a lawyer who specialized in matrimonial disputes. Even the most sophisticated and intelligent persons who are not lawyers have difficulty in coping with the arcane procedures of the law. A layperson does not know the rules of evidence, when to object to prejudicial questions, how to cross-examine opposing witnesses, how to testify, and how to question his or her own witnesses.

In such a situation the judge often has to ask the questions and rule on questions that are not objected to. This gives the appearance of prejudice. It is an undesirable practice because the judge soon is acting as counsel for one of the parties and participating in the trial in an improper way. I decided to delay the trial in the hope that Emily Williams could obtain an lawyer.

Emily rose and was sworn. She was a small, trim young lady with smooth ash blond hair. She was wearing a very proper gray Brooks Brothers suit and neatly polished shoes. She looked like the wife of a prosperous young banker, the kind of young woman who would be active in the Junior League and neighborhood good works. During the following months, as I came to know Emily, I found my first impression of her had been correct. This had been her life before her divorce. Now she was a member of the new poor, a person who had to beg, not very successfully, for help to reclaim all that had been important in her life.

I asked Emily why she did not have a lawyer. She told me that the complaint had been prepared by a lawyer friend, a young associate in a large firm. She could not afford to pay him. Because she was not actually indigent, the firm would not permit her friend to represent her without fee. Emily explained that she had been divorced for more than a year. It was an uncontested divorce. She had not had counsel and had been led by Tom to believe that she would have custody of Jessica, their daughter, and that he would return her property when she obtained an apartment of her own.

Tom Williams was obviously a member of the new rich, a yuppie. I observed him closely, as I do all litigants. Juries are instructed to observe the manner and demeanor of the witnesses, to note how they look, what they say, and to evaluate the truth of their testimony in the light of all the evidence. As a judge I, too, observed the manner, demeanor, and appearance of the litigants. Tom was seated between his lawyers, both associated with a wealthy prestigious law firm. Tom was easily the best-dressed person in the courtroom. From his carefully blow-dried chestnut hair to his Bally shoes he was a model of sartorial splendor. From time to time he adjusted the shirt cuffs, protruding exactly one-quarter of an inch below his jacket and fastened with gold knot links. Occasionally he glanced at Emily, who scrupulously ignored him. Then he turned to his lawyers with raised eyebrows and a shrug of his well-padded shoulders, as if to say, "What can a man do when his ex-wife is foolish enough to sue him!"

Emily stated that both her parents were dead. She had no siblings. Her only relative was an aunt, who lived in Minnesota. In a low, clear voice she began to describe her acquaintance with Tom.

"We met," she said, "shortly after the death of my parents, who were killed in an automobile accident. We had no friends in common, only two mutual acquaintances. In fact, I now realize, we knew very little about each other. But he seemed to be kind, and I was very sad and lonely. We were married within six months.

"After the marriage I began to learn many disquieting things about Tom: his drinking, his expulsion from college—"

"Objection, objection." Tom's lawyer was on his feet. "These people are divorced. Any testimony relating to their marriage is irrelevant. I move that these highly prejudicial, unsubstantiated statements be stricken from the record."

"The objection is sustained. The motion granted." I turned to Emily. "Whatever problems you may have experienced in your marriage are irrelevant to this proceeding, unless you are attempting to set aside the divorce—a most difficult action in view of the fact that Mr. Williams has remarried. We shall confine the evidence to the property claims alleged in the complaint."

"No," Emily replied slowly, "I don't wish to contest the divorce. If he had not filed for divorce, I would have done so. But aren't the lies he told me before and after we were married relevant? If I had known the true facts about his character and his past life not only in college but the jobs he had been fired from for dishonesty, I should never have married him."

Before Emily was through, Tom's attorney was on his feet again, shouting, "Objection, objection. I move that this—this woman be held in contempt of court for willfully and deliberately violating this court's order."

"Counsel, please be seated. I shall try again to explain to Mrs. Williams the limits of admissible evidence. We have not begun the trial. We are exploring Mrs. Williams's ability to obtain counsel."

"Your Honor, Emily Williams is a very cold, calculating, intelligent woman. She understands the English language. She has a master's degree in English with highest honors from Bryn Mawr. She was an editor at Doubleday for some six years. If anyone understands the English language, it is Emily Williams. I renew my motion that she be held in contempt of court, for blatant violation of Your Honor's order."

I looked to Emily for some response. She stood before me in utter bewilderment.

"If I said something wrong, I apologize. I was simply trying to explain how this miserable, sordid situation came about."

"Counsel, your motion is denied. It is obvious that the violation of the order was unintentional. Your characterization of the plaintiff will be stricken. There will be no character assassination of any party in this courtroom." I continued: "Mrs. Williams, your lawsuit is for the return of property that you allege is yours. What is the basis of your claim?"

"All these items of furniture, art, antiques, jewelry, and other things of value are mine. I inherited them from my parents. Nothing in that list was purchased by Tom or owned by him. When we were married, all he had was a list of debts that I paid off, and I paid for his tuition to get his M.B.A. when he was fired from his job for dishonesty."

Tom's lawyer was apoplectic. "Objection, Your Honor. You have been too patient with this woman. She simply refuses to abide by the court's ruling. I renew my application for an order of contempt and move that all of her maundering, slanderous statements be stricken."

"Mrs. Williams and gentlemen, we are having great difficulty proceeding because Mrs. Williams does not have counsel. Will you please tell me, madam, why you do not have an attorney?"

"Your Honor, I brought this lawsuit in order to gain possession of my property so that I could sell it and raise enough money to retain a lawyer in my lawsuit to regain custody of my child. When I agreed to the divorce, I was in the hospital. Jessica, my daughter, was three years old. I had just had a very difficult pregnancy, a dreadful surgical delivery. The baby was defective and died after six weeks. After his death I still had not recovered. Mr. Williams told me he wanted a divorce. I inquired of several lawyers and learned that whether or not I agreed, he could get a no-fault divorce. I thought that at least I would refuse until he paid my medical bills. But I was told that there was no way I could prevent him from getting a divorce. So I told him I would sign the papers if he would agree that I have custody of Jessica, and he did so agree. He was never fond of children."

"Objection, objection."

"Please, counsel. All the inadmissible statements will be stricken. Just let Mrs. Williams explain why she cannot obtain counsel in this matter without any further interruptions. Continue, Mrs. Williams."

"I have absolutely no funds whatsoever. During the first two years of our marriage I earned a good living as an editor. Of course, the book industry is not highly paid, not like stockbrokers and financiers. All my earnings were used to support us and to pay Mr. Williams's tuition so that he could obtain an M.B.A. After Jessica was born, I decided not to work full-time. I preferred to stay home and care for her myself. I did some part-time editing, but these earnings were also used in partial support of the family.

"When I received a notice from Mr. Williams's lawyers that he would no longer be responsible for my medical care, even though he had health insurance as part of his employee benefits, I left the hospital against the advice of my physicians. I am not well enough to work full-time, but I have been working part-time to the best of my abilities and supporting myself in an extremely modest life-style.

"On leaving the hospital, I immediately asked for the return of Jessica. Mr. Williams adamantly refused. He attempted to deny me even the right to see my daughter. I went to family court to assert what I thought were my parental rights. After one hearing at which Mr. Williams's lawyers objected to all my testimony, I realized that I would have to retain counsel. My aunt, who is a widow supporting two college-age children, lent me a thousand dollars. The attorney I retained explained that I would need substantially more money to obtain expert witnesses, Mr. Williams's records, and other vital pieces of evidence. Mr. Williams is alleging that I am emotionally unstable, an unfit parent. He wants to deny me all access to my child. There is no one from whom I can borrow three thousand dollars. I have no bank credit because all my money was in a joint account and Mr. Williams removed all the money from that account. The lawyer who is handling the lawsuit against the drunk driver who caused the accident of my parents informs me that it will be at least a year before I will collect any money. The jury awarded me five hundred thousand dollars, but the insurance carrier appealed and refused to make any offer of settlement. I do not know where to turn for help, Your Honor."

I suggested the bar association lawyer reference bureau, the young lawyers' committee, a women's law center, a child advocate organization, and Community Legal Services and said I would continue the matter for two weeks.

"Please, not two weeks," Emily implored. "I shall diligently attempt to obtain counsel. But the custody hearing in family court is scheduled for three weeks from today. I must have some assurance that I can obtain my necessary witnesses before then."

"Very well. This matter is continued for one week. My clerk will give you the names and phone numbers of the legal agencies I mentioned." I also suggested that Emily bring to court with her her medical bills, her income statements, and any information she had with respect to the property that was in issue.

The courtroom was filled with workmen, employees on strike who were opposing their employers' request for an injunction against their picketing. These thirty or forty rough men had listened to Emily with rapt attention. There were mutterings: "She got a raw deal . . . what a bastard he is . . ."

Emily gathered her papers and without a glance at Tom walked out of the courtroom. Tom was whispering happily to his two lawyers. He had not said a word. The burden of proof and of going forward with the case was on Emily. She, in effect, not he, was on trial. She was required to bare her entire life to a stranger in judge's black robes. And she had to do it not only in the presence of her former husband and his new wife but also a roomful of strange men.

After the case of *Williams v. Williams* that was before me had been settled, I learned what had happened in family court. As soon as Emily left the hospital, she had seen Jessica daily. Tom and Jessica were living in their old apartment. Emily went there every morning and took care of Jessica while Tom was at work. She took Jessica with her when she went looking for an apartment. At night she did her editorial work in a cheap rented room. During these few weeks Tom never mentioned that he would oppose giving custody of Jessica to Emily, nor did he tell her that he was contemplating remarriage. In fact, Tom asked Emily to come back and sleep at the apartment with Jessica for two weeks while he was out of town. She subsequently discovered that he was on his honeymoon.

Shortly after his return with his new wife, Charmaine, Tom refused Emily permission to see Jessica, claiming that she upset the child, that she was too emotional. Emily immediately went to family court to obtain a legal order granting her custody of Jessica. The personnel at family court told Emily that she could proceed without a lawyer.

At the first hearing in family court the judge awarded her visitation one day a week and deferred decision on custody until the court could conduct an investigation into both Tom's and Emily's living arrangements, the usual procedure. Tom asked for a psychiatric examination of Emily, which the judge ordered. Emily protested that Tom had agreed that she would have custody of Jessica as soon as she was well, that otherwise she would not have consented to a divorce. The judge told her that such agreements were not binding and that in view of her psychiatric problems the court would have to decide what was in the best interests of Jessica. Emily protested that her illness was physical, not mental, but the judge was adamant.

Every time she tried to speak, Tom's lawyer interposed an objection. When Tom testified that she was emotionally unstable and unfit, she did not know how to refute him. Emily then realized that she needed a lawyer. She consulted her lawyer friend, who explained to her that the judge's statement of the law was correct, as was true, and that Emily would indeed have to prove her fitness to have custody of her own daughter.

The investigator from family court reported that Emily's apartment was neat and clean, though sparsely furnished. She had only one bedroom. Emily told the investigator that Jessica could have the bedroom and that she, Emily, would sleep on a daybed in the living room. There was no separate entrance to the apartment. Emily and Jessica would have to go through the hall of the house, which was occupied by several unmarried adults, male and female. The apartment was in a poor neighborhood in the city. There was no public kindergarten nearby.

Tom and his new wife had purchased a large four-bedroom house in the suburbs. They had a garden with a swimming pool. The local schools were excellent; there was a good nursery school only two blocks away.

Emily's interview with the court psychiatrist was disastrous. Emily became upset and angry when she was asked whether she was thinking more of her own needs than of Jessica's welfare. He reported that she was emotionally unstable and vindictive.

Peter Barnes, Emily's lawyer in the custody suit, wisely advised her that she must retain her own psychiatric expert. He also suggested that they subpoena Tom's college records. Emily knew that Tom had been suspended for smoking marijuana. He had also been on the verge of being fired from his job in a brokerage house for financial chicanery when he decided to go back to school to get a master's degree. These facts might help her case. But it is expensive to obtain this information, which Tom adamantly refused to supply. Barnes suggested that Emily sue to reclaim her antiques and sell them so that she could finance the custody suit.

When Tom and Emily returned to court before me a week after the first hearing, she was wearing the same carefully pressed suit. She looked ill and harried. She was again alone. I wished that she would bring a friend with her, someone to help her through her ordeal, but I did not make this suggestion lest it be a breach of judicial decorum. In rape cases I often summoned a representative of the Women Against Rape organization to be in court with the complaining witness. But there was no similar organization to help women in civil litigation.

Tom was back with his two lawyers. I noted that he was wearing a different elegant suit. His senior attorney customarily charges clients at the rate of three hundred dollars an hour. The younger attorney was probably billed by the firm at a hundred dollars an hour.

Emily reported that Community Legal Services could not help her because she earned too much money. Her pay of two hundred dollars per week for editing on a part-time basis was above its limit for a single client with no dependents. Because Jessica was living with Tom, she could not be counted as Emily's dependent. The bar association lawyers wanted a minimum of five hundred dollars for a retainer and would charge fees by the hour. No one was willing to take her case on a contingent-fee basis—that is, to be paid 40 percent of the recovery if Emily won and nothing if she lost. Clearly no one was impressed with the validity of her claim. A public-interest law firm that Emily consulted told her that her case was not sufficiently important. It was concerned only with matters on the "cutting edge" of the law. The women's legal office was occupied with legislative reform and writing appellate briefs. The child advocate office told her its position was to be strictly neutral in custody cases. A staff attorney suggested that if the court would appoint the agency to represent Jessica, it would make its own independent investigation to determine which parent could better provide for Jessica and then advocate that position in court. Emily inquired whether the agency was interested in the moral character of the parents. She was told, "Only as it relates to the parent's ability to care for the child. Naturally if either parent was a child abuser, the agency would oppose the award of custody to that parent."

"What if you found that one parent was dishonest in his business dealings?"

"We would not be concerned with any of the parent's activities that did not directly relate to fitness to care for the child," Emily was told.

It was evident that Emily had exhausted all avenues for obtaining counsel. It was necessary for her either to represent herself or to drop her claim.

The trial proceeded painfully and haltingly. Emily took the stand. "Where shall I begin?" she asked.

I explained the law to her. The divorce was valid and binding unless she had not received proper notice or unless she was incompetent when she signed the acknowledgment of the complaint. She testified that she had indeed received the papers, she knew what they were, and she did not wish to contest the divorce.

"But I would never have consented to give up Jessica," Emily declared firmly.

"The matter of Jessica's custody is not before me. The family court judge will have to make that decision," I explained.

Even if they had entered into a written agreement with respect to custody, one of the parents could always move to set it aside in the best interest of the child. The court must decide which parent can better provide care for the child.

"Isn't a mother supposed to have custody of an infant?" Emily asked. "Jessica is just three years old. I wasn't even permitted to be with her on her birthday."

For many years American law followed the tender years doctrine, under which custody was presumed to be given to the mother of a very young child unless the mother was proven to be unfit. However, under the rubric of equality and gender neutrality that presumption was abolished. Although some judges still give preference to the mother, the rule in most states is the best interests of the child. The court compares the characteristics of each parent's financial condition, the physical properties of the home, the nature of the caretaker when both parents work, and other objective factors.

"The only issue before this court," I explained to Emily, "is whether the property consisting of the items specified in your complaint should be returned to you. You, as the plaintiff, have the burden of persuading the court that these items are your personal property and not marital assets. If they are marital assets, then it will be my duty to make an equitable division of the goods."

Emily took the witness stand and was sworn to tell the truth, the whole truth, and nothing but the truth. She began going through the list of items in the complaint and stating when and from whom she received each one. After a few minutes of testimony Tom's lawyer rose and stated: "Your Honor, defendant concedes that all these items were the sole property of plaintiff before the marriage. It is his contention that after the marriage, all these goods became marital property."

"Mrs. Williams, you have heard counsel's admission. Is there anything else you wish to put in evidence?"

"I don't know, Your Honor," she replied in bewilderment.

"You will not be foreclosed from putting in further evidence later. If you think of anything you wish to add, I shall permit you to reopen your case."

Emily rose and started to leave the witness stand.

"Please resume your seat, Mrs. Williams. It is now time for defense counsel to cross-examine you."

Emily admitted under cross-examination that everything she claimed as gifts or inheritances from her parents had been in her possession before the marriage and that she had brought all this property to the apartment that she and Tom had occupied when they were married. Clearly all these goods were marital property. That meant under the law they were to be subject to "equitable distribution." The fact that she had supported Tom for the two years he attended graduate school was irrelevant. In a claim in family court she might treat that as a contribution to his earning capacity and claim a larger amount of alimony based on his future earning capacity that she had helped to enhance. But the question of alimony was not before me. That would be heard before a family court judge.

Emily attempted to prove that Tom had brought no assets to the marriage. In fact, he had debts of several thousand dollars that Emily paid out of her earnings and small inheritance. These facts were irrelevant and inadmissible.

On cross-examination Emily painstakingly went through the list of her property and the values she assigned to each item. Many of these things had great sentimental value because they had been in her family for generations. The law does not take cognizance of sentimental value. In an assessment of the value of possessions, the standard is market value. There were many items Emily had forgotten to include in the complaint that she mentioned in her testimony. Tom's lawyer objected. I sustained the objection and suggested that she orally amend the complaint to include them. Tom's lawyer objected on the ground that I as the judge had no right to suggest legal strategy and remedies to Emily. I overruled his objection and granted him an exception. That meant that the issue was reserved for consideration by an appellate court.

Emily was subjected to a grueling cross-examination with respect to the value of each item.

When Tom took the stand, he described her property as secondhand furniture, chipped dishes, old glassware, worthless family portraits, and cheap jewelry.

Emily hadn't the faintest ideas of how to cross-examine Tom. I asked him what property he had bought since the marriage. Again there was objection from Tom's counsel. I ordered Tom to testify. Counsel then asked for a recess, obviously to brief Tom. It was a legitimate request.

Tom testified that he had bought very little household goods in all the years of their marriage. His purchases had been principally Emily's clothes and things for their child.

When he finished, I asked Emily, who was visibly angry, if she wanted to cross-examine Tom. She had learned a lot from her own cross-examination. She went through a long list of items. His purchases had included an expensive stereo set, two television sets, a Cuisinart, a Mercedes-Benz automobile, and other property. The total value was almost seventy-five thousand dollars.

Tom resumed the stand to put in his case on the counterclaim. He

presented a whole sheaf of hospital bills amounting to more than a hundred thousand dollars. Again Emily had no idea as to how to cross-examine him. I reviewed these exhibits. Tom grudgingly conceded that the bills all related to the pregnancy and birth of the second child and Emily's postpartum illness. He also acknowledged that with the exception of the deductible, 80 percent of the bills were paid by the insurance company, that health insurance was one of the fringe benefits of his job. He testified that some of the bills amounting to approximately twenty thousand dollars were received after the divorce. When I pointed out the dates of the services rendered, Tom angrily admitted that they were for medical services supplied before the divorce was final. The bills for services rendered after the divorce had been sent to Emily at his instructions. Tom's attorney rested his case.

I took the matter under advisement and instructed them to be back in court in three days, when I would enter my order. Tom's attorney asked leave to file a brief and requested a month's delay. I granted leave to file a brief but ordered that it be filed within one week. I would enter my order at the end of ten days. Time was of the essence for Emily because her hearing in family court was listed three weeks hence. She would have to have some assurance that she would have available funds in order for her attorney to retain a psychiatrist.

The rules were clear, and I was bound by them. All property brought to the marriage by either spouse is marital property to be equitably divided between them at the dissolution of the marriage. Which party had originally owned the property is irrelevant. The court is not to apportion it in accordance with the percentage that each party had contributed. Although equitable distribution does not necessarily mean equal division, there must be some proportionality.

As for all bills incurred during the marriage, both spouses were responsible for payment. If Emily could not pay, then Tom was obligated to do so. Tom had no legal obligation to pay for any medical expenses incurred after the divorce. The fact that these expenses arose out of health problems that existed prior to the divorce was also irrelevant. Tom's counterclaim was, therefore, denied.

In determining the value of Emily's antiques and other goods, I accepted Tom's lower evaluation of $60,000. But I also included in the value of the marital property the things purchased from Tom's earnings that I had valued at $75,000. From the $60,000 valuation of Emily's household goods I excluded jewelry, portraits, and small items like ornamental vases, antique jades, and other collectibles that I concluded were personal items not part of the household goods. This reduced

Emily's contribution to the marital property to $45,000. The value of all the marital property was then assessed at $120,000. I divided the property equally, awarding $60,000 each to Emily and Tom, and then suggested that the division be in kind—that is, that the actual goods be distributed, that Emily should receive what had originally been hers, that Tom should keep what he had purchased and pay her $15,000 to make up the balance of $60,000.

Emily agreed to abide by this order. Tom's attorney said that he would file an immediate appeal. The automobile, he contended, was not marital property but was used solely by Tom for his business. He objected to the exclusion of any of Emily's possessions from the status of marital property.

Emily then asked how she would ever receive her property if she won on appeal because Tom was planning to move out west and take all her things with him. Tom said that his plans were not certain but that he could not state under oath that he would not leave the jurisdiction within the next year. I entered a protective order restricting him from moving or disposing of any of these items until the appeal had been decided. Emily was advised that she had a right to file a cross appeal, and I entered an order permitting her to do so without paying filing costs.*

Tom's attorney petitioned the appellate court for relief from my protective order. The petition was summarily denied.

Tom's counsel promptly filed an appeal and posted the necessary bond. His attorney then asked for a conference. This meeting was not productive. A few days later counsel requested another conference. At this meeting a settlement was reached. Emily agreed to accept in settlement the property that had belonged to her before the marriage, to make no claim for any property purchased by Tom during the marriage, and to give up the fifteen thousand dollars that I had awarded to her in return for Tom's dropping his appeal. I entered a final order to this effect.

Family court awarded custody of Jessica to Tom, finding that his suburban house was far more desirable than Emily's small apartment. The judge also stated in his adjudication that since Emily would have to work full-time to support herself, she would not be able to give Jessica the care the child needed. Tom's wife was pregnant and assured the court that she would stay home and take care of Jessica and her own baby.

Tom's attorney strenuously opposed any visitation rights for Emily.

*Without such an order Emily would have had to pay at least fifty dollars in filing fees.

He argued that it would be disruptive and emotionally upsetting for Jessica to have two mothers. He quoted at great length an influential book by Anna Freud, daughter of Sigmund Freud, the founder of modern psychiatry. Anna Freud wrote:

In addition, certain conditions such as visitations may themselves be a source of discontinuity. Children have difficulty in relating positively to, profiting from, and maintaining the contact with two physiological parents who are not in positive contact with each other. . . . Thus, the noncustodial parent should have no legally enforceable right to visit the child, and the custodial parent should have the right to decide whether it is desirable for the child to have such visits.[1]

The family court judge refused to terminate Emily's rights. Under the law, unless she was proved to be unfit, she had the right to maintain her parental relationship with her daughter. Emily was awarded visitation one day each week and given custody of Jessica for two weeks each summer. The court retained jurisdiction. If Tom actually decided to move, the judge would reconsider the visitation arrangements.

Emily's lawyer took an appeal. The appellate court affirmed the lower court's decision. In its opinion the appellate court held that Jessica's best interests were served by living in Tom's highly desirable house. Emily's psychiatrists convinced the trial court that she had recovered from her "mental illness," that she was not an "unfit" parent and could not be denied visitation. Any further appeal would probably have been futile. By that time Emily had exhausted all the money realized from the sale of her furniture, household goods, and jewelry.

Emily was awarded five-hundred-dollars-a-month alimony for three years as a transition payment to help her resume her full-time employment. The judge pointed out that Emily was well educated, that she had held good jobs, and that she did not need any further schooling or retraining. Emily's lawyer protested that six thousand dollars was a paltry sum in comparison with Tom's earnings, eighty thousand dollars a year plus stock options and bonuses. Indeed, it was below the poverty level. If Emily should get sick again, she would have to go on welfare. But, the judge pointed out that, Tom had a wife to support. They were expecting a baby. And he would be supporting Jessica. Emily had been married to him for only five years and couldn't expect him to support her indefinitely.

The best thing for Emily to do, he benignly advised her, was to let bygones be bygones and get on with her life.

After a few months Tom ignored the alimony order. Emily went to court three times without an attorney and managed to get fifteen hundred dollars in back alimony. Then Tom, Charmaine, and Jessica moved to California. In order to enforce the alimony order in California, Emily would need a lawyer there even though the law provided that the Pennsylvania court was supposed to take steps to enforce its order. Again Emily learned that she was too affluent for free legal services and too poor to afford counsel.

Just prior to Tom's move the court ordered that Emily have visitation rights with Jessica for two weeks at Christmas and one month in the summer. Tom and Jessica were to divide the expenses of transporting Jessica from California to Philadelphia and back. Emily decided to move to California so that she could be near Jessica and see her every week. She wrote from California to her attorney, Peter Barnes, that she had rented a small apartment not too far from Tom's large house, that she was still working for the publisher and also working as a waitress part-time because the cost of living was so high. She had been offered a position as a teaching assistant in the English department of a local university, but the stipend was insufficient to maintain herself. She was hoping to find a more lucrative night job, so that she could go back to the university and get her Ph.D. in English. With a doctorate she would be eligible for a full-time teaching position that would pay a modest but adequate salary.

After a few months in California Emily again wrote to her attorney, telling him that on her visits to Tom's house she had observed that Jessica was very subdued and unhappy. Jessica told Emily that Tom's wife hit her and made her stay alone in her room. The maid took Emily aside and told her that Charmaine drank, was often abusive to Jessica, and that both Tom and Charmaine doted on their baby son and ignored Jessica. On her weekly visits Emily bathed Jessica and washed her hair. She had seen several bruises on Jessica's body.

Emily asked what would happen if she simply did not return Jessica after her visitation and brought her back to Philadelphia.

The lawyer strongly advised her not to do that. In Los Angeles she would have the maid as a witness to testify for her. He also suggested that Emily talk to the neighbors and to Jessica's teacher and take photographs of any bruises.

On Emily's next visit Jessica wept and pleaded with her not to make her go back to Tom's house.

"I hate him," the child cried. "He's not my real father. A real father isn't mean. I hate Charmaine. Why do I have to live there?"

Emily could not force herself to return Jessica to such conditions.

She thought of taking Jessica away to another community where Tom would not be able to find them. But she had almost no money after paying her rent. She could not afford even the cheapest motel, much less a baby-sitter for Jessica while she worked at a new job in a strange place. She simply kept Jessica with her in her small apartment. For three days she did not hear from Tom. On the fourth day two police officers came to Emily's apartment with an arrest warrant for her and a warrant to seize Jessica. Emily was handcuffed and taken to jail while Jessica screamed and wept.

Emily was allowed one phone call from jail. She called her Philadelphia lawyer collect. Fortunately he was in his office and accepted the call. He promised that he would get her a lawyer. Because she could not post bail, Emily spent that night in the local jail with thieves, prostitutes, and drug pushers and users.

The next day a public defender whom her lawyer had contacted came to the jail to see her. At last Emily was poor enough to qualify for free legal services.

She was given a preliminary arraignment on the charges of kidnapping and recklessly endangering the welfare of a minor.

A part of the transcript of the bail hearing follows:

Public Defender: Let the record note that the defendant's blouse is torn from the neck to the waist, that she has a black eye and numerous scratches on her face and hands. Her skirt is torn. What appears to be dried blood is on her clothing. Mrs. Williams, were your clothes in this conditions when you were arrested?

Emily: No, your honor, my clothes were clean and intact.

PD: Did you have any cuts, scars, or bruises?

Emily: No. I was uninjured.

PD: Who assaulted you?

Prosecutor: Objection, leading.

PD: Were you assaulted?

Emily: Yes, many times.

PD: Where did these attacks take place?

Emily: In the cell. . . .

Court: Counsellor, I don't run the jail. It's unfortunate that this happened. What can I do about it?

PD: You can release this defendant forthwith on her own recognizance.

Court: Look, she's charged with a serious crime, kidnapping.

PD: It's her own child and the father was abusing her.

Court: That's what they all say now. She can't take the law into her own hands. We can't have a lawless society.

Prosecutor: If the court please, the child abuse unit of our office is today filing criminal charges against the father and his wife. The child will be placed in a county shelter pending a hearing on those charges.

Commotion in the courtroom. Child's father and stepmother are admonished to keep still.

Prosecutor: Our office does not oppose the release of this defendant on her own recognizance.
Court: Well, I'll let her go, but I think there should be some kind of protective order to prevent her from seeing the child.
PD: With all due respect, your honor, that is beyond your jurisdiction.
Court: What does the prosecution say?
Prosecutor: We agree with the defendant's statement of the law.
Court: If she goes out and kidnaps some other child, don't blame me. Bail is set at $5000, defendant to sign her own bond.

Emily's Philadelphia lawyer told me that the criminal charges against her were dropped. The charges against Tom and Charmaine were also dropped but only after Tom entered into a consent decree terminating his parental rights. The prosecutor, who had tried scores of similar cases, insisted on this decree. Without it, Tom could always reopen the custody case. Tom also agreed that a support order for Jessica be embodied in the decree.

Emily's lawyer told me that he did not recognize Emily or Jessica when they appeared at his office. Jessica, who had been a pretty, rosy little girl, was wan. Her hair was close-cropped. She clung to her mother's hand. Not once did she let go of Emily, not even when she was offered some candy. Emily seemed to have aged ten years. She had lost considerable weight. Her hair was streaked with gray, and her hands trembled. She told the lawyer that she had obtained a full-time job in New York with a publisher and was looking for an apartment and a day care center. She was worried about money but confident that she and Jessica would make it. The attorney wrote the prosecutor in California that Tom was almost ten thousand dollars in arrears on his alimony and support payments. Suit was filed. Tom resisted, claiming he could not afford the payments. There was a change of staff in the prosecutor's office. Emily received five hundred dollars and then heard no more from the court or Tom. That was the last news I had of Emily.

More than 53 percent of women who have custody of their children do not receive the support payments or the alimony the courts order.[2]

Most, like Emily, give up the struggle to claim their rights. It is too exhausting.

Emily was more fortunate than most women whose husbands obtain no-fault divorces.[3] She is educated, has a job, and has only one child, who is now of school age. Many divorcées have several children and even less money. Thanks to the public defender and the prosecutor, Tom's claims on Jessica have been permanently terminated. Unlike many mothers whose former husbands seek to win their children's affections with money, gifts, and more lavish life-styles, Emily does not have to compete for Jessica's love. Jessica has ceased to be a pawn in the games ex-spouses play. Emily was also fortunate in that she had good legal representation from the public defender, the state prosecutor, and her lawyer, who continued to give her help and advice long after her money ran out and his formal representation of her had ended.

Emily's situation is similar to that of more than ten million American women who are heads of families seeking to retain custody of their children and to rear them without adequate support from the fathers. Under the slogans of equality and gender-neutral laws they have lost both the benefits of hard-won legislation reforming the harshness of the common law and the protections married women had for several generations.

For centuries under British law, the husband had title to the wife's property and custody of their children. Even when the husband died, was imprisoned, or became incompetent, a designee or relative of the husband, not the mother, became guardian of the children. The guardian had control over the marriages of the children, who were wards of the court, as well as over their property. A husband could divorce his wife, but she had no right to divorce him.

These archaic laws of marriage, divorce, and child custody provoked legislative battles in the United States and Britain during the nineteenth and early twentieth centuries. Most reforms were fought by men on behalf of women in an attempt to redress the manifest unfairness of the common law. After much travail the law was radically revised. The property of a married woman no longer belonged to her husband. Both parties were granted equal rights to obtain a divorce. A wife was granted legal rights to the custody of her children contrary to the common law, which gave such authority exclusively to the husband. Grounds for divorce were expanded to include in most states not only adultery and desertion but also incompatibility and irreconcilable differences. Alimony was established so that a man would be required to support his children and former wife.

This was not an ideal situation. Divorce was a painful process in which the party who sued for divorce had to prove that the other spouse was "at fault." When adultery was the only legal ground for divorce, couples who had amicably agreed to divorce had to undergo a degrading, lying farce in which one spouse, usually the husband, arranged to be caught flagrante delicto by the other spouse's detective. *Holy Deadlock,* a novel by English barrister A. P. Herbert exposing the hypocrisy of the law, led Parliament to enact a statute expanding the grounds for divorce.

Before the adoption of no-fault divorce, most American states permitted dissolution of a marriage for what was essentially incompatibility even though the nomenclature differed in the various states. When clients came to me and said, "I want a divorce. Do I have grounds to get one?" I would reply, "You're married, aren't you?" Without any real perjury, any husband or wife could prove instances in which the other spouse had been insulting or humiliating or had made mentally cruel remarks. A gentle push or shove could constitute "cruel and barbarous treatment," legal ground for a divorce in most states. The real problem, of course, was money. Wealthy husbands and wives could buy off the unwanted mate. And the rejected party could use the divorce proceedings and custody demands as a means of holding up the other spouse for a better settlement. Because in most cases the parties through their lawyers arrived at a property settlement and custody agreement, divorce was a formality in which the judge played a ceremonial role of approving these private arrangements.

For people of moderate means whose only assets were a heavily mortgaged house and a steady paycheck, divorce was financially more difficult. Many couples stayed together simply because they could not afford to live apart. However, if one spouse was determined to obtain a divorce, he or she was almost always able to get one.

The working poor, as usual, were the most disadvantaged. Divorce was fairly expensive. Such families rarely had any assets. Often the dissatisfied spouse simply left. Runaway husbands who go to another state can easily escape their obligations. Then, as now, it was expensive to pursue an errant spouse and attempt to collect alimony and child support.

The indigent simply ignored the entire legal process of divorce and remarriage. Most legal aid societies in the mid-twentieth century did not provide free counsel in divorce matters. Divorce was considered a luxury for the rich, not a legal right that should be equally available to all. Consequently, many poor people simply separated and established new relationships without benefit of the law or the clergy. Usually these arrangements were satisfactory. But when one party died leaving some property, difficulties inevitably followed. A person who had lived as husband or wife for years and cared for this unmarried mate suddenly found that he or she had no rights and that a long-forgotten legal spouse had valid legal claims on the property. Children of the second arrangement were often disadvantaged. Social Security and pension benefits frequently went to the legal spouse, who was not the actual spouse.

With the turmoil of the 1960s and new demands for freedom on the part of both men and women, divorce law was suddenly perceived to be an anachronism. No man or woman should be forced to remain in a marital situation that was unpleasant and unwanted. No one should have to engage in deception and chicanery to obtain a divorce. And so the concept of no-fault divorce became popular. Such laws were enacted in a majority of the states. Like no-fault automobile insurance, it was intended to be a cheap, easy way to obtain redress without expensive lawsuits in which one party had to prove that the other party was wrong. It has proved to be far more expensive than the old procedure.

A bright young woman activist who was happily married to a successful attorney asked me to prepare a set of do-it-yourself forms so that any woman could obtain her own divorce without the necessity of retaining counsel. To her astonishment, I refused. I explained that anyone can get a divorce, but it requires the skill and expertise of a good lawyer for a middle-class women to get a decent property settlement for herself and adequate support for the children. I was accused of putting property considerations before liberty.

In the 1990s marriage is no longer the unquestioned norm. In the United States 60 percent of children under the age of eighteen have divorced parents. Children and ex-wives are among the poorest segments of society. One year after divorce the economic condition of the ex-husband has improved 42 percent and that of the ex-wife has worsened by 73 percent.[4]

Prior to gender-neutral divorce and custody statutes, the law presumed that custody of children of tender years would be awarded to the mother. Alimony for an ex-wife was to be paid until her remarriage or death. Mothers of young children and middle-aged housewives were not expected suddenly to become self-supporting.

Had Tom sought a divorce ten years earlier, before no-fault divorce law and the new gender-neutral rules on custody, all the proceedings would have been entirely different. Emily would have been notified that she had a right to contest the divorce. She would have obtained counsel.

Even though she had no funds, counsel would have immediately applied to the court for an award of counsel fees and temporary alimony while the case was pending. Since Tom was obviously eager to marry Charmaine, Emily's lawyer would have used that as a bargaining chip in negotiations for a property settlement. Under no-fault divorce and the best interests of the child doctrine, husbands frequently use the threat of demanding custody to lower support payments.

Prior to no-fault divorce there would have been little doubt that Emily's inheritance was her separate property. Unless she lived in a community property state like California, Tom would have had little likelihood of successfully claiming any part of her furniture and antiques. A good lawyer would have demanded a cash settlement in addition to Emily's property. If he had lacked ready cash, Tom could have raised money by getting a loan on his car.

In most states Emily's alimony would have been fixed at a sum that would have enabled her, insofar as possible, to maintain herself in the life-style to which she was accustomed. She would not have been expected to leave a preschool-age child and get a full-time job. The Supreme Court, however, has held gender-based alimony statutes unconstitutional.[5] Many a successful woman has found that the price of a no-fault divorce is the support not only of herself and her children but also of her ex-husband. Although the wife's possessions are treated as marital property to be divided equitably between husband and wife, the Supreme Court held, despite the Former Spouse's Protection Act, that a military pension (commonly that of the husband) is not part of the community property.[6]

Under the pre–gender-neutral law, Emily would not have had to fight for custody of her young daughter. Every court would have awarded custody of a young child to the mother unless she was clearly unfit. Tom would have had weekly visitations with Jessica and probably two weeks in the summer. But if he had moved out of the state, he would have had to pay for Jessica's transportation to visit him. Tom would also have been required to pay Emily support for Jessica, probably a minimum of twenty-five or thirty dollars per week. He could not have avoided support by the device of demanding and obtaining custody. If he had not paid, Emily could have obtained an order attaching his salary at least until he left the state.

Emily's problems in collecting arrearages from Tom are not unusual. A recent study showed that separated parents frequently move to different states. Three years after divorce 25 percent were in different states, and eight years after divorce, 40 percent. Of the cases sent to other states for enforcement of support orders, only 41 percent had a chance of yielding results, and the average time for receipt of any payment was eleven months.[7]

Clearly children should no longer be considered the property of parents to be disposed of by bargain. However, the best interests of the child rule ignores parental claims. Both the mother and the father, in my opinion, have fundamental human rights to enjoy the custody, rearing, and companionship of their children as well as have legal obligations to support and protect them. The outward indicia of the desirability of the home and the neighborhood unfairly weight the scales in favor of the more affluent parent. This is a facially gender-neutral rule. But in the vast majority of cases it favors the father over the mother.

Rather than seek an artificial symmetry of neutrality, it is time to examine gender differences and adopt a set of rules and presumptions that provides both males and females with an equal opportunity to achieve their parental rights and also furthers societal goals.[8]

At a minimum each spouse should, on the termination of the marriage, be put in as roughly similar a position as he and she had during the marriage. The parent who had assumed primary custodial care during the marriage should have the presumption of continuing that care, provided that it is not deleterious to the child. And society should be protected by laws that require both parents in accordance with their earning capacities and assets to provide their children with an adequate standard of living.

3

Gender and the Criminal Law

When a man is arrested he asks for a lawyer.
When a woman is arrested she asks for her children.

— SARA GAUCH

LORRAINE AND EMILY came from opposite ends of the social spectrum. But the similarities of the problems they encountered in court were greater than the differences in their backgrounds and life-styles. Both were twenty-eight years old when they appeared before me. Each had one child but no husband.

Lorraine, like most defendants in state criminal courts, both men and women, was poor. These courts are where the poor and underprivileged encounter the law. A state trial judge does not see many Leona Helmsleys or Oliver Norths.

Lorraine was born and grew up in a black inner-city slum. As a child she had been the victim of sexual abuse. She was a school dropout.* During her adult life she had had only the most casual employment but acquired a lengthy criminal record. She was in court before me on charges of shoplifting, grand larceny, and possession of drugs with intent to deliver. In lay language she was accused of being a drug pusher, a much more serious crime than being a drug user.

*Despite her deprived background, Lorraine was functionally literate and employable. Unlike the majority of young male offenders, who are functional illiterates, all female offenders who appeared before me were literate. They came from the same backgrounds as the male offenders, attended the same schools, and also dropped out of school in the tenth or eleventh grade. With a little help most of them could be employable and self-supporting.

While we were waiting for Lorraine to be brought to court from the cellblock, the young public defender moved to have the charges against her dismissed because it was more than seven months since she had been in custody awaiting trial. Lorraine had not been able to make bail. It was set at fifty thousand dollars (five thousand dollars' cash) because she was charged with being a drug dealer. Most male defendants who actually are drug dealers have little difficulty in posting bail.

The Sixth Amendment to the Constitution provides that an accused "shall enjoy the right to a speedy and public trial. . . ." In order to implement this provision, many jurisdictions have adopted rules requiring that every accused person be brought to trial within 180 days of arrest or be discharged. There are exceptions and loopholes. If the court calendar is too crowded, then the prosecutor may ask for an extension of time. Such an extension had been sought and granted in Lorraine's case. The extension had not yet expired. I denied the motion to dismiss.

The prosecutor, the defender, and I had a brief conference in which the defender attempted to get the prosecutor to drop the drug charge. "It's fifty thousand dollars' worth of cocaine that dame was carrying, in a baby carriage no less," the prosecutor commented. "I can't walk away from that."

Lorraine was brought into court by the sheriff. At the door to the courtroom her handcuffs were removed. She was a tall, slender, strikingly handsome woman. Her bronze skin was smooth, and her long hair thick and highlighted with a reddish glow. She was wearing skintight black stretch pants, high-heeled boots, and a sequin-encrusted T-shirt. Despite her seven months in jail Lorraine looked reasonably healthy. I looked at her arms and hands for signs of needle marks, but there were none. Clearly she was not on drugs.

Defense counsel requested a jury. Selection went quickly. Both the public defender and the prosecutor were experienced young professionals. The case was of no particular public interest, and they went about their work rapidly and efficiently.

The jury panel consisted of forty people who ranged in age from eighteen to approximately eighty. It was racially mixed. The prosecutor attempted to strike all black members of the panel, and the defender attempted to strike all whites. Neither succeeded. I think both counsel would have been better advised to reverse tactics. Most blacks are all too familiar with the drug trade and hostile to anyone involved in it. I excused two black jurors for cause. One woman whose husband was in prison for drugs said she feared he might be injured if she convicted this defendant or anyone accused of drug dealing. The other was a man whose son had been murdered by a junkie and who admitted he could not be fair to anyone accused of a drug offense. White jurors who are less familiar with the drug trade are more likely to have a reasonable doubt as to guilt than jurors who are daily exposed to its dangers. Both sides exhausted their challenges. By 4:00 P.M. we had a jury of twelve members and two alternates. Nine were women, five men; seven were black or Hispanic, and seven white. It was to all appearances a fair jury. They were seated and sworn. The trial commenced the next morning and was completed in one day.

A judge who has been a trial lawyer always suffers at least a mild case of split personality when presiding over a trial. I cannot help thinking how I would try the case for both the prosecution and the defense. Both attorneys in this case were young, bright, and conscientious. For them it was simply a routine trial. They did not make any serious errors. They presented their evidence straightforwardly and fairly, if not imaginatively or energetically. I could not fault either of them.

Marlene Gremins, the assistant prosecutor, had the easier task. She had all the evidence. Her witnesses were professionals and testified clearly and convincingly. The jury liked Marlene. She wore a simple dark suit and looked both pleasant and efficient.

Sheldon Harte, the public defender, was a nervous young man. He knew he had an uphill battle. He had not seen Lorraine until the morning when she was brought over from the jail and the jury was selected. An investigator had interviewed her in the jail, and a paralegal had prepared the file. Sheldon was first given Lorraine's file along with several others at five in the afternoon of the day before the case was called. If I had been Lorraine's lawyer and if I had had the opportunity to talk with her before the trial date, I would not have permitted her to come to court in the sexy-looking outfit she wore. I would have instructed her to wear something very plain, even dowdy-looking, a skirt and a schoolmarmish blouse and very little makeup. We would have had her baby in court so that Lorraine would appear to be a concerned and loving mother threatened with separation from her only child.

It is easier for a lawyer to instruct a male client as to his attire and appearance. Counsel tells him to wear a shirt and tie and jacket and get a conservative haircut, no long-haired ponytail but not a skinhead cut either. Whether the defendant is a member of the Mafia, one of a gang of teenage delinquents, or a pillar of the financial community is not readily apparent if he is wearing a dark jacket, a white shirt, and a striped tie. A woman betrays her class and origins before she opens her mouth. A pink polyester pants suit and a tight permanent place her on the socioeconomic scale with as much precision as a three-page questionnaire.

Lorraine's artificial eyelashes and inch-long red fingernails as well as her clothing provoked a hostile response among the female members of the jury and a wary suspicion on the part of the men. Lorraine was faced with serious prejudice before the trial even commenced.

The state called as its first witness Sam Wilkins, a department store security guard. He was a regular witness in the court and handled himself with ease. He testified that he was watching a bank of TV monitors in security headquarters when he saw on number seven a hand seize a gold watch from a store counter and stuff it under the blanket of a baby carriage. He immediately called Guard Coleman, who responded on her walkie-talkie. She was on the floor not ten feet from the jewelry counter. He alerted her to keep an eye on the baby carriage. Wilkins continued watching the monitors, and later on number twelve he saw a black female, whom he identified as Lorraine, exit the store, pushing the baby carriage. He saw Guard Coleman make the arrest.

On cross-examination Wilkins testified that he did not see the person whose hand took the watch and stuffed it into the baby carriage; the face was out of range of the monitor. The hand could have been male or female. He couldn't remember any identifying characteristics, no jewelry or nail polish. He was asked to observe Lorraine's hand with its long bloodred nails.

"Wouldn't you remember that hand?" the defender asked.

"Can't say that I would," Wilkins replied. "I was concentrating on the watch that was in the hand."

Security Guard Coleman was a short, stocky, no-nonsense black woman. She, too, was an experienced witness. She testified that she was patrolling a few feet from Lorraine and the baby carriage when she received the phone call from Wilkins. She immediately concentrated on the carriage, keeping two or three feet behind Lorraine until she exited the store without paying for the watch. She then placed her under arrest. Coleman said that she asked Lorraine to remove the baby's blanket from the carriage. Lorraine picked up the baby and wrapped it in the blanket. Coleman then saw in plain view a package that appeared to contain several hundred glassine envelopes of a white substance that she thought looked like cocaine. The watch, which still had the store price tags on it, a $150 man's Movado watch, was also in the carriage. It was exhibited to the jury and placed in evidence, as was the packet containing the envelopes. Guard Coleman testified that she called the city police. Officers Olszewski and Kelly appeared in a few minutes, and she turned over to them Lorraine, the baby, and the evidence.

On cross-examination Coleman admitted that she did not see who had placed the watch or the packet in the carriage. She also said that there were countless customers, male and female, entering and leaving the store at the time Lorraine exited with the baby carriage. Yes, it was possible that one of them could have stuffed the packet and the watch in the baby carriage before she began to watch Lorraine. Anything was possible, she said with a shrug. Several jurors smiled.

The police officers identified the defendant and the evidence. A chemist from the crime laboratory testified that he had tested the contents of several of the glassine envelopes. All those he tested contained a high-quality cocaine. He estimated the street value at fifty thousand dollars. In his expert opinion this quantity was not for individual use but for resale. Even a heavily addicted person would not use more than three bags a day since these would be diluted before being injected or otherwise ingested. The state rested.

Lorraine took the stand. The jury watched her with rapt fascination. They stared at her as if she were some exotic, dangerous bird of prey. She returned their inquisitive looks with a blank, obsidian gaze. Would the jury buy her story that a man had placed the watch and the cocaine in the baby carriage without her knowledge or consent? I didn't think they would unless she identified him as her boyfriend and explained the circumstances of their little shopping trip. Even though I thought it was highly likely that the boyfriend was the drug dealer, there was no doubt that the drugs had been in the baby carriage with her baby. So far there was no evidence of any man involved.

Lorraine's testimony was that she had taken the baby and gone shopping. No one else was with her. She had stopped to look at some earrings when she saw a man lean over the baby carriage.

"That quick I turned back to look at the baby. Y'know how many nuts there are these days. So I pushed my baby away from him. I didn't see him put nothin' in the carriage. I ain't seen the watch or the dope until the guard pulled 'em out of the carriage," she said firmly.

"Where was the packet of cocaine when you first saw it?"

"In the carriage. It was under the blanket and the guard reached in and pulled it out like she knew it was there."

"Was it in plain view?"

"No. Not until she grabbed it." She lifted her wrist. "Look, I got a gold watch. I didn't need that one. Besides, it's a man's watch."

On cross-examination Lorraine was asked again who this mysterious man was. She claimed she didn't know him, wouldn't recognize him if she saw him again. She couldn't describe him—not his race, height, or age.

The prosecutor asked if she could think of any reason why a stranger would want to plant this evidence on her.

"Probably the guard seen him and he tried to unload the hot stuff on me."

Even though that may have been exactly what happened, it was not a very convincing story. The jury deliberated less than an hour and found her guilty on all counts.

The jury's brief acquaintance with Lorraine was over. It had done its duty and was discharged. My involvement with Lorraine was just beginning. As I did in most cases, I asked for a presentence investigation of Lorraine, including her school record, her employment, and her criminal record. She would go back to jail for another six weeks until all this material was assembled. Her lawyer would write a brief and later argue several legal issues that seemed to Lorraine to be quibbling, but the lawyer took them seriously. We were ready to adjourn when the defender made a request. Lorraine wanted permission to see her child.

"Where is the baby?" I asked.

"At my sister's apartment."

"Why didn't your sister come here to court today?"

"She ain't got no phone. I couldn't get in touch with her."

"When did you last see your baby?"

"When I was arrested."

"If you can locate your sister and tell her to bring the child to the courtroom, I'll arrange to have you brought down from the jail so you can see the baby for a little while."

"Thank you, Your Honor," she muttered softly. Then the sheriff came with the handcuffs and she was taken away.

The jail is located a long distance from the courthouse. The female prison to which I sentenced Lorraine is several hundred miles from her sister's home. Lorraine had not seen her child for seven months. If I didn't arrange a visit, she probably would not see the child for three years. The men's prison is within easy commuting distance of the courthouse. There is good public transportation.

Lorraine's life reads like a soap opera or a sociological study of lives of ghetto children. The facts are as true in the objective details as official records are. The reality of her days is more difficult to reconstruct. What is life like for a little girl in a high-rise housing project where danger lurks in every corridor and even in her own home? What is a home where the family never has a meal together but simple wolfs down food standing by the refrigerator? And what is school when the class-room is filled with thirty noisy kids who slap and kick and knife one another when the teacher is not looking? How can a child study in an apartment where no one reads and the TV set blares all day and all night? The violence in the apartment building is more terrible than that on the TV. It is a place where women carry carving knives in their pocketbooks as routinely as upper-class women carry handkerchiefs.

Before imposing sentence, a judge is supposed to have reliable information about the defendant, to determine what is in that person's best interests and what is necessary to protect society and promote the rule of law. Of course, these goals are usually mutually exclusive. Society will feel safer if all law violators are locked in prison for long periods of time. The defendants will probably be better off if they are freed. And that amorphous American deity the rule of law may be propitiated by some innovative penalty like requiring the defendant to help the homeless. But first the judge must at least try to get to know the defendant.

Lorraine was born in the city public hospital to a teenage unwed mother, father unknown. Her mother never completed eighth grade. According to the hospital records, she was a puny, failure-to-thrive baby. Three or four times she was rushed to the hospital and revived. At the age of two she had second-degree burns over her body—an upset teakettle, the mother reported. At five she was enrolled in kindergarten. The school records report attendance, grades, and health. Until she dropped out of school at age fifteen, Lorraine's attendance was apparently splendid. Year after year she missed only two or three days of school. These absences were usually explained by the phrase "baby-sitting younger sister." In first grade she was reading at a third-grade level. In fifth grade she was skipped a year. Her grades continued to be excellent. By seventh grade she must have blossomed into the handsome person I saw. She was already five feet five inches and weighed 115 pounds. She had the lead in the school play, I wished that the school records included photographs. The unknown, never-mentioned father must have been tall and fairly light-skinned. Lorraine's mother, who came to court for the sentencing, was short, dark, and kinky-haired. She told me, "I done my best with that girl. Guess she's just no good."

The court records cast considerable doubt on the mother's view. Lorraine was arrested at age fifteen as a runaway. She told the court personnel that she ran away because her mother's boyfriend molested her. At the juvenile court hearing both the mother and the boyfriend denied the charge. The mother declared that Lorraine was incorrigible. Despite her remarkably good school record, the court sent her to a home for "wayward girls," for six months. There is no evidence that she ever returned to school. There were then, as there are today, compulsory school attendance laws. But apparently the authorities made no effort to reenroll her in school. Where she lived and what she did in the long days and nights from her fifteenth year until she was twenty-two must be pieced together from brief notations.

When Lorraine was eighteen, she appeared in juvenile court as a witness for her younger sister, Doreen, who was accused of shoplifting—stealing a blouse priced at $4.95. Doreen was released to the custody of Lorraine, whose employment was listed as "waitress" at the Black Cat. This was a notorious bar that even in those days was known as a topless establishment. It was shut down as often as it was open. Evidently the court personnel did not recognize the name of the place. The address given by Lorraine was an expensive apartment a good distance geographically and socially from the project in which she had grown up.

Lorraine had probably done what most smart good-looking girls in her position strive to do: She had found a protector, a man who set her up in a nice apartment, got her a job, and kept the other men away. She had the same address for several years, indicating that this was a stable relationship. She told me later that Rocko, her then boyfriend, was murdered by a rival gang. She wisely left town for a year or two. The car and jewelry Rocko had given her were soon sold. She was afraid to sell the drugs he had hidden with her, so she just flushed thousands of dollars' worth down the toilet. Within a year she was back on the street.

There were three arrests for prostitution, two convictions. Each time she had a different address. Two years before this crime she had been arrested in a big drug bust. Her address then was in a good neighborhood. She had evidently found another protector. These charges were dismissed because the drugs were discovered in the common entryway of the building. The well-known lawyer who represented both Lorraine and her friend, a wealthy underworld figure, successfully argued that the entryway was accessible to many people and that there could be no proof beyond a reasonable doubt that the drugs belonged to Lorraine, her boyfriend, or anyone else.

Birth records for her daughter, Candice, name this drug dealer as the father. Since listing her employment as waitress at the Black Cat, Lorraine had had no legal employment and no visible means of support. She differed from countless other single mothers in that she had never been on welfare.

Lorraine told me that her earliest memories were of the welfare workers coming to her mother's apartment in the projects, snooping around, looking for a man in the house. She recalled her mother being berated for having a dirty apartment, junk food, too many babies. Lorraine wanted no part of the welfare system.

She was bitter about this conviction, unfairly blaming the young public defender. "I shoulda had a real lawyer, not a PD."*

Her boyfriend had failed to leave her any money when he rushed out of the department store, leaving her with the baby, the stolen watch, and the cocaine.

The defender valiantly argued that the cocaine and watch were not "in plain view," that the guard searched the baby carriage without a warrant, and that while there might be grounds to seize the watch, the evidence as to the cocaine must be suppressed. The testimony of the two security guards was that Lorraine had picked up the baby and the blanket, thus exposing the cocaine to their view.

The plain-view cases are always difficult. What sensible felon would expose evidence of contraband to the police? Nonetheless, in case after case police testify that as they approached, defendants removed packs of cigarettes from their pockets and dropped them on the pavement. The police retrieved the cigarette packages, which were found to contain cocaine or heroin or angel dust. Time and again the policeman's testimony is found to be credible because "he has no motive to lie."

In this case the guard's story was not so preposterous because Lorraine herself maintained that she did not know the cocaine was in the carriage. It was not unreasonable to believe that she picked up the baby and inadvertently exposed the illegal contraband. There was no arguable ground on which to set aside the conviction. Unless there is insufficient evidence to sustain the jury's verdict, it must be upheld.

I was faced with the unpleasant duty of imposing sentence on this twenty-eight-year-old woman who had been denied all the rights of an American childhood: a decent home, freedom from abuse, a public school education until the age of seventeen, and a fair hearing in juvenile court. She had no skills, no opportunity for lawful employment, and no security from violence.

In eighteenth-century British criminal law there was a strong presumption that when a woman committed a crime, she did so at the direction of her husband or some other man and that therefore, she was

---

*This is a common complaint of poor defendants. In this case it is unlikely that any lawyer could have obtained an acquittal unless Lorraine was willing to implicate her boyfriend. Perhaps more experienced counsel could have persuaded her to do so, but the public defender didn't have the opportunity to go over the case with her carefully before the trial.

not so culpable as he. In Lorraine's case, I was reasonably certain that the boyfriend had placed the cocaine in the carriage. But under American law a female accused of crime is fully responsible for her own misconduct. She gets no presumptions that her will was overborne or that she acted under coercion.

Since Lorraine had two prior convictions for prostitution, she was supposed to be considered a recidivist and subject to a mandatory sentence of five years' total confinement in prison. Because the vast majority of all offenders are males, the reasoning, theories, and justifications for imprisonment are designed with men in mind. One in possession of a large quantity of drugs is sensibly presumed to intend to sell the drugs, not keep them for his own use. It is also presumed that the person in possession is a dealer, not simply a courier. In fact, most men caught with large quantities of drugs are dealers on one level or another. A very few women are also drug dealers. The vast majority of women convicted of possession with intent to deliver are dupes like Lorraine. These women are used as fronts by men who vanish at the first sign of the police.

A second drug offense is certainly more serious than a first and should result in a heavier penalty. In Lorraine's case her prior offenses were for prostitution, a crime that has nothing to do with drugs. Indeed, it is sometimes called a victimless crime. To treat this woman as if she were a hardened drug dealer violated common sense and fundamental fairness. I sentenced her as if she were a first offender. The sentence was reversed by the appellate court, and a five-year sentence was imposed. The fact that a sentence of imprisonment on the mother of a young child imposes a penalty on the child was also held to be irrelevant by the appellate court.[1]

Under the rubric of equality Lorraine was given the same sentence that would have been imposed on a man found guilty of a third drug offense. When she is released, her baby will not recognize her. Whatever ties they had will be broken. Who will drive five hours to bring Lorraine's baby to visit her in prison? Men in prison are regularly visited by their wives, girl friends, and children. The prison is only a short bus ride from the city. There are many work-release programs for incarcerated men so that they can earn money while serving their sentences. In the remote countryside where the women's prison is located, there are no such programs. Lorraine may get some work experience plowing the fields. But how will that fit her for city employment when she is released? In the men's prison there are many educational courses. Some prisoners even earn college credits. Many learn useful skills. Every aspect of imprisonment is different for men from that for women. Only the length of the sentence is the same.

The differing roles of men and women in the commission of crimes is revealed in case after case. But it is not a subject discussed by criminologists or feminist scholars. Except for sex crimes the criminal law on its face (or, in legal language, facially) is gender-neutral. Murder is murder whether the murderer is male or female. Larceny, arson, assault, and the entire panoply of criminal offenses apply to males and females alike. When I charged a jury in a criminal case, the elements of the crimes and the defenses as I explained them were identical regardless of the sex of the accused. And the penalties imposed on the guilty were by law the same whether the offender was a man or a woman.

The fact is, however, that crimes committed by men and women are very different even though the nomenclature is the same. More than 85 percent of crimes are committed by males. Fewer than 10 percent of the defendants who appeared before me were women. More than 50 percent of the victims of crime are females. The motivations for the crimes and the means by which they are committed are in most instances strikingly different. More than 40 percent of the women entering prison have been convicted of larceny, forgery, or fraud, compared with 15 percent of the men.[2] Women rarely commit crimes of violence against strangers. But the law takes no account of these differences between men and women in any aspect of the criminal process from arrest through trial and sentencing.

Like Lorraine, Rita and Janine were co-opted into crime by a man. They were defendants in a case of armed robbery of a bar. Both were charged with robbery and conspiracy. If they were found guilty, I was required by law to impose a mandatory five-year prison sentence on each.

In a brief pretrial conference with counsel I was told that this case was a routine armed robbery of a bar. In examining the bills of indictment, I noticed that the defendants' first names were Janine and Rita.

"Where is the man who put them up to it?" I asked.

"He was killed in an unrelated incident," the prosecutor calmly replied.

My young law clerk was astounded. Later she asked me how I knew that a man was involved. Of course, I didn't know. I had never heard of the incident or Janine or Rita. But through long experience I learned that men and women commit different types of crime. Armed robbery is a typical male offense. If a woman is involved in such a crime, it is usually at the behest of a man. Everyone in the criminal justice system accepts that elementary fact of life. But the law takes no account of it.

A coconspirator is as guilty as the ringleader if he or she knowingly participated in the crime. This is true even if one conspirator does not know that the other has a weapon. Neither Janine nor Rita had a gun. The man did, and he used it. According to the testimony of the patrons of the bar, the three went into the bar together. The two women seated themselves on stools and ordered drinks. The man stood near the door, drew his gun, and announced that this was a holdup. He ordered the bartender to empty the cash register and place the contents on the counter. The bartender did so and pushed a silent alarm button on the floor. The patrons were ordered to place their wallets, watches, and jewelry on the bar. As the women picked up the loot, the police rushed in. The man fired his gun and escaped. The women who were left holding the evidence were arrested. Rita was the girl friend of the man and the mother of his children. Janine was her sister, who lived with them.

In case after case I saw women who had been used, and often abused, by their husbands or boyfriends in the commission of crimes. Lovida was a prostitute who supported her pimp, Shorty. She was young, pretty, and soft-spoken. He was a bald, stocky middle-aged man whose weapon of choice was a sawed-off billiard cue. He never hesitated to use his powerful fists if the cue was not handy. He was on trial before me for aggravated assault against another of his prostitutes, whom he suspected of holding out money. The eyewitness was her "john," who was so horrified by the attack that he summoned the police.

I pronounced the verdict of guilty and set bail at fifty thousand dollars. Under the usual practice, cash bail of 10 percent is sufficient. When Lovida, who was sitting in the front row, opened her purse and began counting out the money, I announced that I wanted the entire amount of bail in cash. Shorty turned around and struck Lovida so hard that she was knocked off her seat before the astonished sheriffs could subdue him.

Prostitution, shoplifting, and welfare fraud were the most common female crimes before the spread of crack. Women addicts steal, rob, and commit violent assaults to obtain crack. Unless women are drug addicts, they rarely commit violent crimes against strangers, and they seldom engage in drug dealing except at the behest of a man friend.

Carol was also a prostitute. She appeared before me because she was the courier for her boyfriend, a drug pusher. He was tried, convicted, and sentenced to prison by another judge. I sentenced her to probation for three years. She had two small children. This was her first drug offense. I did not want to subject the children to the uncertainties of foster care. As a condition of probation I required Carol to get a job. Although she was a high school graduate, she had never had any lawful employment. She had been supported by a series of men. I do not know whether Carol was an abused child or whether she had a good, loving family. Nor do I know whether her boyfriend, the drug pusher, was a man she loved, a pimp, or a bully. I do know that she exhibited concern for her two young daughters. Faced with the choice of work or prison, Carol opted to work. With the help of the probation department, she found a job in a factory. She arranged for a neighbor to care for the children while she was at work. The first five monthly reports I received were satisfactory.

Then one day, while I was on the bench, I received a message from a court officer that Carol wanted to see me. She said it was "a matter of life and death." I sent word that she should wait and I would see her as soon as possible. When we took a brief recess in the trial over which I was presiding, Carol came to the robing room. At first I did not recognize her. In court she had been wearing high-fashion clothes, spike-heeled shoes, and lots of makeup. Now she was dressed in a simple skirt and blouse, no eyeshadow, very light makeup. Her hair was no longer teased and dyed. She looked much younger and prettier, even though she was obviously distraught.

She told her story in a rush and somewhat incoherently. Her male probation officer at first had been very nice and helpful. He was a middle-aged married man. She looked on him as a father figure. Then he wanted to have sex with her.

"I didn't like it," she said. "But it was no big deal. He would pick me up after work a couple times a week. I would go with him for maybe a half hour, and then he would drive me home. But lately he's demanding all kinds of kinky sex. Last time there were three men. If I don't do what he wants, he says, he'll give me an unfavorable report. I just can't take it anymore. Being on the street is better than this. If I have to see him again, I'll kill myself."

"Have you told anyone else about this?" I asked.

"Who could I tell?" she replied.

And if you did, who would believe you? I thought. It would be the word of a convicted felon against that of a corrections officer. It would be folly for her to bring such a charge. The man might, of course, be innocent. His career and his family life could be ruined. There would be no way that a hearing officer, a judge, or a jury could ever really ascertain the truth. I was reminded of Shakespeare's Isabella in *Measure for Measure.* When the deputy offers to pardon Isabella's brother if she will have intercourse with him, she refuses, declaring, ". . . with an out-stretched throat I'll tell the world aloud/What man thou art." To which the deputy replies, "Who will believe thee, Isabel?"

The only practical remedy I could devise was to permit Carol to report to her probation officer by mail. I notified him of my changed order, explaining that according to his reports, she was doing well and that he was, as I knew, overworked and could better spend his time on more difficult probationers. Carol completed her three years' probation without further incident.

Juries are admonished by lawyers and judges not to leave their common sense outside when they go into the jury room to deliberate. They are told to bring to their difficult task all the experiences of their collective lifetimes in deciding the questions of credibility of the witnesses and the ultimate issue of guilt or innocence.

In imposing sentence, judges also try to bring to that painfully sensitive duty their common sense. They know that despite gender-neutral sentencing laws, sentences have a different impact on women offenders, from that on men. Although male probationers are sometimes subject to extortion by their probation officers, few are sexually abused by them, whereas many women are. Women prisoners are also sexually abused by male prison guards. Mistreatment of offenders, whether males or females, by correction officers is difficult to control. Some individuals when given power over vulnerable people will abuse that power. It is virtually impossible for supervisors to monitor these one-on-one contacts.

Until the 1970s and the demand for elimination of discrimination against women in employment in the corrections system, women probation officers supervised female probationers and women guards staffed female prisons. But the Supreme Court in the name of equality held that height and weight requirements for guards in prisons were unconstitutional.[3] Consequently, women can now serve as guards in male prisons, and conversely, men serve as guards in female prisons. Probation officers are also assigned on a gender-neutral basis.

Most judges recognize that mothers are the primary caretakers of their young children. If a mother is sentenced to prison, in most cases her children will be turned over to the state and placed in a series of foster homes. Children lose contact with their mothers. Brothers and sisters are separated. Families are permanently destroyed. When a father goes to prison, his children will be brought to visit him by their mother. She will hold the family together.

Two factors have caused a sudden surge in the number of women in jails and prisons: the widespread use of drugs and the adoption of gender-neutral sentencing guidelines and mandatory sentencing laws. Public outrage over the plague of drugs and its terrible effects on the unborn and the physical abuse drug-addicted parents inflict on their children has caused many courts to sentence women convicted of drug charges to prison without considering the terrible personal and social costs or optional penalties. Most of the women convicted of possession of drugs or possession with intent to deliver are not big pushers engaged in the lucrative drug trade. Like Lorraine, they are caught up in drugs through their boyfriends. The desire to punish rather than treat these women has led to bizarre results. Of the women in custody, 75 percent are mothers of young children. In the first six months of 1989 the male prison population increased by 7 percent, and the female population by 13 percent. This unfortunate trend will undoubtedly continue because gender-neutral laws prohibit judges from taking into account the special needs of women and children when imposing sentence.

Although there is legal protection for the fetuses of drug-addicted pregnant women, the law has done little to provide care for their children. In 1989, for example, under a statute designed to punish drug dealers, a woman was convicted of delivering a controlled substance to her newborn baby through the umbilical cord. Pregnant women have also been convicted of abuse of a fetus, a crime not specifically designated by statute and unknown to the common law.[4]

Few judges who are aware of prison medical services would send a pregnant woman to prison unless she was found guilty of a truly heinous crime or a prison sentence was mandated by law. The problems of caring for infants who are born in prison are complex. All solutions to date are unsatisfactory. Should the child be taken from the mother at birth? Some say that this practice prevents the necessary bonding between mother and infant essential to proper emotional stability. If the newborn is left with the mother, at what age should the child be removed? And what emotional scars will this separation leave on the child and the mother? America is certainly not going back to the Dickensian era, when entire families were incarcerated to remain with the malefactor or debtor who was imprisoned.

American jails and prisons were established and are operated on plans designed for male inmates because the vast majority of inmates are men. Accordingly few have appropriate facilities for prenatal care, childbirth, and infants. The problem gets little attention because the numbers involved are comparatively small. Since women inmates are unlikely to engage in violent riots and prison breaks, their needs are not given a high priority. With the increasing number of women in prison caused not only by a more violent society, teenage pregnancies, and drugs but also by changes in the law mandating prison sentences for certain crimes and more stringent guidelines for sentencing, more babies will be born in America's jails and prisons.

The impetus for these new sentencing laws was twofold: frustration with the inability to control crime and a belief in equality. A felon's sentence depended, in many instances, on the chance assignment of cases. Each judge has his or her philosophy of penology. Some judges are notoriously believed to be hanging judges. Others are considered bleeding hearts. A New York judge was popularly known as Turn 'Em Loose Bruce. Undoubtedly there were disparities in sentencing. But many of these gross inequities could have been corrected by the appellate courts under less stringent standards for taking appeals. The disparities in sentencing probably have been exaggerated. Gross statistics do reveal differences in the length of prison sentences imposed by different judges. In my court we had the usual spectrum of judges, ranging from those who believed strongly in punitive sentences to those who believed with equal firmness in rehabilitation. But a careful analysis not merely of the length of sentences imposed but also of the nature of the crimes for which these felons were sentenced revealed an extraordinary consensus. Homicides, on the whole, were given long prison sentences, car thefts relatively light sentences, with appropriate penalties for crimes in the middle range.

In the belief that the same sentences for crimes with the same nomenclature ensure equal justice regardless of the personal characteristics of the offender and the circumstances under which the offense was committed, the legislatures of most states and the Congress have established strict guidelines for the imposition of sentence.[5] A judge must consider only a limited number of factors relating to the crime—was a weapon used, the location of the crime, the amount of property taken, and the like—and a limited number of factors relating to the offender. These include the prior criminal record of the offender but not sex.*

In the past few decades the law has been substantially reformed with respect to sex offenses such as rape and spousal abuse.[6] Judges and juries are more likely to accept a plea of self-defense when a woman kills an abusive spouse or lover. But the criminal law with respect to other

---

*Federal judge Frederic N. Smalkin of Maryland refused to follow the guidelines of eight to ten-year prison terms in sentencing two young mothers for drug offenses, stating that the sentencing commission "did not adequately take into account the family situation of mothers who are the sole custodians of their small children" (*New York Times,* March 19, 1989, p. 23). Few judges have followed his example.

offenses has not been reexamined to determine if it impacts with equal severity on men and women. The women I have seen in criminal court cause me to question the assumption that gender-neutral criminal laws do provide equal protection for women.

I do not suggest that all women offenders are naive innocents who have been railroaded to prison by a brutal sexist system. In each case tried before me the woman was charged with an offense because there was probable cause to believe that she was guilty. Like accused men, indigent women were provided free legal counsel. Each woman who pled guilty did so only after a legally sufficient colloquy informing her of the charges, the elements of the crimes, the maximum penalties that could be imposed, and her right to a trial either with or without a jury. These women defendants were represented by counsel as adequate as those provided for male defendants. The juries were fairly selected and included approximately half women; sometimes they were predominantly female. I, the presiding judge, was certainly not hostile to women. Many of the prosecutors were women. There was no taint of sexism in the trials. I am as certain as one can ever be in these matters that the women who were convicted were, in fact, guilty of the offenses with which they were charged. Like men defendants, they were informed of their right to appeal. The entire criminal process was gender-neutral. But in every phase of these prosecutions from arrest through imprisonment the law impacted more harshly on women offenders than on men.

4

Civil Litigation and Gender

Marriage is the only actual bondage known to our law.
There remain no legal slaves, except the mistress of every house.

—JOHN STUART MILL

IN MOST CIVIL ACTIONS the plaintiff is seeking money damages. A case may arise out of an accident, a contract claim, or some other dispute over property. In these matters the law is gender-neutral on its face. The decisions in many civil cases, however, are biased against women claimants on the basis of old common law doctrines and also under recent doctrines mandating equal treatment of the sexes. Such routine, uncelebrated cases are among those that I found denied women equal protection of the laws.

Police Officer Patty Parsons had been a plaintiff in a famous case establishing women's rights to equal treatment under the Constitution. That case commanded a great deal of attention. She had the assistance of several women's law projects. Her victory was hailed as a milestone achievement in women's quest for equal rights. But she learned, as so many women have, that great victories in theory often defeat women in the actual day-to-day activities of life.

When I saw Patty Parsons, her famous case had already been decided.[1] She was a police officer assigned to general patrol duties. By a decision of the court, based on the Constitution, she was entitled to the same assignments of duty as any other police officer. Women were not to be restricted to office tasks or the juvenile division of the police force, as had been the practice for decades.

Police Officer Patty Parsons was a witness in an ordinary armed robbery case tried before me. She was patrolling on foot a main street in a well-known high crime area at 4:00 A.M. She was alone. She saw the defendant, Spike Brown, who was twenty-two years old, was six feet tall, and weighed two hundred pounds, approach an elderly man, pull a knife, and take the victim's wallet and wristwatch. Officer Parsons blew her whistle, drew her service revolver, and ordered the defendant to put up his hands. "You're under arrest," she yelled. The defendant whirled around, knocked her to the ground, and grabbed her gun.

A passing motorist, who saw and heard what was happening, drove his car onto the sidewalk, pinning the defendant against the wall. The defendant fired several shots with Officer Parsons's gun, and the motorist backed off. Meanwhile, some unknown person called the police. In less than a minute a squad car with two male police officers drove up, surrounded the defendant, and handcuffed him.

It was almost nine months after the incident that I heard the criminal case against Brown. Patty Parsons, who was called as a prosecution witness, came to court in a wheelchair. Two of her vertebrae had been fractured and her spinal cord damaged when she was knocked down. Her prognosis was not good. Patty retired from the police force on medical disability.

After the testimony was completed, I asked her what plans she had for her future.

"I'd like to be a schoolteacher," she said. "I'm taking courses at home. That's a more suitable job for a person like me."

"What do you mean, more suitable?"

"I'm five feet four inches tall. I never weighed more than a hundred twenty pounds in my life. What chance did I have against a six-foot two-hundred-pound man wielding a knife? You know I asked the police sergeant to assign me a partner. But all the men had seniority, so they got to ride two in a patrol car and we few women walked our beats alone."

"Why did you join the force?"

"I was a feisty kid two years out of parochial school. I got caught up in the women's rights movement. Why not be a police officer? If I could pass the test, I had a right to the job. It paid much better than the secretarial job I had. Besides, I thought it would be challenging and exciting working in a man's world. Frankly I was an experienced secretary, and I thought they'd give me office work in police headquarters. You've been there, haven't you?"

"Yes. Many times."

"You see all those guys sitting at typewriters, doing their reports hunt and peck with two fingers. It takes them hours. A good secretary could save the city so much money and keep the patrolmen out on the beat instead of doing paper work. Well, they didn't want me on the force. But I passed the test number one, and I threatened to sue if they didn't hire me. As you know, I did sue and I won. I was hired. But I got the meanest, most dangerous assignments. I was planning to quit just before I was injured. But I didn't want to leave while I was still a probationer. When I think about it, what did I prove? That a woman can be injured the same as a man?

"In the old days they used to assign the women officers to the juvenile squad. They were usually paid less, but the kids were smaller and easier to control than the adult criminals. But someone decided that we were being discriminated against, that women had to have the same assignments as men. It was my bad luck to come along just then and become a test case."

One of the male arresting officers who testified at the criminal trial remarked, "Brown is a lucky bastard. Any man on the force would have shot first and talked later."

Patty Parsons told me that she did not think she was at fault in failing to shoot Brown. "He had his back to me," she said. "He didn't have a gun. I was a police officer, but not a killer.

"The other day I saw an old documentary about the sixties and the civil rights movement," she said. "When I was watching those little black girls with their hair done up in ribbons being jeered at by all those red-faced men, I wondered what those kids thought. They didn't ask to be test cases. Neither did I. I guess it just happened. But I don't want any more men's jobs carrying guns or mining coal or working as a stevedore. I haven't sorted out my thoughts yet. I'm still struggling with these concepts.

"When I protested that I didn't want that assignment walking the beat alone in that dangerous neighborhood, the sergeant said, 'Officer Parsons, you wanted equal rights. You've got equal rights.' But I'm not sure that I did."

Many women who on principles of equality and for patriotic reasons have entered the armed forces, like Patty, have learned the hard way that some tasks requiring great physical strength and brutal acts unfairly jeopardize their health and safety.[2] They are painfully questioning whether they have in fact received equal rights.

Mary Lou Higgins knew that she had been denied her equal rights because she was a woman. She fought her case through the courts without help from any organizations. She lost. After the appellate court denied her appeal, she came to see me because I had known her mother when I was a practicing lawyer. I had represented the hospital where she was employed. In Mary Lou's case, as in so many others, the law had been faithfully adhered to, but a woman was hurt.

Mary Lou was known in the small coal-mining town of Homegate* as Little Mary Lou. Her mother was Big Mary Lou, the rotund, cheerful nurse who saw the entire community through their medical problems. People knew that they were really sick when the doctor said, "We'd better call in Mary Lou."

From earliest childhood, Little Mary Lou had planned to be a nurse like her mother. When Mary Lou was graduated from high school, she applied to the school of nursing in Philadelphia that her mother had attended.

When Big Mary Lou had gone to nursing school, it was one of the few professions that offered free education for women. Young women students did not pay tuition. They were given room, board, uniforms, and a small stipend in return for the work they did at the hospital. For a young girl with no money, no special talents, and average scholastic ability, this was the only means of becoming a professional. For farm girls, nursing school offered a way of coming to the city and earning a respectable living. For city girls, it was an opportunity to rise above the low-status, low-paying job as a factory worker or a salesgirl. For a girl from the mining country, nursing school was one of the few ways of escaping the hard, brutal life of a coal miner's wife.

After several years in the big city Mary Lou was "capped," the graduation ceremony at which she was awarded the right to wear her white nurse's cap. The starched, ruffled scrap of cloth placed on her auburn curls signified that she was a professional, a registered nurse. From that day forward Big Mary Lou knew that wherever she went she could earn a living, support herself and her daughter.

Although she returned to her hometown, she had left the world of jobs in the local five-and-dime, the two textile factories, and the local bar. Her high school classmates who were not pregnant were working at these jobs, earning only minimum wages with little hope of advancement. Most of the girls were already married and worn down by several pregnancies and a constant round of laundry, diapers, and scrubbing floors in a town where coal dust continually seeped through closed windows and doors. Mary Lou, however, was a professional. She

*This is a fictional name but a real community.

earned a good livelihood. And she had status in the community. She was a respected person.

When Little Mary Lou was graduated from high school, conditions in Homegate had not changed very much. There was still little opportunity for a girl in that town unless she was the daughter of one of the few wealthy families. She knew that her only hope of advancement was to get a professional education like her mother's. She was determined to go to nursing school.

In Homegate very few middle-aged men had had jobs since Big Mary Lou was a child. These defeated men sat on the porches of houses with peeling paint or hung out at the corner bar nursing a beer for several hours. The kids left town as soon as they could. Most of the boys went into the military service. The girls simply disappeared into the big cities. Sometimes a girl would come home with a baby but no husband. If she was lucky, she would get a job at minimum wages in the local five-and-dime just as the women of her mother's generation had done.

Although life in Homegate remained the same, the nursing profession had drastically changed. Nursing school was no longer free. Nurses had insisted on upgrading the profession. Now a registered nurse was supposed to have a bachelor's degree from the university. Little Mary Lou was a conscientious girl like her mother, but not a brilliant student. Her college board scores were only mediocre. She was not eligible for a scholarship. The student loan program had been cut. Big Mary Lou could not pay three or four thousand dollars, which was the cost of tuition and living expenses in the cheapest college they could find. Big Mary Lou also had to help support her younger children. Overtime for her husband had been cut. The factory where he was an assistant manager might close any day. But Big Mary Lou was determined that her daughter would become a nurse. She went to her old nursing school, seeking help. The registrar told her that there was one scholarship for "the daughter of a nurse." Little Mary Lou applied and was awarded full tuition and a stipend.

Then disaster struck. Little Mary Lou was notified by the attorney for the nursing school that a young man, the son of a nurse, had applied for the scholarship. Under the law it was illegal to give a preference to a female despite the provisions of the scholarship. The nursing school was almost 95 percent female in violation of federal law.[3] Because it was important for the school to increase the number of male students, that man was being awarded the scholarship. The school apologized and said perhaps student loan money might be found.

Big Mary Lou went to a meeting of the nurses' alumnae association and protested. The association consulted an attorney, who informed them that the school's interpretation of the law was correct. They consulted a women's law reform office. The attorneys there suggested that Mary Lou did not understand the importance of equal rights. "What's equal about this?" Mary Lou demanded. "The scholarship says it's for a daughter and they're giving it to a son? How many scholarships are there in all the universities in this country that are for men and not women? Nursing is our profession, and now the men want to get in on it after keeping women out of medicine for hundreds of years!"

Big Mary Lou through the help of a doctor found an elderly male lawyer who brought suit against the nursing school. A half dozen civil rights organizations filed amicus briefs on behalf of the school. No one supported Mary Lou's position. At the hearing Little Mary Lou testified that she had been graduated twentieth in her high school class of sixty, that she had participated in sports and extracurricular activities, that she had been voted the most determined girl in her class and the one most likely to succeed. She had also been active in local charities as a volunteer nurse's aide in an old-age home. Two of her teachers testified that she was an outstanding girl and would be an asset to any profession.

Her lawyer had subpoenaed the young man's high school records. At best, he was a mediocre student in the bottom third of his class. He had had several disciplinary infractions but nothing serious. He had not participated in any school or community activities. He had submitted a letter of recommendation from a family friend who wrote that he thought the discipline of nursing school would do the young man good.

The registrar for the school testified that it was important for nursing no longer to be seen as an exclusively female occupation, that it was trying to get away from the pink ghetto by having more male students. He conceded that it was difficult to get male applicants who had good records. "They all want to be doctors," he remarked plaintively. He admitted that there were very few male applicants whose records equaled Mary Lou's. He said that the school was sorry to lose Mary Lou. But what can we do? We are acting in accordance with our lawyer's advice.

The lawyer's advice was correct. In 1982, in the case of *Mississippi University for Women v. Hogan,*[4] the Supreme Court decided that a man had been denied admission to the university school of nursing. The Court held that Title IX of the Civil Rights Act must be applied free from fixed notions of roles and abilities. Justice Sandra Day O'Connor, writing for the majority, stated, "Thus if the statutory objective is to exclude or 'protect' members of one gender because they are presumed to suffer from an inherent handicap or to be innately inferior, the object itself is illegitimate." In Little Mary Lou's case her claim that this was affirmative action to compensate for historic discrimination against women was rejected although affirmative action plans for nonwhite males had been upheld in countless cases. The trial court, which was obligated to follow the Supreme Court decisions, refused to apply the test of strict scrutiny as it did for claims of racial discrimination. Accordingly allegations of gender discrimination would be dismissed if there were any reasonable grounds on which the school based its decision. The court concluded that having a student body with more males would benefit the female students and improve the school. How the profession would be improved or the public be better served by having less able and less dedicated nurses, questions raised by Mary Lou's lawyer, were never answered. Nor did the court consider the question of whether Mary Lou was being denied equal protection of the laws because a less able male student was given a preferred status over her. Since the nursing school had presented a plausible reason for its decision, the court would not interfere. The fact that Mary Lou had been denied the opportunity to follow the career of her choice was deemed to be irrelevant.

The Supreme Court has agonized over questions of affirmative action, quotas, and setasides as to nonwhites. Myriad arguments on both sides of this sensitive issues have been discussed, analyzed, and subjected to intense legal and moral arguments.[5]

The American legal system, which casts all conflicts in a bipolar adversary format, has pitted blacks against whites, women against men, the elderly against the young. Particularly in times of economic stringency a preference for one inevitably displaces another. Mary Lou was displaced by a man who admittedly was less qualified. It is such patent unfairness practiced in the name of equal opportunity that rankles many who would like to see historic wrongs redressed. Perhaps another approach that considers not merely two parties but also the public interest might offer a more satisfactory solution. In a pluralistic society institutions should reflect in some measure the general population. Certainly no person should be excluded by reason of race, gender, age, religion, or any other characteristic. But once these long-standing artificial barriers to education, employment, organizations, and communal institutions have been removed, it may be appropriate to consider whether the affirmative action or preference is in the public interest.

A court might well ask whether societal goals are advanced more by increasing the number of men in a nursing school or by admitting the most capable individuals. In some situations the need to demonstrate that an institution is in fact open to all segments of society may be more important than selecting the most able among qualified individuals. In other instances the balance may be tilted the other way. For example, athletic teams, symphony orchestras,[6] museum curators, brain surgeons, and other occupations that require great skill and training as well as that indefinable quality talent should not place affirmative action above the search for very best.

It may be that it is more important for students to be taught by members of groups that have been historically barred from such employment. Schoolchildren should see that blacks and other minorities can be teachers. Law students should also see that women can function in this traditionally male occupation. Once the barrier has been effectively broken, however, it may be that not only the students but also society in general will be better served by having the very best teachers without consideration of what should ideally be extraneous factors, such as sex, age, and ethnicity. Had a court been given the legal mandate to factor into the equation the public interest, Mary Lou might very likely have received the scholarship.

There is no obviously fair and right answer under present law. Perhaps in another generation racial and gender inequalities will have been sufficiently mitigated that preferential treatment will no longer be demanded or desired.

What offended Little Mary Lou the most was not losing the scholarship but the fact that the law ruled that her claims to equal treatment were entitled to a lesser standard of accountability than those of nonwhite males. That in itself, she declared in a letter to the editor of the local paper, was blatant discrimination.

At the suggestion of her lawyer, Mary Lou applied to a university that has a work-study program. One semester she works and saves her money, and the next semester she attends school. In this way Mary Lou will get a degree in library science. But the nursing profession lost a promising student. And Mary Lou lost her belief in the justice of law.

In many instances old legal doctrines are followed blindly with little thought to either the rights of the individuals involved or social goals. In such situations the disadvantaged woman does not realize that she has been discriminated against by the law itself. In the contest over the will of Mrs. Anspach both she and the two young women she intended to receive a portion of her estate were the victims of what I can only describe as the gender bias of the common law.

When Evelyn Anspach died at the age of eighty-six, she wanted to do something nice for her closest neighbors, John and Mary Miller and Robert Armstrong. By the time Mrs. Anspach's estate was settled, both John and Mary were dead. Her legacy had caused a rupture in the Miller family and neighborhood hostility toward Armstrong. The money was not awarded to those she intended to benefit. The decision was based on time-honored common law principles.

Mrs. Anspach was a frugal, wealthy widow who saw no reason to waste money on druggists, doctors, or lawyers. She died peacefully in bed without having seen a doctor in more than ten years. Her medicine cabinet was bare, except for a package of Band-Aids and a bottle of iodine. She had not consulted a lawyer since her husband died more than ten years before her own death. In her desk drawer was a will handwritten in her copperplate script. The provision that caused so much difficulty consisted of just sixteen words. It read: "I leave $30,000 to my friends and neighbors Robert Armstrong, John Miller and his wife Mary."

Ralph Everett, the manager of the branch bank where Mrs. Anspach kept her funds, was named executor of the will. He knew the Millers and Armstrong because they were bank customers. He considered them nice, quiet people. They didn't spend much money and kept their properties in good repair. The bank held the mortgage on the Miller house. Both John and Mary Miller had been previously married. She had two daughters from her first marriage, Jane and Margaret Wilmot. John had one son from his first marriage, John Miller, Jr. Everyone in the neighborhood, including Mrs. Anspach, knew these three young people. They frequently stayed in the Miller home. All of them spent their holidays together.

In this quiet, modest neighborhood property did not change hands often. Mrs. Anspach had lived in her house for more than fifty years. Armstrong had lived next door to her for much of that period. He had inherited the house from his parents. The Millers had moved next door to Mrs. Anspach ten years before her death. At that time all the children lived at the Miller home.

To the amazement of the neighborhood, Mrs. Anspach left an estate of $250,000. Shortly after her death Robert Armstrong sold his business for more than $100,000, a sum that also astonished the neighbors. Mary Miller had only a tiny legacy from her first husband. John Miller had an accumulation of debts.

Although Mrs. Anspach was unaware of it, Mary Miller was killed in an accident the night before Mrs. Anspach was found dead in her bed.

At the reading of the will, Mr. Everett, who was not a lawyer, suggested that because the residuary estate went to the church and there were no heirs or other legatees, the parties could save themselves a lot of trouble and receive their legacies at once if they all agreed that he distribute ten thousand dollars to each of the legatees. This simple solution was not to be. Counsel for the bank was called in. Mr. Armstrong consulted his attorney. Mr. Miller's son consulted his lawyer. And the bank advised the Wilmot girls that they should retain counsel.

On advice of his lawyer, Armstrong claimed that the thirty thousand dollars should be divided in half—fifteen thousand to him and fifteen thousand to the Millers. At first Mr. Miller argued strenuously that the money should be divided in thirds. When his son reminded him that he had executed an antenuptial agreement with Mrs. Miller providing that neither would inherit from the other and giving up all rights to her estate, he changed his mind.

The Wilmot girls were the sole heirs of their mother and were advised that they should claim her share. At this point the time of Mrs. Miller's death became critical. If Mary Miller had predeceased Mrs. Anspach, then Mrs. Miller's share would lapse. By the time these complications came to light Mrs. Anspach had been buried for several months. Mrs. Miller's car had been involved in the accident that caused her death in the afternoon, but she did not expire, according to her death certificate, until 4:36 A.M. Mrs. Anspach's body was found by her day worker about 8:30 A.M. This elderly woman said that when she touched the body, it was icy cold.

At the hearing before the register of wills, the surprise witness was Mrs. Anspach's clergyman. He testified that he had discussed the provisions of the will with her many times. Her primary beneficiary was the church. She gave him very explicit instructions as to how she wanted her money spent. Her particular interest was the education of girls and young women. She wanted the money to be used for scholarships and living expenses for young female members of the church. She also discussed her neighbors and her reasons for leaving them legacies. Mr. Armstrong was a lonely man. She thought that he was in straitened circumstances. Although he was considerably younger than she, they had spent much time together. Many evenings he came to her house. They would watch television and discuss events of the day. He often mentioned his desire to marry and have a family. He had been very good to her, often driving her to stores and on other errands. She thought a small amount of extra money might enable him to pay for dates and find a lady friend.

Mary Miller was her closest friend. She knew that John was somewhat of a wastrel and that Mary had almost no money of her own. She worried about Mary's daughters, both of whom were working their way through college. Mrs. Anspach considered leaving money outright to the girls but decided that it would be preferable to let Mary give the girls what she thought they needed from time to time. Mrs. Anspach knew that John Miller, Jr., was a wealthy and successful young man who did not need her money. She hoped that John, Sr., would use his bequest to pay off the mortgage on the house and other debts, but she felt that it would be presumptuous of her to tell him what to do with the money. The register divided the money in three parts. With not too much evidence, he concluded that Mrs. Anspach had predeceased Mary and, therefore, that her ten thousand dollars was to go in equal shares to her daughters. Mr. Miller and Mr. Armstrong would each receive ten thousand dollars. John Miller, Jr., would receive nothing.

This tangled tale wound its way slowly through the courts at considerable expense to all involved. During the three years following the death of Mrs. Anspach a trial judge, three intermediate appellate court judges, and a panel of seven appellate court judges deliberated over these sixteen words of Mrs. Anspach's will. Five lawyers filed briefs and presented oral argument.

The appellate court reached a unanimous decision. It struck all the testimony of the clergyman as to Mrs. Anspach's intent because it found that there was no ambiguity in the will. The phrase "to John and his wife Mary" meant not two individuals but one couple. Under English common law, a married couple was one person, and that one person was the husband. Armstrong received fifteen thousand dollars, and John Miller received fifteen thousand dollars. The court did not know that when its decision was issued, John, Sr., was deceased. His son was his sole heir. Thus the fifteen thousand dollars went to the son. The court did not decide whether Mary survived or predeceased Mrs. Anspach because that was irrelevant in its view of the law. All that the Wilmot girls, who needed money and were supposed to benefit from the legacy, received was a substantial bill from their lawyer.

This decision was reached under estate law that is presumably gender-neutral. Statutes that prohibit a woman from serving as an executrix and otherwise preferring males over females have been stricken in landmark cases as unconstitutionally denying women equal protection of the laws. The will of Mrs. Anspach occasioned no comment from any legal scholars. It was but one of many uncelebrated cases in which the ancient biases of the common law continue unchallenged in American jurisprudence.

5

Gender and Equal Protection of the Laws

Why can't a woman be like a man?

—ALAN JAY LERNER

VIRGINIA WOOLF in *Three Guineas* posed a question pointedly accusing female judges. It is a charge I find difficult to defend. Woolf wrote that she was asked to contribute a guinea each to three worthy causes: peace, cultural advancement, and the education of women. Observing that the persons who would administer the funds for the first two causes were the same men of property who had brought Europe to the brink of disaster in World War I, she refused to contribute. To the young woman who requested funds for the education of women, she replied, "If we encourage the daughters to enter the professions without making any conditions as to the way in which the professions are to be practiced shall we not be doing our best to stereotype the old tune which human nature is now grinding out with such disastrous unanimity? . . . Think, one of these days you may wear a judge's wig on your head [an unthinkable thought in Britain in the 1930s] . . . . . . where is it leading us, the procession of educated men?"[1]

Unfortunately in the day-to-day operations of the courts as the case histories described in the preceding chapters demonstrate, women judges, like their male colleagues, continue to grind out the same old tune with the same disastrous results. We do so because judges are bound by their oaths of office to uphold the laws and the Constitution as interpreted by the decisions of the appellate courts.

American judges are now faced not only with common law precedents but also with a multitude of statutes enacted in the past quarter century designed to obtain equal treatment for minorities and women. Either by their terms or by the decisions of the appellate courts these statutes ignore both the biological and societal differences between the lives of men and women. As a result, to paraphrase Supreme Court Justice Abe Fortas's remark that children receive the worst of both worlds,[2] American women in 1990 receive the worst of both legal worlds. They are still subject to common law doctrines denying them equal jural personhood, and also, under the rubric of equality, they are denied common law protections and presumptions under the fallacious assumption that identical treatment of men and women despite their differences will provide equal protection of the laws.

To understand the present unsatisfactory legal status of women in the day-to-day operations of the courts, it is necessary to take a very brief backward glance at the law and the lives of women in earlier times. The lineage of the common law reaches back to the Bible. During these millennia society was patriarchal, and the role of women subservient. Their rights were severely limited; they had few protections or remedies.

The passage in Genesis attributing the fall of man to woman and God's statement to Eve that "thy husband . . . shall rule over thee" has been the predicate for much of the law that determines the rights of women today. Although feminist biblical scholars have promulgated different interpretations of these famous lines, they have been taken rather literally by judges and legal authorities for centuries.[3] The *Corpus Juri Canonici* specifically requires a husband to chastise his wife, both verbally and physically. In the Middle Ages, according to *Customs of Beauvoisis,* a husband may beat his wife, but only reasonably. In England, although women held rank as great ladies, none was ever summoned to Parliament as a peeress. A wife had only such testamentary power as her husband was pleased to allow her. Under the common law of England the word of a woman could not be admitted in proof in the court of law because of her "frailty." Sir Edward Coke's famous *Commentary upon Littleton* (1764), a text for British and American lawyers for centuries, states that "in some cases women are by law wholly excluded to bear testimony. . . ."

In medieval times the lady of the manor was doctor, lawyer, teacher, and chief executive officer of the self-contained world of a feudal estate. While the lord was fighting battles, intriguing at the royal court, hunting, and engaging in masculine pleasures, his wife was in charge of the farm, the production of goods, weaving and spinning, and the care of a multitude of peasants and tradespeople. She was also an important preserver of intellectual life. Many noblewomen were learned in the classics and sciences.[4]

Although women were herbalists and doctors among the people, they were not permitted to become physicians. In 1335 the London guild of bracemakers prohibited women other than wives and daughters of members from working in the trade. One must assume that the profits of those women's labors accrued to the male members of the guild.

In Sir Thomas More's *Utopia,* published in the early sixteenth century, children and wives are bracketed together in their duties of obedience to the husband/father and his right to chastise them.

From the classical period until almost modern times in the Western world women were largely excluded from participation in the affairs of public life and were confined to activities in the home. They had little choice in the selection of spouses and no rights with respect to their children.

The Industrial Revolution took workingwomen out of their homes to toil in factories and mines. But their labor, although essential to the work force, did not improve their legal status.

In colonial America women were subject to British law. While men were fighting the Indians, fighting the British, sailing the high seas in search of whales and booty, and debating the political future of the nation to be born, women were carrying on the day-to-day activities necessary to maintain a functioning society. They raised the children, worked the farms, operated the small workshops and markets. Like contemporary women in West Africa, colonial American women were responsible for much of the local commerce. They were midwives and provided much of the medical care on farms and southern plantations. They were also active in the local lawcourts as attorneys in fact representing themselves and their absent husbands.[5] Until professionalism, educational qualifications, and licensure became widespread in the nineteenth century, women practiced these professions without legal restrictions. An unmarried woman, whether spinster or widow, had the legal status of a feme sole trader and could engage in commerce in her own name. A married woman, known as a feme covert, under the common law had no jural identity. A married couple was legally one person, and that person was the husband.

In the nineteenth century women began to demand juridical rights, the right to vote, the right to serve on juries, and the right to practice law. These demands were denied by American male judges, who based their decisions on the precedents of British common law. When Belva Ann Lockwood attempted to gain admission to practice law in the United States Court of Claims in 1874, the Supreme Court of the District of Columbia denied her petition, declaring, "As this court knows no English precedent for the admission of women to the bar, it declines to admit."[6] Nonetheless, Mrs. Lockwood successfully practiced law for many years without being admitted to the bar. Significantly in the court's decision there was no reference to the equal protection clause of the Fourteenth Amendment.

The first national movement for women's rights in America, particularly for suffrage, was sparked in the mid-nineteenth century by Susan B. Anthony and Elizabeth Cady Stanton. Although northern women activists were strong supporters of abolition, they were unable to obtain the vote after the Civil War. During World War I women's activities as nurses, factory workers, and white-collar employees brought recognition of the fact that women were productive and competent members of society. Finally, at the end of the war, they obtained the right to vote by adoption of the Nineteenth Amendment to the Constitution. Women did not obtain the right to serve on juries until 1964.* The right of suffrage did not materially improve the educational, economic, or familial status of women.

Both male and female critics of the women's movement often have a nostalgically false rosy view of the past. In fact, in the first half of the twentieth century the lives of many Americans, both men and women, consisted of long hours of toil with few pleasures and compensations.

Before the New Deal almost a third of American farms were without electricity. Farmers' wives had to draw water from wells, wash clothes by hand in large pots over open fires, and work in the fields. Many had only rare contacts with the communities outside their own farms. Poor urban women worked in factories, in offices, and as domestics without union benefits, job security, or pensions. Most women, including public schoolteachers, were paid less than men who held the same positions. Job advancement for women was the exception.[7]

Married women were often denied employment on the ground that men as the family breadwinners were entitled to job preferences even though many women were the sole support of their children and aged parents. Women had difficulty obtaining mortgages, bank credit, charge accounts, and a new device—the credit card. Qualified women were denied admission to universities and professional schools. They

*By statutes in many states women were earlier granted the right to serve on juries.

were denied academic advancement in all but women's colleges, and often there also. The political parties relegated females to women's committees that had no policy-making powers. Few women held either elective or appointive public offices.

Sexual oppression existed, as it had for millennia. Married women in all strata of life were subject to economic, social, and often physical abuse by their husbands without legal recourse or remedy. Single women lived on the fringes of society. Like Jane Austen, many were unpaid servants for their parents and married siblings. As the novels of Edith Wharton and Henry James poignantly depict, the only attainable goal of a middle- or upper-class young woman was to obtain a husband, preferably one with adequate financial resources. Economic independence was not possible for most women, single or married. As Virginia Woolf bitterly observed, girls were usually denied the formal educational opportunities lavished on their brothers. They were also sexually abused with impunity by male relatives. Such abuse occurred in the rarefied atmosphere of Bloomsbury as well as the slums of teeming cities, hardscrabble farms, and lush plantations. An Appalachian adage defines a virgin as a girl who can run faster than her father. Sexual harassment in school, the home, the workplace, and public areas was a fact of life. There was no one to whom a female could complain and no avenue of legal redress.

In the marital relationship a wife was required to accept the decisions of her husband as to the place of the family home and all economic matters. A wife's refusal to move was ground for divorce in many jurisdiction, and if the wife was at fault, she could be denied alimony. A man had the right to force his wife to have sexual relations with him against her will. The police routinely refused to arrest wife beaters on the ground that wife beating was a family matter, not a crime.

Women also saw that the criminal law was blatantly biased against them in the treatment of sex offenses. In rape prosecutions not only was the testimony of the woman complainant entitled to less weight than that of the accused man, but also her prior sexual history was admissible to show consent whereas his prior record of sex offenses was not admissible to show his propensity to commit the crime.[8]

Thoughtful women and men recognized that the law that sanctioned these practices was unfair. Women demanded equal pay for equal work, equal access to employment, and equal educational opportunities. They wanted to end discrimination against women in commercial and credit practices, pensions and insurance, and the criminal law. And they wanted to share in American life.

In the 1950s American women again began a concerted effort to obtain full participation in American life. The publication of Simone de Beauvoir's *The Second Sex* in the United States in 1953 excited the attention of educated middle-class Americans. This book by a leading French intellectual, a woman who was the lover of the noted French philosopher Jean-Paul Sartre, had found a wide and receptive audience in Europe, particularly among affluent, educated women. During World War II American women had been urged to leave their homes and children to replace male factory workers who were serving in the armed forces. Rosie the Riveter, apotheosized in popular song, was the epitome of the patriotic female. Barely a decade later these women, who had contributed so much to the war effort, were back in their homes in Levittowns all over the nation, producing children and leaving the conduct of the world to the men. Behind the white picket fences and the green lawns women were restless, resentful, and dissatisfied. Those who had the leisure and historical perspective to contemplate their individual roles in society looked about and did not like what they saw.

The Second Sex seemed to me in 1953, as it does now after a second reading, to be not only a shrill denunciation of a male-dominated society but also a total misreading of the needs of the vast majority of Western women and of the serious economic, professional, and educational discrimination that most of these women suffered. The cry of de Beauvoir was for "equality" and a demand that in this quest gender difference be ignored. In the introduction she stated that woman "was denying her feminine weakness, but it was for love of a militant male whose equal she wished to be." These characteristics of men as militant and women as weak I find fantastically exaggerated and wrong. De Beauvoir denigrated marriage as a status in which woman was inevitably subordinated to man. Similarly, Andrea Dworkin and Catharine MacKinnon in the late 1980s asserted that sexual intercourse is not a mutual voluntary act but male oppression of women,[9] a statement with which many women disagree. De Beauvoir further stated apodictically, "A woman supported by a man—wife or courtesan—is not emancipated from the male because she has a ballot in her hand." Women who were supported by their husbands she called "parasites."

De Beauvoir was also shockingly elitist. She acknowledged that the "milliner's apprentice, the shopgirl, the secretary will not come to renounce the advantages of masculine support." The needs, interests, and wishes of such women were of no concern to her. The Soviet Union was seen as the ideal society because it promised women the right to work at the same jobs as men and for the same pay. In a footnote she observed:

"That certain too laborious occupations were to be closed to women is not in contradiction to this project." Thirty years later under the rubric of equality women are denied many of these protections.

I had visited the Soviet Union and seen women working at hard, dirty labor in fur-tanning factories, old women bent nearly double sweeping the streets with short-handled brooms, and all of these women at the end of their long, hard days of work standing in lines to do the shopping, then going home to cook, wash the dishes, clean the apartment, do the laundry, and care for the children. This was not my vision of a female utopia. Unfortunately it is the reality for many American women in 1990.

A decade after de Beauvoir's book was published in the United States Betty Friedan's *The Feminine Mystique,* based in part on de Beauvoir, had a wider and more enthusiastic reception. The women's movement was launched. If Susan B. Anthony was, as Gertrude Stein wrote, *The Mother of Us All,* [10] Betty Friedan was her twentieth-century incarnation. Female professors at women's colleges, their students, clubwomen, and celebrities marched down the major thoroughfares of the big cities of the United States demanding equality for women. What they had not achieved through the Nineteenth Amendment, they now sought unsuccessfully to attain through another constitutional amendment, the Equal Rights Amendment.

Not only did 1953 mark the birth of the women's liberation movement, but it was also a significant year in the ongoing struggle to abolish both gender and racial discrimination in the legal profession. The Harvard Law School admitted its first female students that year, and the American Bar Association admitted its first black members.*

The following year a unanimous Supreme Court rendered the landmark decision in *Brown v. Board of Education* [11] abolishing racial discrimination in the public schools. It was a heady time of hope when women, blacks, and other minorities looked forward confidently to a nation in which for the first time all people would be treated equally and all would reap the fruits of their own labor.

*In 1953 there were no women on the Board of Governors of the American Bar Association, no tenured female professors on the faculties of any leading law schools, and barely a handful of female partners in leading law firms. The employer of first and last choice for female attorneys, regardless of their academic records, skills, and experience, was the government. The Voluntary Defender Association of Philadelphia (precursor of the public defender) refused to hire women attorneys because they might have to defend rape cases. The year 1953 was a significant one for me in my understanding of discrimination against women. That year I was the first woman to win the prestigious American Bar Association Ross Essay Prize, but the award did not give me tenure at the law school where I was teaching or membership on the board of governors of the bar association to which I was nominated. Women did not attain these positions until more than two decades later.

The expectations of women were not realized for many political, social, and economic reasons. Their hopes were blasted by forces over which they had little control and also because the articulated aims of the leadership were not shared by a majority of American women.

Although most women wanted equal pay for equal work, equal educational opportunities, and equal access to better jobs, they recognized that regardless of laws, they would still be wives, mothers, and homemakers as well as employees. Unlike many of the leaders of the movement, most women wanted to retain their roles as wives and mothers even though they were dissatisfied with discriminatory practices. They feared to lose the legal protections they had won with much difficulty. They did not want to go back to working in low-paying jobs or to working night shifts. Nor did they want to forfeit support from their husbands and the right to alimony in the event of divorce. These fears were exaggerated and manipulated by many large corporations that employed women in factories, offices, and retail stores at minimum wages with few job benefits and little security. The women's movement was fractured by those with selfish interests, both male and female, and by much of the rhetoric of its leaders.

The undisputed facts reveal that in the decade of the 1980s American women were still in a position woefully inferior to that of men. A *New York Times* survey disclosed that in 1989,[12] 55 percent of women were in the work force, as compared with 76 percent of the men. But the average woman earned only 70 percent of the wages of the average man. The average female college graduate earned less than the average male with just a high school diploma.

Women made up 20 percent of all doctors and lawyers but only about 6 percent of engineers and 14 percent of police officers. Almost 50 percent of bus drivers, not the most desirable occupation, were female. In schooling, women fared better, having approximately the same number of years of formal education as men. But in 1986 women were presidents of only three hundred of the nation's three thousand colleges and universities.

Like their Russian sisters, most American women not only work outside the home but also do most of the household chores, such as cooking, cleaning, laundry, food shopping, and child care. Almost half the husbands questioned in the *Times* survey admitted that their wives did more than a fair share of chores, whereas only 11 percent of the wives said that their husbands did a fair share of chores. More significant is the fact that 48 percent of the women and only 33 percent of the men believe that women have had to give up too much for better jobs and job opportunities. The greatest complaint was that women have insufficient time for themselves. This is to be expected when one considers that women are really working two jobs. Although in their outside employment women earn less than men, it was estimated in 1984 that the annual market value of labor performed by the American housewife was $40,288.04.[13] In 1990 the value would be much greater. If women were compensated for both jobs, their average earnings would far exceed the average earnings of men.

These figures give only a partial and distorted view of the lives of American women. According to them, 40 percent of American women are single, divorced, or widowed, 53.3 percent of black women, 25.6 percent of Hispanic women, and 15.5 percent of white women are the primary caretakers of their children; 53.5 percent of female-headed households are living in poverty; and 50 percent of fathers ordered to pay child support do not do so.[14] Many more fathers are not even subject to support orders.

Although the law is only one factor of many responsible for these economic and social conditions, it cannot be ignored. In the past the law exercised a pervasive influence on women's lives. In the present time of rapid change it also plays a significant role.

In the 1960s women joined with blacks in demanding an end to the pervasive racial and sexual discrimination that was permitted to flourish under common law doctrines. With not too much opposition legislation prohibiting racial and sexual discrimination was enacted by Congress, notably the Civil Rights Act of 1964. Most state legislatures also enacted similar laws.

Despite the passage of this legislation, the ferment of the 1960s achieved disappointingly small improvements in the status of women. As recently as 1975 only four women were members of Congress. In 1988 there were two women senators and fifty-five women in the House, still a shockingly low number. Few hold any positions of leadership in Congress. A few women were with great fanfare appointed to visible positions of prominence in government and industry. But the power structure of the United States continues to be dominated by men. Washington correspondent Helen Thomas noted in 1989 that few women in the federal government were involved in policy making.[15]

Some discriminatory economic practices have been abolished. Women are now entitled to obtain credit. But pensions for women lag behind those of men. Insurance rates have not been adjusted to meet the realities of the differences in risks between men and women. Equal pay for equal jobs is mandated by law, but traditionally female positions are paid substantially less than those of traditionally male occupations. Most courts have refused to recognize the principle of comparable worth.

Despite the difficulties of quantifying the values of dissimilar jobs, most people would concede that at least in the public sector there are gross inequities that should be adjusted. For example, public school-teachers, mostly female, should be paid as much as janitors, who are mostly male and receive higher wages. Sociological techniques of opinion surveys and job analyses could furnish legislatures and courts with guidelines to determine whether predominantly female occupations are grossly undercompensated. In the 1950s and 1960s courts relied on statistics and expert opinion as predicates for redressing racially discriminatory practices.[16] If courts recognized gender-based discrimination as a denial of equal protection of the laws, judicial remedies could be devised.[17]

In sex crimes the law as to testimonial credibility and the admissibility of the sexual history of the complainant have been abolished by statute in most jurisdictions. Criminologists now recognize that the most effective way to stop wife beating, in gender-neutral terminology "spousal abuse," is by vigorous criminal prosecution.[18] But neither equal educational opportunities laws nor anti-job-discrimination laws have succeeded in obtaining equal economic benefits and employment advances for women.

In the learned professions, gender discrimination was rampant throughout most of the twentieth century. Most professional schools either barred women or admitted only a few adamant and determined female students. Doctors treated their female patients like children who had no right to be informed or to participate in decisions concerning their own treatment.[19] Lawyers rarely consulted the wishes of female clients but instructed them as to the disposition of their property and their investments. The increase in the number of women doctors and lawyers as well as the education of both men and women as consumers of professional services has ameliorated many of these evils. Probably more significant factors have been the legal requirement of informed consent to medical procedures and the prevalence of malpractice suits against doctors and lawyers.

As the cases described in the preceding chapters reveal, the law is still subject to many old illogical conceptual dogmas, and equality is used as a ground to deny women the benefits of protective legislation, custody of their children, adequate support, and equal economic benefits.

There are many differences between the lives of men and women in America today. The most intractable one is the biological fact that only women can become pregnant and bear children. Nonetheless, under the rubric of gender-neutral laws the courts have blatantly denied equal benefits to women. For example, the Supreme Court upheld the exclusion of health benefits to pregnant women under a statute gender-neutral on its face.[20] Thereafter Congress enacted the Pregnancy Discrimination Act.[21] Decisions permitting denial of health insurance coverage for pregnancy were nullified by the Civil Rights Restoration Act of 1988.

Historically abortion was not a common law offense. It was banned by statute in order to save the lives of women who frequently died as a result of unsafe procedures. In the Western world contraceptive devices did not become readily available and somewhat but not wholly reliable until the mid-twentieth century, thus freeing women from unwanted, frequent, and dangerous pregnancies.

Under the common law a fetus had no separate identity. Injury to the fetus was treated as an injury to the pregnant woman. Advances in medical technology that now make early abortion a safer procedure than carrying a pregnancy to term should have obviated the need for restrictions on abortion but have had the contrary effect. The heroic medical measures by which premature infants are enabled to be kept alive (although often mentally or physically deformed) have spawned new legal concepts that have no precedent. The novel doctrine granting potential life equal or greater rights than a life in being is used to deny women the benefits of both common law and modern science.

Until the Supreme Court decision in *Webster v. Reproductive Services*[22] no common law court had ever even inferentially held that the law could compel the body of one human being to be used for the benefit of another.* In fact, the law had always been that no person is under any obligation to rescue another even though the danger to the potential rescuer is minimal and the risk to the other extreme. No father has ever been ordered to donate a kidney to his child in order to save the child from certain death. Even so relatively risk-free a procedure as donating blood has never been required in order to save the life of a person who

---

*In the cited case a statute giving "potential" life priority over the health and rights of the pregnant woman was upheld. Recognition of bodily integrity as a liberty interest guaranteed by the Constitution would be consonant with the common law and avoid many of the difficult problems raised by judicial reliance on privacy, a relatively recent concept that has been frequently disregarded by the Supreme Court. See, e.g., *Bowers v. Hardwick*, 478 U.S. 186 (1986), and *Cox v. Cohn*, 420 U.S. 469 (1975). The distinction between affirmative invasive actions taken against the bodies of women, such as judicially mandated caesarean operations, and negative actions, such as the denial of abortions, is, I believe, specious. No man has been judicially prevented from having elective surgery regardless of his reason for wanting the procedure or the risk.

needed a transfusion. The notion that one human being can legally be used as an incubator or a source of body parts to benefit either potential life or an actual life is fraught with ethical as well as legal and medical hazards. Poor people now sell their blood and marrow. Poor women rent their wombs. The possibility, indeed, the probability, that poor persons will sell their body parts as well as their corpses is not an Orwellian nightmare but a likely consequence of a novel legal doctrine that compels the use of the body of one human being, a pregnant woman, to serve the needs of a "potential" life, a term unknown to the common law.

Ignoring the reproductive biological differences between men and women under the guise of gender-neutral laws has already led to absurd results detrimental to women. The courts have also ignored other important differences between the lives of men and women. Whether these differences are solely biological or significantly societal is, I believe, an unanswerable and irrelevant question.* Law should deal with the facts of contemporary life. Biologically there is probably no reason why men should not be the nurturers and caretakers of their children. In fact, most are not. It is women who have this responsibility. In 1985 fewer than 3 percent of all children whose parents did not live together lived with their fathers, although many men in divorce actions use a claim for custody to punish their former wives or to reduce support payments. The percentage of families headed by females has increased in the succeeding five years. Whether the cause of the broken home is death, divorce, desertion, or the fact that the parents were never married, it is an undeniable fact that it is the mothers, not the fathers, who in most instances care for the children and in most instances support them. And it is women, not men, who are economically disadvantaged by parenthood.

Elijah Anderson, a sociology professor at the University of Pennsylvania who studied the effects of pregnancy on poor black teenagers, concluded, "In each sexual encounter, there's a winner and a loser. The teenage mother is rarely the winner."[23] It is she who must drop out of school, care for the infant, and lose the opportunity for education and satisfying, well-compensated employment. For white teenage girls the same sorry situation obtains. For the adult married woman who

---

*Whether maternal love is a natural attribute or a societal construct, as French philosopher Elisabeth Badinter contends in *Mother Love: Myth and Reality* (New York: Macmillan, 1981), is, I believe, irrelevant in view of the fact that most women by choice or default assume the responsibility for child rearing in the United States. Nor is the current concern over alleged gender bias in scholastic aptitude tests a matter that can be definitively proved as indicating either genetic or social and educational differences.

chooses to have a child, whether or not the marriage remains intact, career opportunities are limited.

Although some women choose not to have children and others are unable to bear children, motherhood is a central fact of life for most women. Pregnancy, childbirth, and child rearing probably occupy less than a fourth of the life-span of the average woman and only a portion of those years. But they are the crucial period for her education and economic future. These undeniable differences between the lives of most American women and men are not reflected in the laws. Those women who can afford to take time off to rear young children forfeit their places on the economic ladder. Those who cannot afford child care services work under an enormous strain of worry and labor. Both the women and their children pay the penalty. The care of the sick and the elderly most often devolves on women. In most Western European nations the law and social institutions recognize that women do in fact bear and nurture children and care for the elderly and recognize as well the value of these vital functions. Free or affordable good public day care is readily available in most European countries. Tax laws are structured to provide not only realistic deductions for the cost of child care but also subsidies for those who do furnish care for their children or for elderly or sick family members. In the United States most of these caretakers are women. Many have to give up gainful, satisfying employment when they assume these burdens.

American law fails to recognize these differences in the lives of men and women. No-fault divorce and equitable distribution treat men and women the same. Affirmative action laws do not take into account these differences. Nor do tax laws. Business deductions for child care are limited to approximately one dollar an hour, whereas other business expenses are deductible with few limitations. Women are twice discriminated against: first, as the mother who pays for child care that is not deductible, and second, as the child caretaker (who is almost always a woman) because she is paid so little as a result of the limitations on deductibility. Neither tax laws nor insurance and pension plans are structured to take into account the needs of women who are the primary caretakers of the young and the elderly and thus usually have shorter working life-spans.

Other statistically verifiable differences between men and women are equally striking.[24] Among men suicide is the cause of death in 20 per 100,000 population. Among women it is only 6.6. Homicide is the cause of death in 10.1 men per 100,000, but only 3 women per 100,000. Motor-vehicle accidents are the cause of death in 51.14 males per 100,000, but only 13.0 females. But gender-neutral auto insurance has been ordered by the courts.

The criminal behavior of men and women is also significantly different. Males commit 90 percent of all violent crimes. Women have nearly a 50 percent chance of being a victim of rape or attempted rape. More than one in three girls will experience some incident of incestuous or extrafamilial abuse by the age of eighteen. One in three women will be victims of violence in their own homes. On the other hand, women rarely commit violent crimes against strangers.[25] It is almost always a relative, friend, or paramour. Even though women offenders are much less a danger to the public than men offenders, they are subject to the same penalties.

These inequities persist because the law has assumed that identical treatment of the sexes constitutes equal protection of the laws. By ignoring gender differences, the law has applied the same rules to different persons. The result has been actual discrimination against women, not equal protection of the laws.

Except for the institution of lawsuits attacking specific gender-discriminatory rules and practices and sexist attitudes in the treatment of women lawyers, judges, and litigants, women in the legal profession have shown little interest in the endemic gender biases of the law.[26]

In almost every other discipline feminist scholars are examining old texts anew from their own points of view rather than the received wisdom. From reading Scriptures to writing history and biography and reexamining biology and archaeology women are bringing a different perspective to beliefs that have been the received wisdom for generations. Carol Gilligan, in her seminal work *In a Different Voice,* has effectively pointed out the differences between men and women in moral values. It is precisely these moral values, male-dominated and male-imposed, that tacitly permeate the law. Male perception appears to be that racial discrimination is inherently morally wrong and legally prohibited but that discrimination against women is of lesser significance. Many black women find that sex discrimination is more pervasive and deleterious than racial discrimination, probably because it is not so apparent.

This view permeates the thinking of even the most liberal and concerned men. I recall a meeting of CORAL (Committee on Religion and Law), a Harvard-based organization composed of men and women of all races and religious persuasions whose purpose is to bring a sense of moral values to the law. One of the activities was in response to requests from educational and civic groups to present panel discussions of legal and moral issues.

In the early 1980s CORAL received an invitation from a civic organization in Missouri. All the members of CORAL voted to accept the invitation except the late Dr. Pauli Murray, a distinguished black female lawyer and clergy person, and myself. We explained that because Missouri had not ratified the ERA, we did not wish to go to that state. The men were aghast.

"You're not serious?" we were asked.

"Would you accept an invitation to present panel discussions in South Africa?" was the rejoinder.

"But that's different," we were told.

"I don't see the difference," Dr. Murray replied.

Finally the Reverend William Sloane Coffin, who belatedly recognized the similarity, managed to persuade a majority to decline the invitation.

Many aspects of the common law enshrined for generations in the decisional law of the United States accord with the perception of right and justice of men but are counterintuitive and contrary to the responses and beliefs of most women. When these common law substantive and procedural rules are applied to cases in which women are litigants, the results, as has been shown in the preceding chapters, are often shockingly unfair and inappropriate.

One such doctrine is the duty to rescue. The law as it has been for generations is that no one is obligated to come to the aid of another. The classic statement of the law is found in the 1971 edition of *Prosser on Torts,* a leading textbook:

The expert swimmer, with a boat and a rope at hand, who sees another drowning before his eyes, is not required to do anything at all about it, but may sit on the dock, smoke his cigarette, and watch the man drown. A physician is under no duty to answer the call of one who is dying and might be saved, nor is anyone required to play the part of Florence Nightingale and bind up the wounds of a stranger who is bleeding to death, or to prevent a neighbor's child from hammering on a dangerous explosive, or to remove a stone from the highway where it is a menace to traffic, or a train from a place where it blocks a fire engine on its way to save a house, or even to cry a warning to one who is walking into the jaws of a dangerous machine.[27]

I seriously doubt that more than a minute percentage of women would agree that this statement of the law reflects their views. Perhaps some men also disagree with this legal doctrine, but they have done little, if anything, to abrogate it.

A parlor game that I have participated in many times illustrates the strong gender difference in approach to values. The problem presented is this: Two persons are trapped in a cave with a small aperture that admits enough air for only one to breathe. They have a gun with one bullet. If one person is killed, the other has a chance to survive until rescue comes. Otherwise both will die. You are one of the persons in the cave. What do you do?

Each time we have played this game the males have given one of these responses. Most reply, "Shoot the other person." A few say, "Draw straws to see who shall die." Occasionally a man will say, "It depends on which person is younger, more valuable to society, et cetera."

Women have two standard responses: "I'd shoot myself" and "I would do nothing."

The male attitude is reflected in many aspects of the law. The law requires that a woman victim of rape prove that she offered resistance. The fact that physical violence is anathema to the majority of women and that most male rapists are bigger and stronger than their victims is legally irrelevant.

The common law also permits a person in his own home to use force, even deadly force, against an intruder. There is no duty to retreat. If one is not at home, there is a duty to retreat rather than employ force. I believe that most women do not accept such conceptual differences. If violence is safely avoidable by retreat, then most women believe that is the prudent, humane, and lifesaving course of action and that this should be required by law.

For centuries it was the law that one was entitled to use force in self-defense but not in the defense of others. That rule has been expanded in most jurisdictions to permit defense of one's family. I suggest that perhaps most women would prefer a law that permitted a stranger to use force in defense of a person who was being attacked. Indeed, some states by statute require bystanders to come to the aid of endangered persons.

For many years it was accepted law that a person could recover damages for emotional harm only if there was a physical contact between the wrongdoer and the person allegedly harmed. The rule was enlarged to permit recovery for a parent who sees his or her child being injured, run down by an automobile, for example. However, if the parent does not actually see the accident but is simply told about it and suffers a heart attack, there can be no recovery. I suggest that this rule also is counterintuitive to most women's sense of justice. There are countless other common law tenets devised by male lawyers and judges in past centuries that do not reflect the norms of behavior and concepts of morality of most women who constitute a majority of the population.

In the past three decades women have become a visible and growing presence in the legal profession. But disappointingly they have not made many significant changes in the practice of law or in many legal doctrines that are not overtly gender-biased but that prejudice countless women. It is worth examining the role of women in the legal profession for two reasons: First, it is well documented, and although it may not be typical of all formerly predominantly male occupations, it provides a gauge of women's progress or lack thereof; second, the legal profession has special significance to all who have been denied full participation in American life because law is both the barrier to true equality and the weapon to fight official and unofficial denial of equal protection of the laws. It is also the area that judges and lawyers know best and to which they can most easily relate.

In 1950 only approximately 1 percent of American lawyers were women even though the first woman lawyer in the United States, Arabella Mansfield, was admitted to practice law in 1869 in Iowa. In 1970 women constituted 3 percent of the bar. In 1989, 20 percent of American lawyers and more than 40 percent of all law students were women; 20 percent of all doctors also were women. As recently as 1978 only two women had been appointed to the United States courts of appeals, Florence Allen and Shirley Hufstedler. The first woman member of the Supreme Court of France, Charlotte Lagarde, was appointed in 1946. Sandra Day O'Connor, the first woman on the United States Supreme Court, was not appointed until 1981.

In 1988 only 8 percent of all American judges were women although women constituted 53 percent of the population. Approximately 8 percent of all American judges were nonwhite. Nonwhites, according to the 1980 census, constituted only approximately 20 percent of the population.

Despite their numbers, few women have reached the top echelons of the legal profession. What is called the "glass ceiling" on advancement has not been shattered. Patricia Wald, chief judge of the United States Court of Appeals for the District of Columbia, points out that only 8 percent of the partners in the 250 largest law firms are women.[28] Only 6 percent of the law school deans and 10 percent of the tenured faculty are women. In a recent survey twice as many women lawyers as men expressed dissatisfaction with their work environment. Discriminatory treatment of lawyers and court personnel has been noted and documented. Bar associations have passed resolutions to ban these practices.

But the endemic discrimination against women litigants and witnesses of all socioeconomic strata in the daily operations of the courts has not received the attention it deserves from either women lawyers or women judges. What I call the Mameluke psychology unfortunately prevails among many professional women. The Mamelukes were enfranchised slaves who became the sultans of Egypt. Although they had suffered bitter hardships under their former masters, they acted with equal cruelty when they obtained power. All too many successful business and professional women adopt the mind-sets of the males who dominate these fields of activity and perpetuate practices that are seriously prejudicial to women. A notable example is Felice N. Schwartz, who suggests a two-track career path for women: the fast track for those who forgo parenthood and a limited advancement for those who choose to have families.[29] Similar division of males into fathers and nonfathers has never been suggested.

Most women lawyers and judges, including those who are mothers, see themselves as persons on the fast track. Unfortunately too few have viewed their role as being that of protectors or advocates for other women.

A study by the American Judicature Society of the voting records of President Jimmy Carter's male and female appointees to the federal bench confirms this observation.[30] (President Carter appointed more women to the federal bench than had been appointed in the entire history of the nation.) This study analyzed the votes of male and female and black and white judges in cases involving crime, prisoners' rights, and sex and racial discrimination cases and found that there was no statistical difference in the decisions of male and female judges. However, there was a decided difference between black and white male judges on issues involving criminal defendants. Black men evidently perceived the injustices of the legal system as to blacks and voted to correct them. Women either did not recognize the injustices of the law in those areas with respect to women or did not identify with the females subject to legal discrimination. A study comparing the sentencing records of male and female judges discloses that women judges sentence female defendants more harshly than do male judges.[31]

This attitude can be explained in part by the Mameluke mind-set and in part by the expressed expectations of social analysts who assume that toughness and aggressiveness are desirable and necessary qualities for successful women who engage in predominantly male occupations. Many questionnaires addressed to women judges ask what qualities are necessary for success. In these multiple-choice answers "aggressiveness" is always included. Rarely is "diligence," "intelligence," "dedication," or "compassion" listed.

Many significant victories for women have been achieved in the courts. Sexual harassment in the workplace has been banned. The Supreme Court has held that women can no longer be subject to sex discrimination in becoming members of law firms and cannot be excluded from such organizations as the Chamber of Commerce and Burning Tree Golf Club,[32] organizations whose members are high-powered, high-income males. Important political, business, and professional contacts are made there. Members have many advantages, both social and economic. These decisions have primarily benefited fast-track women who are educated and have reasonably good jobs.

Far too few advances have been made in abolishing the day-to-day inequities that afflict the majority of women who are poor and struggling to meet the demands of supporting themselves and caring for and supporting their children.* These are the neglected areas of the law that a trial judge sees and is powerless to rectify. Many leaders in the field of women's rights have failed to recognize the special burden that women bear in contemporary American society and are wedded to a gender-neutral legal approach.

Typical of this viewpoint is the report "New Directions in Women's Rights," prepared for the 1987 Biennial Conference of the American Civil Liberties Union. The authors, three women lawyers, write that "the selective recognition of pregnancy related disability and the needs of mothers is a constitutionally inappropriate as well as a strategically unsound step towards that goal [granting leave for medical conditions or parental responsibilities.]"

John Kenneth Galbraith commented that "economics rejects as fact what it cannot accommodate readily to the theory."[33] Similarly, many who are dedicated to principles of equal justice under law reject those facts that cannot be accommodated to a gender-neutral theory. The facts are that only women become pregnant, that the overwhelming majority of women are the primary caretakers of children and the elderly, that single mothers constitute two of every three clients of the Legal Services Corporation, which provides legal aid for the poor, and that 85 percent of all food stamp recipients are women and children. Until the law recognizes these gross differences between the lives of men and women, it cannot provide equal protection for women.

*Women lawyers in Philadelphia obtained an agreement in September 1989 from the major law firms that they be given maternity leave and compassionate leave to care for their sick children. The same rights were not requested for female employees of these law firms who suffer the same problems and have lower incomes.

6

The Child as Defendant

In every infant's cry of fear
In every voice, in every ban
The mind-forged manacles I hear.

— WILLIAM BLAKE

JUVENILE COURT is where most American children learn about justice and the majesty of the law. It is not a forum where a child goes to assert rights or claim remedies. When a child is injured or deprived of property, suit must be brought in adult court by an adult who is the plaintiff on behalf of the child. This individual may be a parent, a guardian, or a person known as next friend. Most prosecutions for child abuse are also brought in adult court, where the accused receives constitutional rights and protections.

Juvenile court is the place where children are brought by the police, their parents, or their custodians to be punished when they are accused of crime, delinquency, or dependency. Under juvenile law a child can be brought to court not only for acts that are violations of the criminal code that applies to adults but also for many acts that are not crimes, such as running away from home, truancy and incorrigibility—a catch-all term that includes disobedience, mischief, and annoying behavior. Children are also brought to juvenile court when it is charged that they are dependent—that is, that their parents or guardians are inadequate. As a result of a finding on any of these charges, a child may be removed from his or her home and placed in an institution that has many of the characteristics of a prison.

Robert Wilkins and Eldred Clark were two of the more than two million children arrested in the United States each year. Like most children accused of delinquency, they were poor and undereducated. And like the majority of children and adults accused of street crime in large metropolitan areas, they were nonwhite. The crime, robbery, was also commonplace. Legally a robbery may be a purse snatch, a demand for a wallet, the grabbing of a gold chain, or an armed holdup of a bank. The nomenclature, the procedures, and often the penalties are the same.

During every stage of the proceedings from arrest through appeal Robert was denied the constitutional rights to which all adults are entitled and also denied the protections that should be afforded to all children. I, the trial judge, was bound by the mandates of the common law as interpreted by the appellate courts. As so often happens when children are prosecuted, I found myself presiding over legalized injustice.

When these boys were arrested, they were brought to the police station and then turned over to juvenile court.* Four months later they were certified to be tried as adults because that court found they were no longer amendable to the rehabilitative treatment of the juvenile process.

I expected to see big bullies, the kinds of hostile, overgrown youths who beat up younger children and cause trouble in juvenile institutions. I have seen many such boys who have the bodies and angers of grown men but the emotional and intellectual development of preadolescents. Neither juvenile courts nor juvenile institutions want to deal with them. But despite their size, these youngsters are not adults. They are ill equipped to deal with the procedures of adult courts. The law has only two options: to treat such youngsters as the children they are or to employ a legal fiction and treat them as adults. The latter choice had been made.

I was astonished when Robert was brought into court by two sheriffs and the handcuffs were removed from his slender wrists. The boy was only about five feet three inches tall and weighed at most 120 pounds. He looked to be not more than thirteen years old although he was sixteen. One of the sheriffs patted his head and gently showed him to his seat. The public defender whispered briefly to him. Robert's eyes were downcast. He did not speak, only nodded assent to what his attorney told him.

Eldred was much bigger, a tough, surly-looking boy who slouched into the room, glaring angrily at me. He was represented by a court-appointed lawyer. Because there might be a conflict of interest between

*When a middle-class child is arrested, if a concerned parent comes to the police station to claim him or her and the offense charged is not too serious, the matter is simply "adjusted" and the child goes home. He or she does not have a juvenile record.

the two boys, the same lawyer could not represent both.

Robert and Eldred were charged with armed robbery and conspiracy. The documents before me indicated that they had held up a man at knife point and taken eight dollars. The victim was not harmed. I would have liked to have returned both children to juvenile court. But the law does not permit a judge in felony court to enter such an order overruling the decision of a family court judge.

Neither boy had been arrested with a warrant. If they had been adults, the arrests would have been quashed and they would have been freed because no adult may be apprehended without a warrant unless the officer actually sees a crime being committed or arrives on the scene shortly thereafter. Children may be arrested without warrants for crimes and noncriminal acts known as status offenses, such as truancy, runaway, and incorrigibility. A child who is alleged to be neglected, abused, or in need of treatment can also be detained (held in a jaillike institution) without a warrant for his own good.

Both Robert and Eldred had been in detention (a juvenile jail) for nine months before I saw them. If they had been adults, they would have been entitled to a bail hearing. But juveniles are not entitled to bail.[1] The boys were charged with serious offenses. Since the taking involved only a small sum and the victim was not injured, nominal bail would probably have been granted to an adult accused of these crimes. In most jurisdictions there are bail projects that arrange for an adult accused of crime to be released on his or her own recognizance.

The purpose of bail is to secure the presence of the accused at trial. The usual criteria are ties to the community, a stable home, and employment. Few children are likely to flee the jurisdiction. They have no money and no place to go. The Eighth Amendment, which prohibits excessive bail, does not extend to children because by another legal fiction, they are accused not of crime but of delinquency. The boys were in detention for nine months, waiting first for juvenile court to decide what to do with them and then to be tried as adults. If they had remained under the jurisdiction of the juvenile court, in all likelihood they would have been sent to a correctional institution. But at least, they would not have had criminal records.

This, however, was adult criminal court. In 1987, 61,253 children of the more than 2,000,000 who were arrested were referred to adult criminal court and tried in proceedings like those to which Robert and Eldred were subjected. All the requirements of due process of law were meticulously observed. Both boys were sworn. The charges against them were read aloud by the court crier. "Robert Wilkins and Eldred

Clark, you and each of you are charged with Count I, feloniously and unlawfully robbing James Gubbins of a wallet containing eight dollars at knifepoint on the eighteenth day of July . . . and Count II, unlawfully and feloniously conspiring together to rob the aforesaid James Gubbins on said date in the City and County of Philadelphia all of which is against the peace and dignity of the Commonwealth." The two defendants were then asked how they were pleading. The two attorneys whispered to them, "Say not guilty." They dutifully muttered, "Not guilty."

This was to be a waiver trial, counsel informed me. All persons accused of crime in adult court are entitled to a jury trial. Children tried in juvenile court, the Supreme Court has held, have no right to a jury trial.[2] Nor do they have a right to a speedy public trial. Because this was adult court, the children had to be informed of their right to a jury trial.

"Please qualify your clients to waive a jury trial," I instructed counsel.

One of the lawyers assumed this task. "Robert and Eldred, I'll ask you both the same questions. Both of you must answer to each question. D'ya understand?"

They nodded.

"When I ask you a questions, you gotta say yes. Don't nod."

I interposed an explanation: "You must respond either yes or no to each question. If you don't understand the question, please say so, and we will explain it to you. Do you understand?"

Both said, "Yes." Neither asked any questions throughout the entire proceeding.

The attorney then rattled off the prescribed colloquy. Everyone understood that this was just a formality. It was already eleven-thirty. This was the third case on the list, and there were seven more to go. The preliminaries were to be gotten through as quickly as possible. The lawyer consulted his dog-eared sheet and read rapidly.

"You are entitled to a trial by jury. D'ya understand?"

Both defendants said, "Yes."

"A jury consists of twelve people drawn from the voting lists of Philadelphia. These people will decide your guilt or innocence. In order to be found guilty, all twelve people must agree that you are guilty beyond a reasonable doubt or you cannot be found guilty. If even one disagrees, you cannot be found guilty. The verdict must be unanimous. If the jury cannot agree, you cannot be found not guilty. And you cannot be acquitted. That is a hung jury. The commonwealth will have the option to try you again. D'ya understand?"

"Yes."

"A reasonable doubt means an honest doubt arising out of the evidence. It does not mean proof to a mathematical certainty. D'ya understand?"

"Yes."

"In choosing a jury, about thirty people will be brought into the courtroom, and we as your lawyers will have the right to question them. So will the district attorney. If any of these people is biased or prejudiced against you or cannot give you a fair trial, that person will be excused. By 'prejudice' we mean if anyone says he thinks all young people are guilty or that he doesn't like blacks, that person will be excused. D'ya understand?"

"Yes."

"Conspiracy means that you two agreed together to rob this man. To prove conspiracy, the district attorney doesn't have to prove that you actually said, 'Let's go rob this guy.' It's enough if they prove by circumstantial evidence that you agreed to rob him. D'ya understand?"

"Yes."

I gave them a simple explanation of circumstantial evidence.

"The maximum sentence you can get for each crime is five to ten years, consecutive—that means one after the other, not concurrent. That doesn't mean that this is the sentence the judge will give you. It's the maximum that can legally be imposed. D'ya understand?"

"Yes."

"Now if either of you has a prior record, if you have been convicted of another felony, then the judge will have to impose a mandatory sentence of five years' total confinement. D'ya understand?"

Again I interposed. "That means that you will have to go to prison for five years if you are found guilty and if you have previously been convicted of another crime." I did not pursue this because it appeared to be legally impossible that either boy could have had a prior adult conviction.

The attorney rattled on, reading his sheet.

"Now you also have the right to be tried by a judge without a jury. The judge will hear the evidence. And before you can be convicted, she must find you guilty beyond a reasonable doubt. But because the judge cannot disagree with herself, there cannot be a hung jury. You will be found either guilty or innocent. There will not be a possibility of a second trial. D'ya understand?"

"Yes."

"How do you want to be tried?" There was silence.

"Do you want to be tried by a jury or by the judge sitting alone?"

Both boys looked bewildered. The other lawyer whispered to them, "By the judge alone."

They duly repeated, "By the judge alone."

"Just a minute, counsel," I objected. "These defendants are minors. Are the mothers here?" I looked around the courtroom.

Counsel consulted with the boys. "No, Your Honor."

"Is any friend or relative here?"

Another whispered colloquy. "Robert's mother is here. There is no one here for Eldred, Your Honor."

"How long have you had to consult with your clients? Have you seen them before they came into court this morning?"

Robert's lawyer said, "No, Your Honor." He was the public defender who had to represent eleven cases listed before me. I knew that a paralegal had probably interviewed the boy and a clerk had made up the file which was given to him the day before, perhaps at 5:00 P.M.

Eldred's lawyer said, "Yes."

The prescribed formula for waiver of a jury trial had been read rapidly. With my interruptions it was completed in little more than five minutes. How much did either of these boys understand? Even a literate, sophisticated adult has difficulty in deciding whether to give up his right to a jury trial. If the evidence against an accused is persuasive and the law is clear, a jury may be the only hope for acquittal. Perhaps one of the twelve jurors will have a reasonable doubt. The odds of finding one favorable person in twelve are better than relying on one judge who hears similar cases every day. This might be the most important choice these boys had. On what basis could they make this decision when they knew nothing about the entire process?

"I suggest we take a short recess while both of you discuss the case with your clients and Robert's mother," I told the attorneys. The crowded courtroom was restless during the brief recess. Jaded court watchers realized that the boys would know little more after they spoke to the lawyers than before. Meanwhile, all the other cases were being delayed. Perhaps counsel would indicate the advisability of a jury trial. And if there should be an appeal, the transcript would show that all the requirements of due process had been met.

When the boys and their lawyers resumed their places at the bar of the court, counsel again asked them whether they wanted to be tried by a jury or by a judge alone. This time both promptly answered, "By the judge alone."

They were then asked, "Can you read, write, and understand the English language?" to which both hesitantly replied, "Yes."

"Are you satisfied with my representation of you thus far?"

Again silence. After my brief explanation the boys were told by counsel to answer, "Yes," and they did.

The court crier gave each of them a jury waiver form to sign and a pen. The boys dutifully and with some effort began to sign their names.

"Just a moment. I want you to read the form before you sign it," I told them.

Eldred's lawyer began to read it to the boys.

"No," I interrupted again. "Let him read it aloud."

The form consists of four lines stating that the undersigned has been informed of his right to a jury trial and knowingly and voluntarily chooses to be tried without a jury. Eldred could not read a word. The form was then read to him.

Robert read the form haltingly.

And so we proceeded to trial. Mr. Gubbins, the victim, was an elderly black man who testified that he had been walking down the street when he was approached by two teenage black males who demanded his money. He immediately gave them his wallet, which contained eight dollars and his Social Security card. No wallet was ever found.

"Did either of the boys have anything in his hand?" the prosecutor asked.

"One of them had a knife."

"Which boy?"

"The big one." It was admitted for the record that it was Eldred.

Gubbins had gone to the corner bar and called the police. Within a few minutes a patrol car with two officers came. Gubbins told them his story and pointed to the direction in which the boys had fled. He had described them as two young black males, one about sixteen or seventeen, the other younger and smaller. The big one was wearing a black sweat shirt; the little one, a jeans jacket. Both were wearing jeans and sneakers. At least ten thousand youngsters in the city of Philadelphia would fit that description. The police rode around the neighborhood for some time but did not see the two defendants. Two days later they saw Eldred and Robert on a corner a block from the bar where they had seen Mr. Gubbins. They stopped the car, and the boys began to run. The officers quickly apprehended them. They did not ask the boys any questions other than their names and ages. When they learned the boys were juveniles, they took them to the juvenile detention center, where a court employee, not a judge, decided that they should be detained until their court hearing.

The police then brought Mr. Gubbins to the detention center, where he identified both boys. If they had been adults, they would have been entitled to a lineup (sometimes called a stand-up), where they would have been placed in a line with four or five other persons of the same race and approximately the same age, size, and appearance. Mr. Gubbins would have been required to pick out his two robbers from such a group. The police would have been required to keep photos of the entire array of individuals in the lineup so that the judge could decide if the lineup was fair. If, for example, Robert, who was very dark-skinned, had been put in a lineup with all light-skinned boys, the identification would have been quashed.

If Robert and Eldred had been adults, they would have been entitled to discovery. Their attorney would have had the right to examine the police records to learn the exact time Mr. Gubbins had called the police and the precise descriptions he had given. But because they were juveniles, none of this discovery was undertaken.

According to the testimony of the arresting officer, when Mr. Gubbins was shown the two boys three days later at the detention center (where there was no lineup), he immediately said, "That's them." Then he pointed to Robert and said, "That's the one with the knife." Robert immediately protested. "I didn't have no knife. It was Eldred who pulled the knife." Gubbins then corrected himself and said it was the big one who had the knife. Had the boys been adults, their lawyers would have been present at the identification and probably would have warned them not to say anything.

All this had taken place nine months prior to the trial before me. Learned legal discussion then took place at sidebar, while the boys dozed off. The room was stuffy. They could not hear what was being said, and it is most unlikely that if they had heard the argument, they would have understood it. The law was clear. An adult must be brought to trial within six months of arrest or the charges will be dismissed unless the prosecutor has requested and been given an extension of time. The Sixth Amendment requires a speedy public trial in all criminal prosecutions. Because of the legal fiction that acts of juvenile delinquency are not considered crimes, this provision does not apply in juvenile court even though a child may be deprived of his liberty.

In this case no request for an extension of time had been made. The boys had not been certified to be tried as adults until five months after arrest. Under decisions of the appellate courts the operative date to begin the six months is not the date of arrest of a juvenile but of the certification that the child be tried as an adult. I was bound by this ruling although I indicated on the record my disagreement. Alert counsel would have taken this issue as ground for appeal. Clearly there was a constitutional equal protection issue. If an adult had been arrested the same day as these boys and not brought to trial until the date of their trial, the prosecution would have been dismissed and the accused would have gone free and could never be tried on those charges. But because Robert and Eldred were children, this constitutional provision did not apply to them. The weary defender saw no point in making more work for the office by taking an appeal or an issue that had already been decided. Robert was clearly guilty anyway.

It was settled law that the statement Robert made to the police could not be used against Eldred, his coconspirator, and that it was admissible against Robert as an admission against interest. Robert had placed himself on the scene of the crime. An adult need not be warned of his right to remain silent until the police are about to question him. A volunteered statement, however, is admissible. This is known as a blurt out. When children are tried as adults, adult law is applied to them. Even though it was highly unlikely that Robert knew that he had a right to remain silent and that anything he said could and would be used against him, his unwary remark was legally admissible and sufficient, in this case, to convict him.

All authorities on constitutional law recognize the cardinal importance of time in the criminal process. Every day spent in pretrial detention not only deprives the accused, who is presumed to be innocent, of his or her liberty but also makes it far more difficult to find witnesses and evidence that is exculpatory. These same considerations should prevail with respect to children. Time is a far more critical factor in the life of a child than in the life of an adult. The loss of a few months of schooling may necessitate repeating a grade. The forcible wrenching of a child from his or her home and placing the child in a jail removed from family and friends are very traumatic experiences. The longer the child remains in custody, the more deleterious its effects.

The American Bar Association has established time standards for juvenile courts. These require a detention hearing within twenty-four hours of apprehension, then an adjudicatory hearing or transfer (to adult court) within fifteen days if the child is in detention. If the child is at liberty, the hearing (trial) must be held within thirty days and a dispositional hearing within fifteen days after adjudication. These sensible standards are rarely met.[3] In many urban communities children may be in detention for months both before an adjudicatory hearing and more months after the hearing while awaiting placement.

Neither Eldred nor Robert took the stand. There were no witnesses on behalf of either child. An adult accused of crime, unless he or she had a prior record, would have brought an array of character witnesses to court—neighbors, the local minister, family members, anyone who knew the person and could say a good word for him or her. Character witnesses can make the difference between conviction and acquittal. Despite even the evidence of eyewitnesses, testimony that the accused is a good person and has led a law-abiding life can be sufficient to raise a doubt in the minds of the jury or judge as to whether such an individual really did the criminal act. Eyewitnesses can be mistaken in their identification. Most crimes happen very quickly. The victim rarely has a good opportunity to see the criminal. Certainly in the case of two strange teenage boys the victim could be mistaken. If neighbors had testified that Robert and Eldred were good, upstanding young boys, helpful in the neighborhood, kind to older people, and the like, this might have raised a doubt.

Robert's lawyer had not had the opportunity to get in touch with his mother and ask her to find character witnesses. She did not have a telephone, and he could not reach her the night before trial. There was nothing in the evidence before me that was favorable to these boys. The prosecutor also pointed out that the crime was committed on a school day during school hours. On the record I could do nothing other than to find Robert guilty of armed robbery and conspiracy. Even though Robert did not have a weapon, as a coconspirator he was as guilty as Eldred of armed robbery. Again this common law rule does not take into account the actions and the intentions of youngsters like Robert.

After finding Robert guilty, I informed him of his right to file exceptions within ten days, and that if he did not do so, it would be more difficult to take an appeal, and that if he wanted to file exceptions, his lawyer would do so at public expense. Robert's eyes were downcast, as they were during the entire brief trial. I had no way of knowing whether he paid attention to what I told him or whether he understood the significance of posttrial procedures.

Because Robert's testimony was inadmissible against Eldred, the only evidence against him was the identification by Mr. Gubbins, which was, under the circumstances, not convincing. I found him not guilty.

I was then handed the juvenile court records of these boys. Often juvenile court judges look at children's records *before* they hear the evidence. Eldred's was about ten pages. Robert's was the size of the Manhattan phone book. Sentencing was set for the next month. Eldred was released. Robert was handcuffed and taken back to the courthouse cells. Later that evening he was returned to the juvenile detention center where he had spent the preceding nine months. During the past five months, because the boys were being treated as adults, neither had had even the hour or two of schooling occasionally provided to children in detention. The school system was thus relieved of its obligation to teach them. Their days were spent playing cards, watching TV, and getting into trouble. No physical exercise or intellectual stimulation was provided in the detention center, which is no better or worse than those across the entire nation.

Adult prisoners are required to have yard privileges every day. They are also entitled to the use of a library. Children do not have these rights. At least for most of the nine months each of the boys had had a bed. When the center is overcrowded, as frequently happens, some of the children sleep on the floor. The boys were given three meals a day. Neither boy was seen by a doctor, a psychiatrist, a counselor, or a clergyperson during his entire stay at the center.

After presiding over the trials of two more robberies and a rape, I adjourned court at five-thirty. I took Robert's file home with me because I wanted to know what heinous offenses this sad-looking little boy had committed during the first sixteen years of his life.

The file began when he was seven. His mother was hospitalized; his father was unavailable because he was in the military service. So Robert was temporarily placed in a foster home. After two weeks he ran away. Robert was picked up by the police at the hospital where his mother was a patient (he had gone to visit her) and charged with being a runaway, an act of delinquency. Because runaway is not a crime, Robert was not provided with a lawyer. He had no opportunity to tell the judge why he ran away. Was he beaten, starved, or mistreated by the foster family? No one will ever know. Nonetheless, in a hearing that probably took less than five minutes he was adjudicated delinquent. At the age of seven his record of crime and delinquency had begun. He was a difficult child to place because he already had been found delinquent. So he was held at the detention center for a month until his mother was able to care for him. By the time he returned home he had missed two months of school.

At age nine he was back before the court on the complaint of a neighbor that he stole fifty cents from her kitchen cookie jar. Robert was held in detention while this case was being processed. It was listed for trial three times. Each time the neighbor failed to appear and the matter was continued. Each time Robert was represented by a different public defender, none of whom moved to dismiss the charges so that

Robert could go home and go back to school. Had he been an adult, the charges would probably have been dismissed the second time the complainant failed to appear. On the fourth hearing the neighbor appeared, and Robert was adjudicated delinquent. At his mother's insistence Robert was returned home.

The following year Robert was back in court for truancy. The file noted that his father had died in an accident and that thereafter the child stayed home from school for several months. After a death in the family most adults are given leave from work. Every religion recognizes a period of mourning and the need to recover from the loss. The record does not indicate that any plea in extenuation was made on Robert's behalf. The court file states: "adjudicated delinquent—truant." A letter from Robert's teacher was in the file. She wrote that the child cried in class, could not concentrate, and needed help. He was referred to a court psychiatrist, who examined him and reported that Robert was of average intelligence but that he was grieving "abnormally" for his father and needed help. It was suggested that he be referred to a big brothers organization. The record did not indicate that this was done. After three weeks in the detention center Robert was returned home. His record then showed three adjudications of delinquency.

At age eleven he was brought to court by his mother and her paramour as a runaway and incorrigible. The cryptic notes indicate that Robert and the new man in the house did not get along. He was again placed in a foster home. During the next four years he was in six different foster homes and attended six different schools. He ran away twice. Once he was found guilty of assault for hitting his foster mother. After this adjudication of delinquency he was committed to a correctional institution for children euphemistically known as Fenton Farms.* It is a farm in the country. It is also a jail. The inmates are city slum children who are terrified of the woods, the animals, and the isolation. There is little schooling and no counseling there because it is difficult to get qualified people to work in this inconvenient location. After six months Robert was released and placed in yet another foster home, where he was living when he was arrested for the robbery of which I convicted him. This foster mother did not appear in court at either the trial or the sentencing. Robert's own mother appeared both times. Robert had a younger brother who was put in foster placement when their mother was arrested on a drug charge. Robert had not seen his brother for some four years.

By chance I recognized the name of the foster mother who had

*This is a fictitious name but a real institution.

brought assault charges against Robert. About a year before Robert's trial this woman was convicted before me of child abuse of two foster children. They had been taken to the hospital with several fractured bones.

In all but the first of his appearances in juvenile court Robert had been represented by counsel. He had been seen by three court psychiatrists or psychologists, all of whom recommended counseling, which was never provided. The last family court judge who had seen Robert certified him to be tried as an adult because after all these years under the aegis of the family court he was found to be no longer amenable to its treatment. He had failed the juvenile court. Robert had never been given any treatment. I believe the court had failed him.

The judge who certified Robert is a man with a notoriously short fuse. The children who appear in his court call him the terrible Judge Toland. He is a politically ambitious man who served his time in party politics. Before going on the bench, he was an undistinguished, unsuccessful lawyer. For years he has been seeking appointment to a higher court and is embittered by his assignment in family court, where he gets little media exposure. He has no children. He is, however, a popular speaker at political ward meetings and service clubs, where he discusses the problems of crime and delinquency and vows to make the city streets safe for honest, law-abiding people.

Although I no longer had jurisdiction over Eldred, I looked at his juvenile file. Eldred had only one prior adjudication of delinquency. This was for knifing another child in a school playground. For this offense Eldred had spent six months in a juvenile correctional institution. He was released two weeks before the robbery that was the case before me. Eldred was the eldest of seven children, most of whom had different fathers. The identity of Eldred's father was unknown. The mother and children lived in a notoriously dangerous housing project. The mother had not appeared in court. There was no information in the file about her.

I had no way of knowing where Eldred would go on his release or what would become of him. Would he go back to his mother, who had shown no interest in him? Would he attend school? What would become of this violent youngster?

If Eldred had been convicted before me, he would have had a presumptive sentence* of only two to four years even though he had a

---

*Under sentencing guidelines established by statutes in most states and under federal law, a judge is required to follow a point chart prescribing a certain number of months' imprisonment for each offense. If the judge deviates, an opinion detailing the reasons for the deviation must be written. It entails extra work, which many judges are reluctant to undertake.

weapon and had one prior adjudication of delinquency that involved violence. The court psychologist who had examined Eldred for juvenile court reported that he was of low normal intelligence, IQ 85, probably depressed by his total illiteracy. There was every reason to believe that he would commit another crime simply because he was unemployable and apparently no family member took an interest in him. He was certainly a child in need of care. Despite my requests to the prosecutor, the school system, and the welfare department, no one filed a dependency petition for Eldred. Had such a petition been filed, the juvenile court could have ordered him to attend school. On an appropriate petition the school system could have been ordered to place him in a special literacy class. Such actions might have prevented his adult life of crime, which began a few months after I found him not guilty.

If Eldred had been treated like the child that he was and been tried in juvenile court, he probably would have been adjudicated delinquent. Juvenile courts rarely observe the niceties of the rules of evidence. Eldred would most likely have been sent to a correctional institution until he was eighteen. He might have learned to read, and he might have been taught a trade. This last opportunity to help a troubled child was missed because he was treated like an adult but denied the protections assured to adults. If Eldred had been sent to a correctional institution, at the expiration of his commitment (it is not called a sentence) he would have been released. Most modern prisons for adults have careful prerelease programs, during which the prisoner is monitored while he works at a job that has been found for him. The social services departments get in touch with his family and help make arrangements for a place for him to live. The days when a prisoner was given a suit of clothes and two dollars and let out of the prison gates to find his own way are happily over in many communities. But similar prerelease programs for children have not been instituted in most communities.

Because Eldred was acquitted and I was sitting as a judge in adult felony court, my jurisdiction over him ended. There was nothing I could do to help this child.

Robert was my responsibility. I had convicted him, and I had to impose a sentence under adult law on this child. Sentencing even the most willful, knowing intentional adult criminal is the most difficult and painful duty of a trial judge. One is torn between trying to make the punishment fit the crime and making it fit the criminal. The court is given mutually incompatible goals: to rehabilitate the offender and to deter other potential criminals. In addition, sentencing is supposed to uphold the law and to protect society. Not one of these aims is likely to be achieved. Certainly not all of them. Prisons are the last place where an offender is likely to be rehabilitated.[4] To deter crime effectively, one would have to impose the kinds of penalties that are popular in Iran, such as cutting off the hand of a thief. Some writers suggest that vengeance is a proper motive.[5] In this case old Mr. Gubbins, like many crime victims, was not interested in vengeance. Even though he had not recovered his eight dollars, he simply wanted to be let alone. What happened to the boys was of no concern to him. He was notified of the date of Robert's sentencing but did not appear.

The maximum penalty for armed robbery was ten to twenty years, and the same for conspiracy. Under the law the two sentences could be imposed consecutively. If the maximum penalty were imposed, Robert could spend a good part of his life in prison.

Claude Lévi-Strauss, the noted anthropologist, observed that the criminal law "is the height of absurdity, since we treat the culprit both as a child, so as to have the right to punish him, and as an adult, in order to deny him consolation. . . ."[6] In this case a child was being treated as an adult under a legal fiction in order to punish him more severely than would have been permitted if he had been treated like the sixteen-year-old that he really was. And there was no consolation for him.

If I were to prefer the goal of rehabilitation, then what this child really needed was intensive schooling. By some miracle Robert had learned to read, probably at only a fourth-grade level. He was better off than 13 to 17 percent of American children, who in 1990 are functional illiterates. I knew that he would not get much of an education in prison, except in the ways of crime.

The prosecutor was ready with his charts. In my state, as in most jurisdictions, judges no longer have discretion to fashion sentences appropriate to each case. They are required to follow sentencing guidelines[7] that weight a limited number of factors. Aggravating and mitigating circumstances are added and subtracted, and a mathematical formula gives the number of months and years that the offender must serve in prison. It is supposedly fair and unbiased. It is untouched by a human brain or heart. The numbers for Robert came to four to eight years in prison because of his juvenile record, even though the crimes were one theft at age nine, one assault at age thirteen, truancy at age seven, incorrigibility at age eleven, and two runaways at ages seven and twelve. Truancy, incorrigibility, and runaway are not adult crimes. Therefore, I reasoned, that they should not be considered in an adult sentencing of the child.

Because an adjudication of delinquency is not technically conviction of a crime, I believe that no juvenile record should be considered in calculating the presumptive sentence. However, since the Supreme Court had ruled that in juvenile court the act of delinquency must be proved beyond a reasonable doubt, not by a mere preponderance of the evidence, as was the practice for many years,[8] the appellate courts of my state, like most other states, held that judges must include delinquency in arriving at the presumptive sentence even though the other constitutional safeguards of adult criminal trials do not apply in juvenile court. Because the record in Robert's case established clearly that he never had a due process trial in juvenile court, I decided that I was legally justified in ignoring the presumptive sentence. I placed Robert on probation for four years, conditioned upon his attending school and obtaining a high school equivalency diploma. The probation office found a group home for him and an after-school job delivering pizzas. He regularly attended school and reported faithfully to his probation officer. I also required him to repay the eight dollars, and he did.

Robert did not file exceptions or take an appeal from the conviction. The prosecutor appealed the sentence on the ground that I had ignored the sentencing guidelines. These guidelines were devised for adult criminals, not children. Prior record when considered by those who established the guidelines was believed to be an adult criminal record based on a trial in which all constitutional rights were observed. Neither the fact of childhood nor the severe deprivation of Robert's life was a mitigating factor included in the guidelines.

Three years after sentence had been imposed, the appellate court set aside Robert's sentence, remanded the case to me, and ordered me to impose the guideline sentence. By that time Robert had attained his high school equivalency diploma. He was not on welfare; he had not been rearrested. By all criteria he was rehabilitated. The sheriff was unable to locate him. Robert is still at liberty. However, he is subject to arrest and to be brought back to serve a prison sentence of four to eight years whenever he is found. If he applies under his own name for a driver's license or for a license to work as a bartender or other employment that requires a security check, or if he should try to enlist in the armed forces, he will undoubtedly turn up on some computerized crime list and be returned for sentencing. If Robert had been treated like the child that he was, he would now be a free man without a criminal record and able to pursue any career for which he is qualified.

All the procedures to which Robert was subjected were legal even though many of the juvenile court hearings in which he was adjudicated delinquent did not conform to the constitutional standards required for adult courts. In each instance Robert was accused of a delinquent act, given a hearing, adjudicated delinquent, and placed in a foster home or correctional institution.

Many children are deprived of their liberty by juvenile courts not because they are found to have committed delinquent acts but solely because it suits the convenience of their parents.

Kimberly is one of many children who are turned over to the juvenile court under the rubric of incorrigibility. Like many other families, her parents did not want to cope with the problems of an adolescent child. Usually the family is poor. The mother is often overburdened with other children. Frequently the children and her paramour do not get along. The mother gives up the struggle to rear a troublesome child. The court rarely looks at why the child disobeys the parent. It is sufficient if the mother says, "Judge, I can't do nothin' with Tyrone. You take 'im." I have never known a judge to refuse jurisdiction over such a child.*

Kimberly's parents turned her over to the juvenile court. Even though they were middle-class, educated people, they shifted their parental responsibilities to the court, and the court accepted jurisdiction to the detriment of the child.

Kimberly Price was almost nineteen when I saw her in adult felony court. She was holding her six-month-old baby. The charge against her was shoplifting. Usually such an offense would be tried not in felony court but in misdemeanor court, where one harried judge would attempt to dispose of forty cases in a series of quick guilty pleas. Unless a defendant has a long record of crime or is violent, most judges will place these offenders on probation. What was this pretty young girl doing in my court, where serious crimes like rape, armed robbery, and commercial fraud were the daily fare?

Kimberly was angry. Her public defender told me that she insisted on a jury trial even though he assured her that I was most unlikely to send a young mother to prison. But Kimberly had no faith in judges or courts. After I heard her story, I could understand her hostility.

When Kimberly was seventeen, she became pregnant by her high school sweetheart, Scott. Kimberly was in love with the boy and wanted to marry him. Her parents wanted her to give up the child for adoption. They proposed sending her to another city until after the baby was born. An illegitimate child would be a blot on the escutcheon of this

---

*In Manhattan family court a mother told Judge Judith B. Sheindlin, "Place him somewhere. I can't have him at home." The boy had not committed a crime, but he was ordered to be held in custody (*New York Times,* December 15, 1987, pp. B1, 10).

nice, respectable family. Kimberly adamantly refused. She wanted her baby. She threatened to elope with Scott. Scott, who was the illegitimate son of a domestic employee, was considered an unsuitable son-in-law. After the parents consulted friends, a family therapist, and the family lawyer, it was decided that juvenile court was the solution. Mr. and Mrs. Price filed an incorrigibility petition in juvenile court. They assumed that after a couple of weeks of detention Kimberly would relent and accede to their wishes.

Kimberly was represented by a public defender, who valiantly argued that getting pregnant was not a crime, that she was entitled to her liberty and to finish her senior year in high school. The judge tried to reason with the Prices, but they stubbornly refused to permit Kimberly to come home. The judge refused to adjudicate her delinquent and continued the case for thirty days, hoping that Kimberly and her parents would come to an amicable resolution of the problem. At the end of thirty days the matter was listed before the court again. Kimberly's lawyer again made a forceful plea for her liberty. And the Prices again refused to take her home.

This time the lawyer argued that the Prices had an obligation to care for their minor daughter. They simply could not abandon her to the court to provide food and shelter for her.

The judge was sympathetic to Kimberly, who was by this time visibly pregnant and distraught. He asked counsel for legal authority. What precedent was there for him to order the Prices to take Kimberly home? The lawyer admitted that he could find no cases that supported his position.[9] But, he suggested, the Prices could be held in contempt of court if the judge entered such an order and they refused to obey. Without the authority of precedent, the judge refused to enter such an order.

Kimberly's lawyer then argued that it was unconstitutional to deprive Kimberly of her liberty when she had not been found delinquent.

"But where will she go if I release her?" the judge asked.

"We'll find her a place to live," the lawyer promised.

The court continued the matter for another two weeks so that Kimberly's lawyer could find housing for her.

At this point the welfare department became involved. The department filed a petition alleging that Kimberly was a child in need of care. That petition was granted, and the welfare department was ordered to find a foster placement for Kimberly.

A girl who is six months pregnant is difficult to place. And so Kimberly remained in detention until after she gave birth to her baby while the harried social workers looked for a home for her. Shortly after the baby was born, Kimberly became eighteen and the juvenile court lost jurisdiction over her. Kimberly applied for and received welfare for herself and the baby. The allotment was insufficient to pay for the food and clothing that Kimberly was accustomed to. When she needed Pampers and baby supplies, she simply went into a cut-rate store and took the items. This time she was arrested. Shortly thereafter at a bail hearing she was released on her own recognizance.

Kimberly had her jury trial before me. She was convicted of theft by a jury composed of seven women and five men. I placed her on probation. Where was her boyfriend, Scott? He was not in court. Her lawyer told me he had tired of waiting for Kimberly and had a new girl friend.

Although Kimberly was understandably angry at the juvenile court judge, he could not be faulted for failing to make new law. Nor could he be criticized for refusing to release a seventeen-year-old pregnant girl who had no place to live and no one to care for her. The fault, as I have so often discovered, was the law. When parents abandon an infant in a railroad station or a department store, they are arrested and imprisoned for child abuse. When parents abandon their teenage children under the rubric of incorrigibility, it is the child, not the parents, who goes to jail.

Fictions are not facts. Everyone recognizes that fiction is fantasy, not reality. But legal fictions permit courts to do what fact prohibits. The fiction that Robert and Eldred were adults because they were tried in adult criminal court gave an imprimatur of legality to a trial and an order of sentence that would otherwise have been illegal if applied to children. The fiction that juvenile delinquency hearings are not criminal trials permits the law to deny to children like Robert, Eldred, and Kimberly the rights established by the constitution.

If Kimberly had been eighteen instead of seventeen when she became pregnant, she could not have been deprived of her liberty unless she had been charged with a crime.

When children are treated like children in juvenile court, they are denied constitutional rights and equal protection of the laws. When they are tried in adult court, they are treated like adults and denied the protections accorded to children. In both instances they are subject to legalized discrimination. By failing to acknowledge the real physical, developmental, and emotional differences between children and adults, courts deny children substantive equal protection of the laws.

7

The Boy Who Didn't Know His Name

*And the king said, Divide the living Child in two,
and give half to one, and half to the other.*

—I KINGS 3:25

AFTER AMERICAN TROOPS left Vietnam, a United States Army major explained why the town of Ben Tre had been razed, stating, "It became necessary to destroy the town to save it." Most people wondered whether the outcome justified the painful and deadly battle. Often after protracted custody fights are concluded and the children are destroyed, I wondered whether this process can be justified as upholding the law.

The parents of one such child had been divorced for seven years before they brought their battle to my courtroom. The mother, Sandy, had remarried and had a child with her second husband, Arnold Bloomer. The father, Marvin Wellman, had not remarried. All he asked was to see his child once a week, which is known as visitation.

Assertation of visitation rights often causes as much feuding as claims for custody. The parent who has the responsibility for the care and rearing of the child resents the disruption and divided loyalties caused by the other parent, who may seek to bribe the child with gifts and activities forbidden by the custodial parent. Life-styles and goals differ. Holidays and vacations, instead of being joyous occasions, precipitate crises. Old hostilities flare anew as the battling ex-spouses fight over who shall have the physical body of the child and who shall pay the expenses. Traumatic as these episodes are for the parents, it is the child who pays the price.

Courts have not yet adjusted to the dramatic changes in the composition of the average American family. It is no longer what we know as the nuclear family, with working father, homemaking mother, and several children who all live together in the same house. In 1980 one in two marriages ended in divorce. In 1990 the rate is much higher. The children of divorce live in a fractured world torn between their parents, shuttled from one to the other. Many children live with a variety of paramours and subsequent spouses of their biological parents and the children of these other persons.

The prevalence of these various arrangements was revealed in a casual remark by Jason, a third grader, who told his mother that he had been invited to Adam Reder's house for dinner. Jason's mother wanted to call and confirm that her child was actually expected. She asked the boy the name of Adam's mother. Jason replied in a tone of astonishment, "In that family every one is named Reder." In this child's world an intact family unit was the exception, not the rule.

As is my practice in all cases involving custody and visitation of children, I met with the parties, their lawyers, and the child in chambers, not in the courtroom. I did not wear a robe. I try to meet the child in an unthreatening atmosphere, where I am perceived as a human being, not a fearsome figure of authority. Usually I show the child pictures of my grandchildren and ask the youngster about siblings, school, games, toys, and simple matters of daily life.

Five adults, an adorable three-year-old, and one frightened nine-year-old boy were herded into my chambers. There were two lawyers, the mother, her second husband, and the father. Sandy and Marvin were obviously hostile. Before they entered, I had heard angry, raised voices coming from the waiting room. Mr. Bloomer was carrying the little child, Jonathan, who was cheerful and laughing.

I turned to the trembling older boy, who was the object of this struggle, and said, "Hi, sonny, I'm Judge Forer. I'm here to help you." He did not take my outstretched hand, nor did he look at me. His enormous brown eyes filled with tears.

"What is your name?" I asked. This should have been a simple, nonthreatening question.

"M-M-Michael," he stammered.

"This paper I have before me says your name is David. Is it Michael or David?

"I d-don't know. My good father says my name is Michael Bloomer; my b-b-bad father says my name is David Wellman."

"What do you want me to call you?"

"I d-don't know." He had already lost the power to choose.

Many children don't know where their homes are or their relationships, if any, to the people with whom they live, but they know their own names.

Anthropologists tell us that among primitive tribes a person's name is sacred. An individual never tells a stranger his real name lest the person do him or her some harm. Name and identity are closely linked. There is no tribe so primitive that its members do not have names. Even animals are given names. In the Bible on the seventh day of Creation, God brought the animals and the birds to Adam to see what he would call them. All the creatures were given names. Every person who has had a pet knows that dogs and cats, even horses and birds recognize their own names and respond. To deprive a person of his name seemed to me a singular form of cruelty that was peculiarly destructive. The United Nations Convention on the Rights of the Child declares in Article 2, Name and Nationality: "The child shall have the right from his birth to assume a name and to acquire a nationality." This child, who had been given a name at birth, had been deprived of it.

I persuaded the boy to sit down. He chose a chair in a corner, away from everyone. His mother and Mr. Bloomer were seated on the sofa with little Jonathan, who was sucking a lollipop. I offered Michael/David some candy. He looked toward his mother for permission, but she was not paying attention to him, and he refused the candy.

Mr. Wellman, the boy's father, walked over to him. As he approached, the boy began to shake violently and cried. All the adults remained seated and silent. I went over to the boy and asked him if he would prefer leaving the room. He nodded and rose. I brought him into my law clerk's office, introduced them, and asked her to give him some paper and colored pencils.

"Will you please draw a picture for me while I go and talk to the lawyers?" I suggested.

The boy burst out, "I hate it when they talk about lawyers."

"Why?"

"Lawyers cost money. They blame me for that. They blame me for everything—everything except eating. I wish I were my little brother."

"Why? He's only a baby, and you're a nice big boy. You can do things—play games, go to school."

"He's always good, and I'm bad."

"What do you do that's bad?"

"Everything."

"Well, tell me something wrong you've done. What's the worst thing you ever did?"

"When my mom went shopping, she told me to take care of Jonathan. But Jonathan won't mind me. He climbed up on a chair and fell down and hurt himself. It was all my fault."

A nervous, unhappy nine-year-old should never have been left in charge of a three-year-old. Given the boy's subconscious hostility to Jonathan, he might well have hit him. On the other hand, it could easily have been an accident. Should I warn the parents of sibling rivalry and suggest that they not leave the two children alone? This well-meant suggestion could be misinterpreted as a conclusion that the boy was dangerous, rather than that sibling rivalry is normal. I am not a psychiatrist, I reminded myself. I should not overstep the bounds of judicial office.

"Why don't you want to see your father, Mr. Wellman?" I asked.

"He's a bad man. He'll hurt me."

"Who told you that?"

"My mother. She says he'll kill me, my brother, my mother, and my good father. Their lives are in my hands," he cried, holding out two grubby, trembling little hands. Much troubled, I returned to chambers to face the parents and their lawyers.

Between angry accusations and heated denials, I learned that Mr. Wellman, the natural father, was a man with many problems. He had been released from the military for psychiatric reasons. Although he was employed, it was in a low-paid, dead-end job. Mr. Wellman stinted himself on clothes, food, and minor pleasures to pay his lawyer. The boy was his only child. Unless he was found to be unfit and dangerous to the child, he had a legal right to see his son.

As I talked with Wellman, the Bloomers, and their lawyers, slowly, painfully the story unfolded. The boy had been told that his name was Michael Bloomer. He did not know that Mr. Bloomer was not his father until he went to school. The mother was required to bring a birth certificate to show that the child was of school age. The certificate listed the child as David Wellman. Mrs. Bloomer had neglected to tell the teacher that the boy was called Michael Bloomer and that he did not know that Mr. Bloomer was not his father. When the child learned the facts from the bewildered teacher, he came home crying. His mother then proceeded to tell him what an evil man his natural father was.

I never learned whether any of her charges were true. Wellman's lawyer said that he had investigated and that they were absolute lies.

Mrs. Bloomer had never made a complaint to the police charging Wellman with terroristic threats or any other offense.

Mrs. Bloomer did not accuse her former husband of wife abuse or child abuse. Until they came to court, Mr. Wellman had not seen the boy for more than seven years. Despite repeated requests, phone calls, and even visits to the Bloomer home, Mrs. Bloomer adamantly refused to let him see his son. Finally Wellman consulted an attorney. Mrs. Bloomer kept repeating that he was "crazy" and "dangerous." She became hysterical at the mention of Mr. Wellman.

Mr. Bloomer denied any knowledge of Mr. Wellman's past. He just wanted to maintain what he described as his "happy family" without interference from Wellman or the court.

The boy had said he was the cause of all the troubles of his mother and her husband. And he was not wrong in his perception. On another occasion I asked him more about his little brother, Jonathan, who was always brought to these conferences. Either the mother or the father would hold the child lovingly, speak softly to him, and offer him candies and toys that they brought with them. Neither of them looked at or spoke to Michael/David. The boy told me that everyone loved Jonathan; no one loved him. He tried to be good. He came home right after school each day and helped his mother with the housework. But he broke things, and she would get angry and yell at him.

The father and his lawyer insistently demanded the father's right to have the boy one day a week beginning immediately. In the disturbed state the child was in, I would not order that he be compelled to spend even one hour alone with Mr. Wellman. I suggested that the father and son should meet in some neutral place with other people so that the boy would not be terrified and gradually they could become acquainted. The three adults claimed there was no neutral place. Mrs. Bloomer began to scream, and so did Wellman.

Feeling that it was an imposition on counsel, I nonetheless suggested that Mr. Wellman, his attorney, and the boy have lunch together for an hour or two and see how that worked. Counsel and Mr. Wellman agreed. The Bloomers protested, but I made it a court order. I also suggested counseling for the boy. The Bloomers had many objections: First, it was expensive; second, Mrs. Bloomer did not drive and refused to use public transportation; third, the boy didn't need it. I countered her objections by pointing out that therapy was cheaper than counsel fees, there were several good child psychiatric clinics in her neighborhood, and this child was obviously in distress.

When I called Mrs. Bloomer's attention to the boy's school reports and his behavior in front of me, she remarked, "He probably has a genetic defect, inherited from his crazy father."

Mr. Wellman yelled, "You're the crazy one, you liar."

Mrs. Bloomer's lawyer persuaded her to enter into a consent decree requiring that the boy be taken to a clinic on a regular basis. They were ordered to be back in chambers a month later to evaluate the situation. Mrs. Bloomer's attorney said that he would furnish the boy's school reports.

After they left, my law clerk showed me a letter the boy had written while we were having our conference. It read, "Dere God, please help me." It was unsigned.

Thirty days passed, and I did not receive a report from the clinic where the boy was to have been taken. I waited another two weeks and then called the clinic. It reported that the mother had made an appointment but had not kept it. I called a conference with the parents and the lawyers and told them I would hold Mrs. Bloomer in contempt of court if she did not take the boy to the clinic. Her lawyer evidently convinced her that I would not accept any further excuses. Mother and child did go to the clinic for several weeks. The school reported further deterioration. Although the boy had an IQ of 115 and in first grade had been already able to read simple words and write his first name, he had regressed badly. He was now in third grade. He cried in class. On occasion he was incontinent. He did not know how to relate to other children. Reluctantly the school had placed him in a special education class with retarded and other problem children. I could not fault the school for this decision. How could a teacher with thirty healthy active children be mother, father, psychiatrist, and nurse for this child and still perform her teaching duties for all the others?

The next meeting was even more hostile and unsatisfactory. The father's attorney reported that they had met in his office. Mrs. Bloomer had brought the boy and admonished the lawyer not to let Mr. Wellman harm the child. Mr. Wellman had brought a toy, but the child would not touch it. They went to lunch, but the boy would not eat. The lawyer had to make conversation because the boy refused to speak to his father.

The father's attorney demanded that Mrs. Bloomer be held in contempt of court for failing to take the boy to the clinic. Her attorney threatened to appeal the consent order. After more heated discussion Mrs. Bloomer agreed to take the child to the clinic regularly. I scheduled another meeting two months later so that I would have an opportunity to receive several reports from the clinic.

The clinic reported that the child had abnormal fears, that he was unduly attached to his mother, that he needed a long course of treatment before he would be able to perform in school at grade level although he was unquestionably an intelligent child. They did not recommend institutionalization. In the psychiatrist's opinion it was important to strengthen the family ties. I also had the child examined by a court psychiatrist, who reported that the child's condition was serious. However, unless the child's life was actually endangered, he could not testify that hospitalization or placement outside the home was required. Without such medical evidence a judge has no authority to remove a child from the custody of his parents. Mrs. Bloomer would not consent to any therapy other than the weekly visit to the clinic. She missed more appointments than she kept.

I saw Michael/David eight times before Mr. Wellman's funds ran out. Despite the able arguments of counsel that the father had a right to see his child, with which I agreed, I would not order the boy to spend time alone with a man he hated and feared. The last time I saw them all together, the boy became physically ill when his father tried to shake hands with him. We rushed the child to the bathroom. The boy's stammer had become more pronounced. He had developed a facial tic. He was even more withdrawn and reluctant to speak with me.

I implored the lawyers to help the child by finding a relative or friend, someone who would give him a quiet, nonthreatening environment in which to heal from this experience. They agreed with me but were unsuccessful in the quest. No one was willing to get involved. Mr. Wellman's parents were dead. His sister lived in another city and refused to have anything to do with him. She had never seen the boy. Mrs. Bloomer's parents had retired to Florida. Her mother wrote to me and said that she had paid for her daughter's divorce and her second marriage. It was time Mrs. Bloomer took care of her own children.

Mr. Bloomer's family disapproved of his wife. They said she was a lazy spendthrift. They agreed that she didn't know how to bring up her children, but that wasn't their problem. In fact, Mr. Bloomer's sister said she hoped the marriage would soon break up and her brother could make a new start in life. Their rabbi, who had taken courses in marriage counseling, said he was meeting with the Bloomers, trying to hold the family together. If he could just keep the marriage intact, he was sure that the boy would be all right. But it was this nice middle-class family that was destroying the child.

The law in most jurisdictions permits a family court judge to remove a neglected or dependent child from an abusive home. In this case there was no evidence that the child had been physically abused. The psychiatrists did not recommend that he be removed from his mother's home. The court investigator visited the home and reported that it was in a good neighborhood, that it was clean and neat. The boy had his own room. He had books and toys. By all objective standards it was a good home. Now that the Bloomers were providing him with therapy, it would be impossible to prove neglect. Because the child was not under the aegis of the welfare department, the government could not file a neglect petition. I appointed a child advocate to represent the boy. After she had read all the reports and visited the Bloomers, she informed me there were no grounds on which to file either a dependency or neglect petition.

I entered an order permitting the father to withdraw his petition for visitation without prejudice so that in the future if he wished to renew his quest to see his child, he could do so. Month by month I had watched the painful disintegration of a small human being. The might of the law was powerless to protect this child from his family.

If Michael/David had been beaten or starved, I would have had the authority to remove him from such an abusive home. He would then in all likelihood have been placed with a foster family, who would be paid perhaps ten to twenty dollars a day to feed and house the boy. Except in very rare instances, foster parents have little training in the care of children with emotional problems. Such children require much more than a bed and three meals a day. Most children who are in foster care have suffered various kinds of abuse and deprivation. Their needs are much greater than those of the average child who has had a normal upbringing and successful schooling. When a child is too difficult, the foster parents simply return him or her, and the overburdened social workers look for another placement, which may be no better than the first.[1] Many abused youngsters spend their entire childhoods in a series of foster placements. I could not conclude that this child would be better off in a foster home. And there were no other options. Neither psychiatrist recommended placing him in a hospital or institution for emotionally disturbed children.

When divorced parents cannot come to an amicable agreement as to custody or living arrangements for their children, they turn to the courts. Countless judges have made tens of thousands of decisions because under the law they are obliged to do so. They hear reports of psychiatrists, psychologists, child therapists, and family therapists. But to date no one has been able to devise clear rules and principles that protect the rights of the parents and the children.

Under the old common law a father had unquestioned right to custody and control of his children. By the end of the nineteenth century mothers had obtained rights. Today under gender-neutral law the presumption that a mother should have custody of a child of tender years has been abolished. To meet the new demands for identical treatment of mother and father, many judges now order shared physical custody. Under this arrangement a child spends perhaps three days a week with one parent and four with the other. Recalling the difficulty my children had in finding their books, papers, and clothes when they lived in one house, I marvel at how these children can shuttle themselves and their belongings between two different places, two different sets of adults, and two different life-styles. There has been insufficient time to study and evaluate the long-term effects of these arrangements on the children. Meanwhile, without the benefit of reliable sociological and psychological findings and operating under obsolete legal doctrines, we judges muddle along. I tell the parents that I do not have the wisdom of Solomon. I cannot divide the child. The best I can do is divide the year and apportion it between them.

The Hippocratic oath taken by doctors requires them to promise to "do no harm." This principle is not a legal doctrine or a canon of judicial ethics. Often with the best intentions and with faithful adherence to the law, courts do serious harm. In the case of *Wellman v. Bloomer,* as in others, I believe that despite my good intentions, the child was harmed.

In most custody cases a judge is forced to choose between two inadequate parents. When required to make such a decision, I felt like a student taking a multiple-choice examination who is given several optional answers, including "none of the above." When I listened to and observed the mother and father and unhappy child, I wanted to say, "None of the above." Occasionally I was able to find a better solution.

In most instances a judge who looks beyond the two inadequate parents is unable to find a competent friend or relative who is willing to undertake the rearing of another child. Usually, if anyone steps into the breach, it is a grandmother. Some grandmothers are as young as forty and physically and mentally capable of caring for a young child and bringing him or her up through the difficult adolescent years. When the grandmother is elderly, the responsibility becomes increasingly burdensome, and often she loses the ability to control a headstrong youngster. With the widespread use of drugs among young parents, grandparents are increasingly being commandeered into assuming parental roles. It is unfair to them and unfair to the children. But if the grandmother is willing, it is often the best option.

In many cases the grandmothers and the children suffer unbearably.

Hattie was a hardworking sixty-eight-year-old nurse's aide. Her husband died when she was a young woman, leaving her to bring up an only daughter. At great sacrifice Hattie put her daughter through high school, sent her to secretarial school, and happily saw her married. Within a year the son-in-law had deserted his pregnant wife. After the child was born, the mother drifted away and became a drug addict.

Hattie brought up her granddaughter, Rosellen, with love and careful attention. Despite her best efforts, Rosellen became pregnant at age sixteen. Hattie was handed a great grandson, Clifton, to rear. It never occurred to Hattie to go to the welfare department or ask for a foster home for the baby. For four years she showered this child with love and care.

Rosellen was very bright and an exceptional athlete. While her grandmother took care of the baby and worked to support both of them, Rosellen went back to high school and was graduated with honors. She won an athletic scholarship to a university in another city. She had completed her first year with high honors when I met her.

Clifton was a very lively, healthy, cute, but somewhat intellectually slow boy, four years old. Rosellen was most attractive, and determined to succeed. Because she was a minor, even though she was a mother, Rosellen could not file a lawsuit. That had to be done by an adult, who appeared as Rosellen's next friend. This adult, the university's women's athletic coach, petitioned the court to terminate Rosellen's parental rights and put the child up for adoption. The great-grandmother at her own expense retained a lawyer and sought to adopt the child.

I appointed a child advocate* to represent Clifton. He was obviously devoted to his great-grandmother, the only family member he had known during his entire life. He did not recognize his mother when they came to court. She did not touch the boy or speak to him. Hattie, the

---

*The child advocate is now a fashionable adjunct to many family courts. Usually the advocates are sincere, well-intentioned young lawyers who are employed by organizations funded by charitable contributions. They would like to help children, but they do not function like lawyers who represent clients. Only rarely does a child advocate present witnesses on behalf of the child. Although these lawyers have no special expertise, they see their role as that of being an adviser to the court, a redundant function because in most instances the judge has more experience than the advocate. In the Baby M case, for example, the court appointed a child advocate to represent the child. Baby M's mother had agreed for a fee to be impregnated by a man whose wife did not want to bear a child, to carry the child to term, and then to give it to the biological father and his wife. When the biological mother, commonly called a surrogate mother, refused to relinquish the baby, the father sued. Both he and the biological mother were represented by counsel. The judge believed, as many judges do, that the child should be represented. In this case the child advocate's recommendation that the biological mother's rights be terminated was wisely overruled. Rarely does a child advocate undertake an independent investigation. Even when the child is of an age to express his or her wishes, the child advocate does not confer with the child but simply presents his or her own view of what is in the best interests of the child, a decision confided to the judge.

great-grandmother, adored the child. He was everything in her life. For him she continued to work all night every night. She needed every cent she could earn for his expenses. I doubt that Hattie had ever had a moment's rest since her granddaughter presented her with this child.

I suggested an open adoption under which the great-grandmother would be allowed to know the adopting parents and visit the child. This would mitigate the pain to her and ease the transition to a new life for this four-year-old child. Hattie agreed to this proposal, but the child's mother was adamantly opposed to the plan. She did not want the child ever to learn of her identity. She foresaw that she had a good, even brilliant, career ahead of her. A bastard child, not too bright, would clearly be an impediment. She recognized that soon her great-grandmother would be unable to care for the child and the responsibility for her son would devolve on her. She frankly told me that now, while the child was cute and his mental slowness not too apparent, was the time to find him a good family. Her analysis of the situation was correct. When the boy reached age eight or ten, it would be very difficult to find a middle-class family of any race that would be willing to adopt him. This young woman was upwardly mobile. She wanted to assure her child's future and her own freedom.

The child advocate, a nice, sensitive young man, got in touch with many adoption agencies and found a suitable couple who were willing to accept an open adoption. These young people recognized that the great-grandmother would not interfere with their parental roles. The mother would probably never appear, and the child would not have the trauma of being wrenched from his great-grandmother.

But this happy ending was not to be. The mother appealed, and the appellate court held that the great-grandmother had no standing to intervene in an adoption. In the eyes of the law she was a stranger, no different from a foster parent, who is paid a per diem rate by the state to care for a strange child. If the mother wanted a closed adoption, that was her right. No one considered the right of the child to maintain ties with the one person who loved him and whom he loved.

Life is not easy for most children of divorce, whether they live in slums, middle-class houses, or wealthy mansions.[2] They have nightmares. Their schoolwork deteriorates. They become moody and withdrawn and refuse to play with other children. In the midst of this turmoil they are brought to court for custody hearings.

Many judges who must decide custody disputes ask the children which parent they wish to live with. I never did so. This is a choice as terrible for a child as that presented to Sophie in William Styron's novel

Sophie's Choice. Sophie, who was in a Nazi concentration camp, was told by the guard that she could save only one of her two children. In effect she was compelled to condemn one to death. For a child the choice of one parent means the rejection of the other, the condemnation of the other to a limbo outside the area of the child's life. This, I believe, is too great a burden to impose on any youngster.

I recall one bright little blue-eyed girl who was asked this terrible question by the court psychiatrist. He reported to me that the child replied, "Let the judge choose. That's his job."

Most children who are compelled to make this choice go through life, like Sophie, with an unbearable sense of guilt.

Of course, I wanted to know if the child had a preference, and if so, why. Some young children rushed into my chambers and immediately said, "I want to live with my mom," or "I want to live with my dad." Invariably after a few minutes of unthreatening conversation about neutral subjects, the child would blurt out, "I promised I would tell you which one I want to live with." And I invariably replied, "Yes, you did tell me. But I am the one who has to make the decision, not you. I will tell your mom [or dad] what you told me." The child visibly relaxed. Whatever happened, the onus was no longer on the child.

Usually a friendly conversation in which the child describes the various activities he or she has with each of the parents will reveal the child's real preference, if there is one, more honestly than a coached statement. I often heard remarks such as this: "My dad is very good to me. He buys me lots of toys." Or "He took me to the ball game or the circus."

I usually asked, "Does anyone help you with your homework?"

The child might respond, "Oh, yes, my mom sits with me every night and sees that I do my lessons. When I've finished, then we have a treat."

"What is a treat?"

"I get to choose. We can watch TV or go to visit my friend or have ice cream. . . ."

A seven-year-old girl who had just told me that she wanted to live with her mom said that her mother yelled at her and hit her when she disobeyed. The disobedience was not scrubbing the kitchen floor clean enough.

It takes patience and a lot of time to talk with a child and try to learn what the life of that youngster is really like. The facile phrase "the best interest of the child" does not provide a judge with much guidance. Unless one parent is really brutal, sadistic, abusive, or emotionally unstable, the judge's choice is a very difficult one. Often the parents who most vehemently protest their love for the child and their adamant determination to have custody do not really want it. A woman often feels that it is a stigma not to have custody of her children. Many a man has used the custody issue as another ploy in revenging himself on the wife who rejected him. In one or two meetings with the parents and their counsel, even the wisest judge cannot be sure who really wants to care for the child and what is in the child's best interest.

I found that a temporary order of a few months' duration was often advisable. The parent who was awarded temporary custody might find that he or she did not really want it and would propose another arrangement. Sometimes the one who was denied custody and given visitation rights was content with the arrangement. If the child was old enough to write a letter or make a phone call, I told him or her to get in touch with me if the temporary arrangement was not satisfactory. I heard from a number of children. When a child was dissatisfied, I notified both counsel, and usually we were able to work out a more satisfactory division of time and responsibility. But this took time and patience. The child must develop a sense of trust in the judge.

Remarriage of one parent inevitably causes problems for the children. So does a move to another part of the country. These are common occurrences in the lives of American children of divorce. No formula or scheme, such as shared custody or permanent custody, can meet these changed conditions and needs. While parents have and should have rights to the care, custody, and companionship of their children, these rights should not prevail over the fundamental right of every person not to be mistreated. Any formulaic statement of the law that places the family in a position of primacy over the child is, in my opinion, not only unwise but also violative of the equal protection clause.

Had the law permitted, I would have had a full-scale hearing in the case of Michael/David. I would have subpoenaed his teachers, the neighbors, and the clinic psychiatrist to testify as to their observations of the child and the changes in his condition. I would have employed experts in developmental psychology and child psychiatry to examine him and make findings with respect to his condition and prognosis, and I would have ordered appropriate treatment despite the objections of his mother and the demands of his father for immediate visitation.

My last glimpse of Hattie and Clifton was when a court officer forcibly lifted Clifton from Hattie's lap and handed him to the adopting father. The child's piteous wails could be heard echoing down the courthouse corridors as he was carried away. Hattie painfully hobbled on her arthritic feet to the door of the room, tears running down her face for one last look at this beloved child. She called my chambers several times to find out how Clifton was faring. But I did not know and, indeed, was not permitted to obtain any information. The privacy of the adopting parents must be protected.

There are many instances in which adults are denied the companionship of their families and loved ones. Often one spouse bitterly opposes a divorce. Innocent families of prisoners are denied the companionship of the wrongdoers. Draftees are involuntarily wrenched from their homes and families. All these acts are taken pursuant to law and, if resisted, are enforced by court orders. The disposition of children by court order is of a different dimension. Adults have rights that the courts must consider. Prior to no-fault divorce, most divorces were consensual or granted on the basis of the alleged fault of one of the parties. An innocent injured spouse could not be deprived of marital rights. Criminals by their own acts have put themselves beyond the protection of their familial rights. In the case of the military, the security needs of the state override the desires of the individual. In cases of child custody and adoption, despite the best interests of the child formula, it is the parents' rights that are protected. Clifton was represented by able, dedicated counsel, but under the law the wishes of his natural mother prevailed over what most people involved in the case considered were the child's best interests.

In the disposition of children, the legacy of the common law, that children are the property of their parents and lack jural personhood, subconsciously permeates much of the law today. In juvenile court, when parents allege that children are incorrigible, few, if any, judges will compel the parents to take home children whom they do not want.

The Supreme Court has held that when parents have their child committed to a mental institution, the child has no right to a hearing.[3] In custody cases the rights of the parents often prevail over the needs of the child. And in adoption cases the child is not represented. No one speaks for the child. Only the adoption agency or the individual who procured the child for the adopting parents knows the facts about the natural parents and the condition of the child. Under American law a judge does not investigate and is not an inquisitor.

The law of adoption has seldom been challenged because the child, who is the object of the court order, really has no standing at law and little access to lawyers to assert rights or claim protection. Occasionally there is a dispute between foster parents who wish to keep a child and natural parents who wish to reclaim their children. One such case reached the United States Supreme Court. The Court was concerned with the process that was "due" the foster parents. It was not suggested that the children had due process rights.[4]

Adoption has been touted as the optimum solution to the problem of unwanted and homeless children. It appears to offer an ideal answer to three unhappy persons: the childless couple and the homeless child. The popular concept of adoption is that of a loving, caring couple who by an unfortunate quirk of nature are unable to have their own child and find happiness and fulfillment in rearing a child whom they love and cherish as if it were their own. The child who, through no fault on his or her part, has been abandoned by parents who either do not want a child or are incapable of caring for the child is given a substitute family. Some adoptions do bring great happiness to the parents and the child. Unfortunately many do not. For these adults and children adoption is a practice fraught with heartbreak and disappointment.

Even when an adopting couple has all the outward indicia of responsibility and caring and the adoption has been arranged through a licensed agency, there are numerous and insoluble tragic problems. When I was practicing law, I represented many couples who adopted children. While there were some happy parents, there were many more who were unhappy with the role of adopted parent and with the child. Recently adopting parents have been attempting to return the children. I do not know whether the children were happy. There are few reliable studies of adoptees. What one does know is that great numbers of adoptees on reaching adulthood spend frustrating years seeking to find their natural parents. The law in most states prohibits this information from being disclosed to the child. Would these adoptees have been better off under some other arrangement? No one knows. However, there is a growing body of information indicating that adults who spent their childhoods in both foster homes and orphanages vastly preferred the latter.[6]

My clients were all middle-class to affluent young couples. They desperately wanted a child. Some went through the long, agonizing wait for their applications to be approved by licensed adoption agencies. They were investigated. Their neighbors were visited. Their homes were inspected, and also their bank accounts. Older couples and interfaith and interracial couples had little possibility of obtaining a child from an agency. Many of them, like some of the young couples I represented, ultimately turned to private sources: doctors, friends, and agencies in other countries. Sometimes the couple was told the backgrounds of the child's parents. There was, however, no way to verify this information.

Those who obtained a baby from an agency were given very little information. It is the policy of most agencies to "match" the baby to the adopting parents as to race, religion, intelligence, and physical appearance, but many times there is a serious mismatch.

Although in all these cases I was retained simply to do the legal work, I insisted on seeing the infant or child before obtaining a court decree. If the infant's appearance raised any question in my mind, I would urge the adopting couple to have the child tested. Sometimes a baby only one week old who appeared to be white was found to have mixed parentage. I recall one baby who was discovered to have Down's syndrome; another who was three months old and exceptionally pretty was later found to be autistic. Others had serious physical defects. Some couples went through with the adoptions; others did not. At least they made an informed decision.

Adoption is a very old practice. In Britain children were adopted to keep property titles in the family. Usually the adoptees were poor relatives. Legal adoption of strange children by childless couples who simply want the pleasure of parenthood is a relatively new phenomenon. In the past, as today, most adoptions were within the family. In 1982 there were 141,861 adoptions in the United States. There are few reliable statistics as to adopting parents and adopted children. But it is estimated that only 50,000 of these were by unrelated persons.[7]

Adoption is regulated by statute in every state. Although most states require that adoptions be made through approved agencies, in fact, many are privately arranged.

In recent years the numbers of persons—couples, single persons, homosexual partners, etc.—seeking to adopt children have multiplied. These prospective adopters have increasingly turned to private sources, including organizations and individuals that obtain infants and young children from other countries, often under questionable circumstances.*

Most white adults want a white child. Almost every adopting parent wants a bright, healthy infant. Public and private social agencies seek in vain adopting parents for older children, nonwhites, and many sick infants. With the rise of drug addiction and alcoholism among teenage mothers, the number of infants and young children with serious physical and mental problems is growing to staggering proportions. Few people, no matter how desperately they want a child, are willing or financially and emotionally able to assume the care of such an infant or

---

*It is believed that some seven hundred Colombian children have been adopted annually by persons in the United States (*Philadelphia Inquirer,* January 27, 1990, p. 4).

child. But these are the majority of children agencies try to place.

Judge Richard A. Posner points out that there are widespread black markets and gray markets in adoption.[8] He would apply economic market criteria to adoptions. In other words, those who want a healthy white infant should openly pay the going rate. In every state the sale or trafficking in children is forbidden by statute. But in fact, even legal adoptions through an approved agency involve a financial transaction. The adopters pay the agency a fee that customarily includes the medical expenses of childbirth for the natural mother as well as the overhead and incidental expenses of the agency. Obviously there is some hypocrisy in these approved arrangements. Posner's suggestion, however, strikes most lawyers and social workers as crass commercialism. Posner suggests that market forces are benign. He states: "If the transaction diminishes the baby's welfare by more than it increases the transactors' [natural mother's and adopting couple's] welfare, the transaction is not efficient. . . ." This is scarcely a standard that courts could easily enforce. And what if the transactors' welfare is 60 percent but the baby's welfare is only 40 percent? What is in the best interest of a child in such circumstances?

Although in custody and adoption cases courts routinely cite the best interest of the child theory to justify their decisions, courts seldom have the necessary facts on which to base an informed decision. No one represents the child. In custody cases, as has been described, the battle is between the parents. The child is an object, like a house, a car, or a pet dog that is awarded to one or the other or apportioned between them. In adoption cases the court has only the facts presented by the person or couple seeking to adopt the child and the report of an agency (if one is involved) approving the adoption. On such a scant and often misleading record in uncontested cases, as the overwhelming majority of adoptions are, a court order of adoption is merely a ceremonial rite demanded by the law. In entering such orders, I always had an uneasy feeling that I was giving an imprimatur to the sale of a child without any reasonable assurance that this was really in the best interest of the child.

The law employs the fiction that adopting parents are the same as natural parents and have all the rights, privileges, and protections of natural parents. Once an order authorizing adoption is entered, the state loses all legal control over the child and is free of any obligation to protect the child unless an abuse petition is filed.

Often when I entered an order approving an adoption and watched the happy couple leave the courtroom with an infant wrapped in a clean new blanket and dressed immaculately, I wondered what would happen when the baby screamed in the night, when it was sick, when it grew up to be a "terrible two" smashing dishes and lamps, when it reached kindergarten and was no longer cute and adorable but might be fat or skinny and withdrawn, when it reached fourth or fifth grade and might be a slow learner, a heartache, and a problem, and when all the difficulties of adolescence and rebellion inevitably arrived.

Lawyers and judges get horrifying glimpses of these problems and disappointed expectations when adopting parents seek to undo the adoptions they so eagerly sought. Recent cases reveal that disenchantment with adoption occurs more often than the public would like to think. Adopting couples have sued to annul adoptions.[9] Most such actions have been dismissed on two grounds: first, that there is no legal authority to set aside or annul an adoption and second, that it is in the best interests of the child not to disturb the adoption but to keep the family together. The Uniform Adoption Act, which has been enacted with minor variations in most states, does not provide for annulment of adoptions. As of this writing, only Hawaii and New York by statute permit the annulment of adoption. One can only wonder how the best interest of a child is promoted by forcing a child to remain with adults who affirmatively want to rid themselves of the burden and expense of caring for the child.

Other adopting parents have sued for fraud because the approved adoption agency knowingly gave false and misleading information about the child. In one case the agency knew the child was mentally defective but told adopting parents that it was normal.[10] In that case the court awarded damages to compensate the adopting parents for the excessive costs of maintaining the child.

More cases will inevitably arise as adopting parents learn of the availability of relief. Neither annulment of adoption nor damage actions provide a satisfactory resolution to these difficult problems, though both remedies are probably appropriate.

It is perhaps time to look at the whole problem of adoption from the viewpoint of the adoptee unclouded by myths and popular notions. Both adoption and foster care are promoted by elaborate, expensive publicity campaigns addressed to adults, painting a rosy picture of the joys of opening one's home and heart to a charming, healthy, loving child who needs a home and parents. The picture is appealing. President Bush extols the virtues of adoption. Few persons in policy-making positions have asked either foster children or adoptees what they think.

Most adoptees think they have a right to know who their biological parents are and to make contact with them. Their wishes, in most cases, run counter to the law and settled adoption policy. The identities of the natural parents in most states may not be disclosed. Most adoption agencies follow this rule whether or not required by law.

If the law were structured to protect and enforce the rights of the child, both adoption and foster parenting would be very different. While I do not agree with Judge Posner's application of economic theory to the disposition of human beings, he forces society to recognize that any placement of a child for money, directly or indirectly, is a trafficking in human beings. When the state, through an order of adoption or foster placement, removes a child from biological parents and transfers custody, permanent or temporary, to another adult, there should be a continuing public responsibility to monitor the placement and protect the child. In every adoption proceeding the child's interest should be the paramount consideration. Under the Anglo-American adversary system the child should be represented independent of the agency and those seeking the adoption. This is an essential role for a child advocate, but one that is rarely assumed.

Despite the florid and benign verbiage surrounding adoption and foster parenting, it is well to remember that these are legal devices by which the state rids itself of responsibility for abandoned, abused, and homeless children. In adoptions the state is also relieved of the cost of maintaining the adopted child. Today, as in the past, these are seen as cheap and expedient practices, beneficial to adults: adopters, who want children, and foster parents, who are paid (far less than minimum wages) for their services. Proposals to pay adults to adopt hard-to-place children (mentally and physically handicapped children) would compound the evils of trafficking in human beings. This is another device for the state to get care for especially vulnerable children at bargain rates without responsibility for oversight and protection.

The law of adoption treats the disposition of a child like the transfer of property. The prior owner relinquishes all rights, title, and interest. The new owner acquires the property and may legally do with it as he or she wishes. It should be recognized that children are persons, not property. Only very recently has the law begun to erode the absolute dominion of natural parents over their children. It was not until the 1970s that child abuse reporting statutes were enacted. They have been enforced by the courts with extreme caution lest the state interfere with parental rights to privacy and control over the rearing, education, and health of the children.[11] In the light of this background, there has been little, if any, supervision or oversight of adopting parents, who by a legal fiction are presumed to be the parents of the adopted child.

I believe this legal sanctioning of the transfer of a child from a natural parent or parents to strangers should entail a corresponding and continuing obligation on the part of the courts. To date the literature on adoption and most of the judicial decisions are designed to promote finality and to treat the adopted child in every way as if he or she were the biological child of the adopting couple. I suggest that while finality is a desirable goal, it should not override the rights of the child to protection and relief from an undesirable home and unsuitable parents given to the child without his or her consent. Adults are no longer chained to unhappy marriages. A status that has been conferred on the couple by the law as a result of their choice can be dissolved. Similar rights should also be available to a child whose wishes were never consulted when the adoption was entered by a court. However, no reported decision has employed standards with respect to protecting an adopted child from parental abuse different from those protecting a child who has allegedly been abused by the biological parents. This is an area of law that should be carefully examined and reevaluated.

Under most state laws a natural mother has a six-month period after relinquishing her baby for adoption to change her mind. I believe that adopting parents and adoptees should also have a six-month period in which to change their minds. During this trial period the state should have the right to oppose the adoption if investigation should find that the placement was not good for the child. In the case of older children, they should have the right to express an opinion as to whether they want the adoption, and that opinion should be entitled to great weight. The Menninger Children's Villages in Topeka, Kansas, have an adoption program for older children. After careful investigation of the adopting parents and their attendance at a course in parenting, the child and adopting parents spend several weeks together on a trial basis to see if both parties are happy. Sometimes they are, and sometimes they are not. A lifetime of unhappiness for three people is averted by this rather simple procedure.

The law employs many fictions. A corporation is presumed to be a person. All adults unless legally insane are presumed to be reasonable persons. The most recent widespread legal fiction is that an adopted child is the same as a biological child. I favor laws that provide that adopted children inherit equally with natural children and grandchildren. But the fiction that after the adoption decree is final, this legally created family is to be treated the same as any other family, to have the same rights of privacy from state inspection and intrusion places many adopted children at risk and harms many children.

The tragedies that have befallen children in custody disputes, foster placements, and adoptions occurred in many instances because the law gives a primacy to the rights of adults over children. As the cases in the next two chapters dealing with abused children reveal, the courts and child care agencies and personnel are wedded to the concept of keeping the family together at the expense of the welfare and safety of the child.

8

The Child as Witness

Children and fools cannot lie.

—JOHN HEYWOOD

WHEN THE COURT CRIER ANNOUNCED, "*State versus Gardner,*" a young woman and a little girl moved to the front row of the courtroom. The child was sucking a lollipop. In a few moments the sheriff opened the door and a middle-aged man walked over to the defense table. When the child saw him, she began to cry and sob uncontrollably. "Take me home," she begged.

The prosecuting attorney hurried over to the child and said, "Don't worry, Mattie. I'm here. Your mom is here. That man with a gun is the sheriff. He's like a policeman. No one can hurt you now."

"I wanna go home. I hate Uncle Mike. Please, let me go," she cried.

I suggested that a court officer take the child out in the corridor while I talked to counsel.

This was not going to be an easy case to try. When a child is the complaining witness, there are usually problems.

Michael Gardner was charged with rape, statutory rape, assault, and contributing to the delinquency of a minor. He and his attorney were at the defense table. Also present in the courtroom were a pediatrician and a child psychiatrist.

A courtroom is an alien, intimidating place even for sophisticated adults. For a child it is terrifying. Most lawyers are not accustomed to questioning children. They use words that are unfamiliar to youngsters;

they demand yes or no answers. The child sits alone on the witness stand in a room full of strange people.

Gardner had demanded a jury trial. Would six-year-old Mattie Armont be able to tell her story under these circumstances? Many women break down under the trauma of rape trials. Others refuse to prosecute because they fear, with reason, the ordeal to which they will be subjected.

Fortunately the prosecutor in this case was an experienced young woman lawyer who had won the confidence of Mattie and her mother. Defense counsel was an older man who in his forty years at the bar had seen much of the sordidness and brutality of life. He would give his client a good, workmanlike defense, but he would not make more objections than were necessary to protect his client's rights. A lawyer who is not cooperative can destroy a child simply by the tone of voice and legally permissible but unnecessary objections, sidebar conferences, and prolonged cross-examination. There is little the trial judge can do in such circumstances without improperly interfering with the defense.

Before the trial commenced, the prosecutor presented the testimony of Dr. David Perry,* a board-certified child psychiatrist. He testified that he had examined Mattie twice for a forty-minute hour each time, that this was his customary practice. The first time he saw her was four months prior to trial. He described his examination. He had asked Mattie the usual questions: her name, address, her age, the names of her parents and her siblings, her school, her teacher. She responded without any difficulty. He subsequently checked with her mother and learned that Mattie's answers were correct. Mattie was six years old and in first grade. She said she liked school and her teacher was "OK."

All her responses were normal and average for a child of her age. When he mentioned Michael Gardner, the defendant, Mattie froze. She refused to answer anything about him. When the doctor persisted and said, "He is your uncle, isn't he?" she wept and called for her mother. He was unable to get her to talk to him at all, and the examination had to be terminated.

Mattie was brought to him because her mother told him that the child had been having nightmares, that she refused to sleep in her own room, that she would not walk to school alone. This behavior had begun immediately following an alleged incident with Michael Gardner.

---

*The testimony is condensed from the trial transcript.

Dr. Perry saw Mattie again a week before the trial. She was more withdrawn and reluctant to answer questions. When he again mentioned Michael Gardner, she burst into tears and said, "I don't want to talk about him. I hate him."

When asked why she hated Mr. Gardner, Mattie refused to answer.

Dr. Perry stated that it was his opinion with a reasonable degree of medical certainty that it would be deleterious to Mattie's mental health for her to have to be in the same room with Michael Gardner, and he had so advised her mother. He further stated that he had discussed with the mother whether it was in the best interests of the child for Mattie to testify at this trial. Dr. Perry said that psychiatrists were divided on the subject. Some believed that the experience was too traumatic for a child. Others were of the opinion that it was therapeutic for a child to tell what had happened to her and that having told about the experience, she would be better able to put it behind her.

On the basis of his testimony, I decided that Mattie should testify by means of closed-circuit television.

Little Mattie would sit in a separate room with a television screen, accompanied by a court officer and a television technician. She would be able to see and hear the lawyer who was questioning her. The defendant, the jury, the lawyers, and I, the judge, would be able to see and hear Mattie on television. But Mattie would not have to be in the same room with the defendant, whom she feared, and with the jury, composed of fourteen strange adults (twelve jurors and two alternates) who would be avidly scrutinizing her.

Defense counsel objected to the procedure for the record, as was his obligation. But when I ruled that we would use television, he was completely cooperative. In fact, when the procedure was explained in open court, the defendant was relieved. He volunteered that he didn't want to see Mattie. "Kids make me nervous," he said.

Until the trial was over, I did not see Mattie except via television. On the screen the jurors and I saw a little girl with big brown eyes and straight black hair tied in a yellow ribbon. She was missing her two front teeth. On the rare instances when she smiled, she was winsome. Most of the time she frowned and wriggled uncomfortably in the hard wooden chair.

The jurors were asked if they had any problems with the proposed procedure. "As long as we can see and hear the child testify, I don't know why she has to be in the courtroom," one juror remarked.

Jury selection was made with great care. As was my practice in child abuse cases, I excluded for cause anyone who had been the victim of child molestation or who had a close friend or relative who had been molested as a child. Of a panel of forty men and women, eleven persons were excused for this reason, not an unusually high percentage. Three women and one man declared that they could not be fair to anyone who was even accused of sexually molesting a child. Whether that was an easy way to avoid jury duty I do not know. But they were excused.

Of the twelve jurors and two alternates who were selected, only two were childless. The prosecutor struck all the unmarried females, and defense counsel struck the schoolteachers. Although all the jurors were literate and had been employed at some time in their lives, they claimed not to have read or heard about any studies indicating the reliability or unreliability of child witnesses and, in particular, children who claimed to have been abused. We seemed to have as unbiased a group of jurors as the process could provide.

The first problem in a case involving a child witness is to establish that the child is qualified to testify—that is, that he or she knows the difference between truth and falsity and the nature of the oath. This requirement excludes most child witnesses under the age of five. Although tens of thousands of little children are abused each year, in most instances it is impossible to prosecute the abuser because the only person who actually saw the act of abuse take place is the child, and she* is legally disqualified from testifying because she does not understand the nature of an oath.

Mattie sat in her little television studio and was questioned gently but thoroughly by the prosecuting attorney.

"Mattie, do you know you're on TV?"

"Yeah, I can see myself. Look I'll wave to you," and she did.

"I'm Lisa Fox, a lawyer. Do you remember me?"

"Sure."

"Do you remember I told you that when we came to court, I would ask you questions?"

"Yeah."

"And did I tell you that you must tell the truth?"

Mattie was busy making faces in the camera and blowing her bubble gum.

"Mattie, are you going to tell the truth today?"

"Uh-huh."

"Do you know what a lie is?"

"It's a story you make up."

*Most abused children are girls.

"It's not the truth, is it?"

"No."

"What happens to you if you tell a lie."

"My mom gives me a lickin'."

"Do you go to Sunday school?"

"Sometimes."

"Do you know what a sin is?"

"Something bad."

"Is telling a lie bad?"

"Yeah."

Defense counsel on cross-examination asked the same questions again and again, and Mattie gave the same answers. The child was clearly becoming restive and reluctant to speak.

"I believe Mattie knows the nature of her oath and is qualified to testify," I told counsel and the jury. "Let the oath be administered."

A squirming, unhappy little girl swore to "tell the truth, the whole truth, and nothing but the truth so help me God."

We were now ready for the evidence as to the crime. It was alleged that like almost all sexual offenses, this one had occurred when no one was present but the offender and the victim. The entire weight of the prosecution rested on the credibility of this unhappy six-year-old child. She was not able to have the emotional support of her mother or father sitting with her. She was alone in a small room with a kindly female court officer and a male television technician. She had not seen either of them before. There was nothing the prosecutor or I, the judge, could do to help her through this ordeal. I wondered then, as I always do in these cases, whether the vindication of the law is worth the hardship imposed on the victim of the crime. Of course, there is always the danger that pedophiles will commit offenses against other children if they are not convicted and incarcerated for long periods. All too often even after conviction such abusers are given probation and released to commit other offenses against children.

My role in this case, as in all trials, was to be the neutral fulcrum on the scales of justice, to ensure that the defendant, who might be an innocent victim of a child's lies, received a fair trial with as little harm as possible to the child herself.

Years ago very few of these cases were brought to trial because the likelihood of obtaining a conviction was so remote. Few children know the vocabulary to describe what had happened to them. I recall a case in which a four-year-old girl testified that the defendant "put his penis in my vagina." Defense counsel on cross-examination promptly asked the little girl, "What is a penis?"

"I don't know," she answered.

"What is a vagina?"

"I don't know."

"Who told you these words?"

"That man," she answered, pointing to the prosecutor.

A directed verdict in favor of the defendant was entered by the court. The prosecutor found himself facing disciplinary charges for coaching the witness.

Most large prosecutor's offices now have special child abuse units in which the attorneys are taught how to try these cases. They show the children anatomically correct dolls and let the children demonstrate by means of the dolls exactly what happened. Careful prosecutors video-tape these interviews so that there can be no question that the children were improperly coached. But these dolls are seldom used at trial. Even with the help of dolls the child herself must testify as to what happened to her and must identify the abuser. An experienced prosecutor lets the child use her own words for the relevant portions of the anatomy. But even with the most sensitive lawyers, such testimony is a brutal ordeal for a young child.

The most simple factual questions, such as the date and time of the incident, are difficult to prove by a child witness. Unless the crime occurred on Christmas or a birthday, the child does not know the day. Children do not keep datebooks and diaries. Time has a different dimension for a four-year-old than for a forty-year-old. But legal time is that of the reasonable adult.

In this case the prosecutor began with the testimony of the police officer who took the complaint made by the mother and the child. He had his records and testified from official reports. Officer Collins of the child abuse unit testified that he received a call from the emergency ward of the pediatric hospital at 8:03 P.M. on a Friday. He spoke to the doctor who had examined Mattie and to Mattie and her mother, Mary Armont.

Mrs. Armont told him that Mattie had come home about five in the afternoon crying. Her clothes were disheveled, and her underpants were covered with blood. She immediately took the child to the hospital clinic, where she was examined. Dr. David Levy, the physician on duty, advised her to file a child abuse complaint. The doctor also filed an abuse report.

Mrs. Armont told Officer Collins that Mattie said she had been playing outside when Uncle Mike—Michael Gardner, the defendant— came by and told her he had a present for her at his house. Although she had been told by her mother never to go to his house, she wanted to get the present, and she went with him. He took her upstairs to his bed-room, pulled down her underpanties, and hurt her with his "thing." Uncle Mike gave her a dollar and told her not to tell anyone what happened. She ran home and went to her room and threw up all over her bed.

Mrs. Armont said that she questioned Mattie and took her to the hospital. Mattie gave a crumpled bloodstained dollar bill to her mother, who gave it to the police officer. The dollar was introduced into evidence. Officer Collins went to the defendant's home with a body warrant and a search and seizure warrant. He arrested the defendant, searched his room, and seized as evidence the defendant's bedding, which had blood and other stains. These items were also introduced into evidence.

The police laboratory technician testified that the stains on the bedding were semen and blood. The blood type was O, which was the type of both Mattie and the defendant. This case was tried before use of the sophisticated blood tests that, it is claimed, now enable technicians to identify an individual by a blood sample as positively as by a fingerprint. At that time it was impossible to tell whether the blood was that of Mattie or the defendant.

Mrs. Armont testified as to Mattie's condition and what the child had told her. The prosecutor argued that Mrs. Armont's testimony as to what Mattie told her was admissible as part of the res gestae. The law assumes that when a person has just undergone a traumatic or unusual experience, he or she will immediately blurt out the truth before there is time to revise or concoct a false story. Ordinarily a witness is not permitted to repeat what someone else has said. This is known as hearsay. The res gestae exception to the hearsay rule has been recognized by Anglo-American law for generations.

Most commonly such testimony arises out of accidents. Immediately after an automobile accident, if one of the drivers says to the other, "I'm sorry, I ran into your car. I just didn't see you," that statement is admissible. Of course, the jury will have to decide if the second driver is telling the truth. In other words, did the first driver actually admit that he wasn't looking? If believed, such testimony is compelling.

The problem in this case was that the incident occurred several blocks away and no one could say how long it was before Mattie spoke to her mother. I ruled that Mrs. Armont's testimony was not admissible as res gestae but only as corroboration. If Mattie testified in court substantially what her mother stated she said, it would be admissible to show the consistency of her story. If Mattie's testimony was not the same, the jury would be instructed that it could not consider Mrs. Armont's testimony as evidence on this point.

In this case everything would depend on Mattie's testimony.

Mrs. Armont was only thirty years old but looked at least forty. She had a strong face with classic beauty, high cheekbones, straight, heavy black eyebrows above a slender aquiline nose. Her slightly graying black hair was pinned tightly back in a heavy knot. She gave her testimony in a low, tense voice. She never looked at the defendant. He sat back in his chair, apparently at ease, his eyes devouring her.

Defense counsel then subjected Mrs. Armont to a grueling cross-examination. He brought out that Mrs. Armont did not like her uncle Mike, that she had forbidden her daughter to go to his home, that she had made derogatory remarks about him to her family and the neighbors.

Mrs. Armont responded angrily. "Yes, I don't like him. Everything bad I've said about him is true. And I'll tell you what I said—"

"Objection, objection."

The objection was sustained, and the jury admonished to disregard her comments.

Sharp cross-examination continued. "Didn't Mattie first tell you that she had fallen on a piece of metal and that's how she hurt herself?" Mrs. Armont admitted that was true.

"So it was only after you told her you didn't believe her that she said Uncle Mike had hurt her."

"Yes. But I know she was telling the truth then."

"And she was lying before?"

"She knew she had disobeyed me by going to his house and didn't want to admit it."

"So, Mrs. Armont, you now tell us your daughter lied to you first. How do we know she's not lying now? And that's what she told the doctor, isn't it?"

"Yes. But he didn't believe her either."

"So now we have you and the doctor admitting that Mattie lied, and you expect this jury to believe the story you told her to tell—"

"Objection, objection." The prosecutor was on her feet.

The question was withdrawn. No further questions.

Dr. Levy was the next witness. He was a board-certified pediatrician. He had worked in the child abuse unit of the hospital for more than five years and had seen several thousand children who were victims of abuse. He admitted that Mattie had first told him that she had fallen on something sharp, but when Dr. Levy told her he didn't believe that story, she admitted that it was a lie. The doctor read from his notes. "I then asked her to tell me what really happened. She said, 'I went to Uncle Mike's house because he promised to give me a present. He took me upstairs to his bedroom. No one else was home. Then he put me on the bed and gave me a dollar. He pulled down my underpants and put his thing in my peepee hole. It hurt, and I cried. I looked down, and there was blood all over me and the bed. I pulled up my panties and ran home.' "

"Why didn't you believe her first story?" Dr. Levy was asked.

"Because the underpants were not torn and there were no jagged edges on the labia, which one would expect to find if metal had penetrated the skin."

On cross-examination defense counsel asked: "Doctor, you didn't find any trauma to the clitoris or the vagina, did you?"

"No, but I wouldn't expect to. Because—"

"That's all, Doctor—"

I ordered that Dr. Levy be permitted to finish his answer.

"I wouldn't expect trauma because in such a young child the body is extremely flexible and will expand to admit a foreign object without any rupture or sign of trauma. Mattie's hymen was ruptured, which accounts for the profusion of blood."

Dr. Levy admitted that many young girls rupture their hymens while riding bicycles and engaging in other sports. There was no way of knowing when her hymen was ruptured, only that a recent rupture was compatible with the bloodstains. There was no other wound or trauma that would explain the blood.

Dr. Perry, the psychiatrist, was the next witness. He testified that Mattie's behavior was consistent with an incident of sexual abuse, that most little girls who had been abused acted the same way.

On cross-examination Dr. Perry admitted that he did not know whether or not the incident had occurred but—

Objection by defense counsel.

"Don't volunteer any information, Doctor," I admonished him. "Just answer the questions."

Dr. Perry was also given a report by Mattie's teacher stating that prior to the date of the alleged incident Mattie had been a normal, happy child. She was talkative and mischievous but not a real disciplinary problem. She was just beginning to recognize letters and numbers. Her school progress was about average for that class. After the incident Mattie seemed to be unable to pay attention in school. She had dropped behind the class and was unable to read even simple words like "go" and "stop." She no longer wrote her name, although she had been able to write her first name without difficulty. She often cried for no apparent reason. If her mother was late in calling for her at school, Mattie refused to leave the room and the teacher had to wait with her until her mother arrived. Mattie also refused to go out on the playground at recess.

Defense counsel objected to Dr. Perry's reliance on the teacher's report. I gave him the opportunity to subpoena the teacher and cross-examine her. But he did not choose to do so.

Defense counsel demanded to see Mattie's underpants. The prosecutor shamefacedly admitted that the underwear had not been kept as an exhibit.

At this point the state had put in all its evidence except the crucial testimony of Mattie herself. I mentally weighed the evidence. The jury might easily find a reasonable doubt. The child had told two incompatible stories. The mother was clearly hostile to the defendant and may have been motivated by vengeance for some unknown reason. The doctor's testimony was clear and precise. But the missing panties would certainly raise a questions in the minds of the jury. Most damaging was the pediatrician's admission that in some 85 percent of the cases of children he had examined for suspected sexual abuse, he concluded that the abuse had occurred.

Defense counsel asked, "You couldn't be prejudiced, could you, Dr. Levy?"

"No," he replied angrily. "I report these cases as abuse because that is what occurred."

"In your opinion, Doctor. Of course, you weren't there any more than I or the jury was there when these things allegedly happened—"

"Of course, I wasn't there. But in my professional opinion, with reasonable medical certainty, I believe that this child was sexually abused."

"Yes, Doctor, we know that is your *opinion*. [The lawyer ironically stressed the word "opinion."] Thank you."

The entire case hinged on the testimony of a frightened little six-year-old girl who was going to be asked to describe what had happened to her more than four months before. Her parents had been told by the psychiatrist not to discuss the incident with her, to let her put it out of her mind. The schoolteacher's most recent report was that Mattie was beginning to be a little more relaxed and willing to talk to the other children although she still refused to go out on the playground. Would this testimony harm her?

We took a recess. The prosecutor and Mrs. Armont spoke to Mattie for a few minutes. The court officer reported that Mrs. Armont had taken Mattie to the bathroom. Mattie had cried and said she didn't want to go back into the TV room, she wanted to go home. The cameraman promised her that if she would be a good girl and talk into the microphone, he would let her play back her testimony on the VCR. At this she cheered up and asked if she could have the tape so she could play it at home for her brother. He promised that he would make a tape for her.

The television sets were turned on in the courtroom, and the lights dimmed. There was a large set for the jury and smaller screens for the defendant and his counsel, for the prosecutor, and for me. With some trepidation the prosecutor told the cameraman we were ready to go on the air. The jury had seen Mattie when she was asked if she would tell the truth. But that was two days ago. We now saw her again. This time she was wearing a green hair ribbon. She looked even smaller than I remembered.

The prosecutor began in a soft, warm voice. "Hi, Mattie. This is Lisa. Can you see and hear me?"

She nodded yes.

"I can't hear you. When I ask you a question, you must answer in words so I can be sure you heard me. Do you understand?"

"Uh-huh."

"Say, 'Yes, Lisa,' so I know you heard me."

"Yes, Lisa, I hear you."

"That's fine. You have a nice voice. I'm going to ask you some questions now. Remember you promised to tell the truth."

"Uh-huh."

"You will tell the truth, won't you?"

"Yeah."

"Do you remember sometime ago you got hurt and went to the hospital?"

"Yeah."

"You saw a nice Dr. Levy, who talked to you and gave you some medicine. He made you feel better, didn't he?"

"Uh-huh."

"Does anything hurt you now, Mattie?"

"No."

"Well, just tell me what happened that hurt you."

"I don't want to talk about it."

"No one is going to hurt you ever again. I promise. But we have to have you tell us what happened so we can take good care of you.

"I already told you."

"Please, honey, just tell me one more time, and I won't ask you again."

Mattie squirmed in the chair. Her hands clutched her private parts, and she squeezed her legs tightly together.

"Now just tell me where you were when this happened."

"In Uncle Mike's house."

"In what room?"

"His bedroom."

"Where in the room?"

"In the room."

"Were you standing up or lying down?"

"Lying down."

"What were you lying on?"

"The bed."

"What happened?"

"He hurt me."

Tears began rolling down Mattie's cheeks. She wiped her eyes and her nose with the back of her hand.

"How did he hurt you?"

"He put his thing in my peepee hole, and it hurt. He made me cry."

"What did his thing look like?"

"It was big and red and ugly."

"Why did you go there?"

"He said he would give me a present."

"Did he give you a present?"

"Yes, a dollar. I gave it to my mom, and she scolded me."

Mattie began to sob.

"That's all. Your witness."

The prosecutor visibly relaxed.

Defense counsel spoke through the microphone.

"Hello, Mattie, can you hear me?"

"Who are you?"

"I'm Uncle Mike's lawyer."

"I don't like Uncle Mike. I don't like you."

"Mattie, I want to be your friend. If you'll just answer a few questions, then you can go home with your mom and you won't ever have to come back here."

"You promise?"

"I promise. So just answer these few questions. Before you went to the hospital, you told your mom you had hurt yourself on a sharp piece of metal, didn't you?"

"Uh-huh."

"And when you went to the hospital, that's what you told the doctor, isn't it?"

"Uh-huh."

"That's all, Mattie. See, I kept my promise."

"I can go home now?"

She climbed out of the chair.

The prosecutor was back.

"Mattie, this is Lisa again. You can hear me, can't you?"

"I wanna go home."

"Mattie, when you told your mom and the doctor you hurt yourself on a piece of metal, were you telling the truth?"

She shook her head no.

"Mattie, please answer me yes or no. Was that the truth?"

Mattie whispered, "No."

"Why did you tell them a lie?"

"Because my mom told me not to go to Uncle Mike's house."

"Are you telling the truth now?"

Mattie burst into tears again.

"Please, Mattie, just tell me yes or no and I'll let you go home. Are you telling the truth that it was Uncle Mike who hurt you?"

"Yes."

She climbed down from the chair and ran to the door.

I ordered the television turned off and announced that we would take a brief recess.

The jury sent me a note by the court officer. It read, "We, the jury, are exhausted. Even though it is only three o'clock, may we be excused?"

I was only too glad to recess court for the day.

I was drained watching and listening to this child being questioned against her will. Although the jury could go home and try to relax, I had to prepare the instructions on the law that I would give them the next day.

At sidebar, out of the presence of the jury, defense counsel moved that the last testimony of Mattie be stricken. The prosecutor was leading the witness. "She knows better than to ask the complaining witness whether it was the defendant who committed the act," the lawyer argued cogently.

If the witness had been an adult, I would have struck the testimony and ordered the jury to ignore it. If there is any principle of evidence that has been accepted for generations, it is that counsel cannot lead his own witness. A lawyer cannot put words in the mouth of the witness. This rule makes sense in most instances. A witness should testify without coaching from the lawyer. If the witness does not know what happened without prompting from counsel, then that person's testimony is likely to be suspect and unreliable.

But this rule was never devised for a frightened six-year-old child. The entire trial was inappropriate. Mattie had told her story so many times by now that it was probably impossible for the child to be sure of anything. She had first told her mother the two versions. Then she spoke to Dr. Levy at the hospital. The next day she was questioned by Officer Collins.

A few days later she was questioned by the prosecuting attorney. She was questioned twice by the psychiatrist and again by the prosecuting attorney the day before the trial. I have no idea what Mrs. Armont told Mattie before and during the trial.

Counsel, the jury, and I knew what she had said on the witness stand. I decided to let these twelve citizens decide for themselves whether Mattie had told them the truth. That is the function of the jury, not the judge. To deprive them of the right to consider this vital piece of evidence would be to usurp their role.

Michael Gardner did not take the witness stand. He presented no defense. Both attorneys made fair and effective closing arguments. Defense counsel argued, "My client stood up here before you, ladies and gentlemen of the jury, and entered a plea of not guilty. He told you then under oath that he did not commit this heinous crime. What else can he tell you? He told you then, and I tell you now, he did not do it. What is the evidence against him? The word of a six-year-old child who has told different stories. We know her mother has an animus against the defendant. It was her mother who said she didn't believe Mattie when Mattie clearly told her she injured herself on a sharp piece of metal. In order to please her mother, she changed her story. We have the testimony of Dr. Levy. But he thinks all injured children are victims of child sexual abuse. He admits he wasn't there; he doesn't know what happened to Mattie. And the one piece of physical evidence that would have helped you decide, Mattie's underpants, mysteriously disappeared. Ladies and gentlemen, I wasn't there, the prosecuting attorney wasn't there, and you weren't there. I submit that under all these suspicious circumstances you must have a reasonable doubt."

Before instructing the jury, I ruled that there was not enough evidence of rape for that charge to be submitted to the jury. There was sufficient evidence from which the jury could infer that there had been penetration, but there was no evidence that Mattie had resisted, a requirement of the law. If the complainant consents, it is not rape. The crime of statutory rape does not require resistance on the part of a minor female. I wondered about the inappropriateness of my ruling. How could a six-year-old who had little idea what an old man intended to do to her resist his advances? What sense did it make to expect such behavior of a little girl? However, if I failed to dismiss the charge and the jury convicted the defendant of forcible rape, the conviction would certainly be set aside for legal error. There might have to be another trial.

I gave the jury the standard jury instructions that apply to all criminal cases regardless of who the defendant is and who the complaining witness is. The jurors were told that in order to convict Michael Gardner, they must be convinced beyond a reasonable doubt that he was guilty as charged. They must consider carefully the testimony of all the witnesses, must resolve any discrepancies in the testimony in the light of common sense, must consider the credibility of the witnesses and all the circumstances of the case. They must consider the manner and demeanor of the witnesses, how they testified, their consistency, and the inherent plausibility of their testimony. I further charged them that the fact that the defendant did not testify must not be held against him and no unfavorable inference might be drawn from his failure to take the stand. Every defendant has an absolute constitutional right not to testify. The jurors must reach their verdict on the evidence they heard, not on any speculation as to evidence that was not presented.

This was standard, boiler plate instructions, tried and true, given by countless judges in innumerable cases over many decades and upheld as proper by the appellate courts. The charge to the jury is the one part of the trial in which it is inexcusable for a judge to make an error unless the law as declared by the appellate courts is confused or in conflict. In the heat of trial a judge must make many rulings. One cannot stop the trial to go research the law. A judge, however, does have time to prepare the charge. This usually has to be done at night after a long day of trial. If the judge gives an erroneous instruction to the jury and the defendant in a criminal case is convicted, the verdict will be set aside. If the defendant is acquitted, he (or she) can never be retried on those charges. All the time, effort, emotional strain on the defendant, the witnesses, the lawyers, and the jury will have been in vain. The cost to the taxpayers is considerable. A charge to the jury is not the time or place for judicial creativity or innovation. One follows precedent unless there is a serious constitutional question at issue. In this case I gave the standard charge. No judge was ever reversed for using this approved instruction. But what relevance did it have to a case in which the alleged crime victim, the person whose testimony was crucial, was six years old?

I refused to give the charge requested by defense counsel based on Wigmore's classic text on evidence. Wigmore states that the testimony of children is unreliable. For authority he quotes Robert Louis Stevenson: "[Children] walk in a vain show, among mists and rainbows; they are passionate after dreams and unconcerned about reality."[1] On such slender evidence, the opinion of a novelist who wrote popular adventure stories for children, courts for generations have concluded that the testimony of children is unreliable and entitled to little credence or weight. A judge who follows these rules will accord weight to the denial by the adult accused of abusing the child but disregard the child's testimony. However, when a child makes an admission against interest, under the law, as stated by Wigmore and followed by most courts, that is admissible in evidence and accorded full weight and credibility.[2] It is interesting to note that Wigmore treats the admissions of "fools" and children identically and in the same section of his treatise.

Wigmore also states that in rape cases prior acts of intercourse by the complainant are admissible to show her consent. This rule has been abolished in most jurisdictions. I believed the rule with respect to the credibility of children was also archaic and not founded on logic or psychology. I was sustained by the appellate court in Mattie's case.

After deliberating for three hours and eating a lunch of two sandwiches each, a piece of pie, and several sodas, the jurors asked to have part of Mattie's testimony on video replayed. They wanted to hear her testimony on redirect examination when the prosecutor asked her if she was now telling the truth. We all listened intently and had some difficulty in hearing Mattie's reply. The technician was asked if he could raise the volume. He said he would do so, and the tape was played again. This time in answer to the question "Are you telling the truth now?" all of us clearly heard her say, "Yes."

The jurors again retired to deliberate. In fifteen minutes they came back with a verdict of guilty.

After the jury returned its verdict, it was excused. Its painful and difficult task was over. But I was plunged into the hostile world of the Gardner family. I then learned that Michael Gardner had a long record of petty crime. It is wrong for a judge to have such prejudicial information before the jury returns its verdict because it will, of course, influence the judge's attitude toward the defendant. Even though nothing is said, the jury may be affected by the judge's tacit response to the evidence. I learned that Gardner was a ne'er-do-well who had been supported most of his life by his aged mother. She was in the courtroom when the verdict was returned. She cried loudly and turned on the weary lawyer for her son, accusing him of selling out to the Armont family. She demanded he return the counsel fee of fifteen hundred dollars that she had paid. The court officers removed her from the courtroom.

In reviewing Gardner's rap sheet, I learned that he had been accused of rape, statutory rape, and child molestation at least a half dozen times but had never been convicted of these charges. One of the complainants was his niece Mary, Mattie's mother. Was he a child molester or was Mary Armont a vengeful woman? Fortunately I did not have to decide this question. The jury's verdict was based on sufficient evidence from which it could have reasonably found him guilty as charged beyond a reasonable doubt.

Michael Gardner owed three years' back time for violation of parole on a robbery charge, which he would have to serve before beginning my sentence. I sentenced him to seven and a half to fifteen years on the charges before me. Even with early parole on these charges for good behavior, it was likely that he would serve eight years before being released again.

Defense counsel had previously argued vigorously that the evidence was insufficient to convict. At sentencing he argued that even if he was guilty, the defendant had a mental problem. Sex offenders are sick people, he declared, citing a wealth of psychiatric authority. He urged that the defendant be sent at public expense to a sex offenders' clinic, where he could be treated and cured of his mental problem. A director of a well-known sex clinic was in the courtroom and testified on behalf of the defendant. This doctor assured me that modern science was able to treat these unfortunate sex offenders. Some studies, however, indicate that very few such offenders are cured. But the director argued that to jail a person with a mental illness is as barbaric as jailing a man who has tuberculosis or cancer. He claimed that these offenders are not responsible for their actions. Whatever the scientific truth of that argument, it did not accord with the law. On the record before me, Michael Gardner had not suggested that he did not know that having sex with a six-year-old was not wrong, nor had he suggested that even if he had known it was wrong, he was unable to choose between right and wrong.

Although it may be true that a man like Michael Gardner is unable to control himself and, therefore, might conceivably meet the legal standard of insanity, he had not raised that issue. I had no evidence of credible scientific studies that prove that even under the most rigorous therapy, a pedophile like Michael Gardner, if, indeed, he had this affliction, could be cured.*

No one except her mother suggested that Mattie was in need of intensive psychotherapy. Mary Armont told me that her entire life had been destroyed by Michael Gardner, who had raped her when she was ten years old. Neither her mother, who was his sister, nor her grandmother believed Mary's story. Mary also claimed that he had raped her sister, Virginia. Immediately after that incident Virginia had moved out of the city and broken off all contact with the family. Although she had been brought up as a good Catholic, Mary had been divorced for several years. "I just don't like having sex," she explained, "and it wasn't fair to my husband. He's a nice man, and he pays support for Mattie regularly." She begged me to find some help for Mattie now so that the child would not have to suffer the same problems that she had endured for so many years.

On further investigation I discovered that Michael Gardner received a disability pension from the army as a result of an old injury. I ordered that this money be paid through the court for Mattie's therapy at a child psychiatric clinic.

After several years the probation department reported that Mattie had been discharged from the clinic and was apparently making a satisfactory school adjustment. I put Gardner and Mattie out of my mind. This was a case that, despite all the difficulties and inappropriateness of the law, had somehow been resolved fairly through the common sense of the jury and the fortuity of an army pension.

A few years later I learned that Michael Gardner had been released from prison because the United States Supreme Court had ruled that a child witness must be present in the courtroom and look at the defendant.[3] The case before the Supreme Court involved two slightly older girls who were permitted to testify behind a screen where they could not see the defendant and he could not see them clearly. Justice Antonin Scalia, writing for the Court, set aside the conviction of the rapist on the ground that he had been denied his constitutional right to confront his

---

*Despite the lack of proof that psychotherapy is an effective treatment for child molesters, they are routinely sentenced to involuntary psychiatric treatment. Note that Gerald Bryant, who was charged with raping a two-year-old, had just been released from a psychiatric hospital (*Philadelphia Inquirer,* January 18, 1990, p. 2B).

accusers. The Sixth Amendment to the Constitution provides that "In all criminal prosecutions, the accused shall enjoy the right . . . to be confronted with the witnesses against him. . . ." This is an important and critical right. It was designed to prohibit the practice enshrined for centuries under British law in which the evidence against an accused person consisted solely of documents. Sir Walter Raleigh, for example, was tried, convicted, and executed for alleged crimes that were proved entirely by affidavits. No live witnesses appeared against him. He was unable to cross-examine his accusers and attempt to show the falsity of their statements. The Supreme Court in 1895 did hold that the purpose of the confrontation clause was to permit the jury to see the witness.[4]

However, in many cases such as the death or unavoidable absence of a witness, if the testimony has been taken and the witness has been cross-examined, that testimony may be used in a subsequent prosecution. In such cases there is no face-to-face confrontation. But with no discussion of the history of the common law of evidence or the original intent of the framers of the Bill of Rights, Justice Scalia, writing for a majority of the Supreme Court, held that this provision requires not merely the right of cross-examination of live witnesses but a face-to-face "look me in the eye" meeting of the accused and his child accusers.

I presided over dozens of rape trials in which the complaining witnesses were fully competent adult women. In no instance did the victim ever look at the man who had allegedly raped her. She averted her gaze. Some defendants also looked away. But many leaned back in their seats and sneered at the women who were forced to describe in detail what had happened to them. I know of no case in which the court directed the complaining witness to look at the accused other than to say, "Look around the room and see if you recognize the accused."

Often a defendant came to court wearing sunglasses. I ordered him to remove the glasses for a few moments when the witnesses made the identification. But I never required the complaining witness and the defendant to make eye contact. That rarely occurs. Except for Justice Scalia's opinion, no court has ever ruled that the confrontation clause was violated because the complaining witness did not make eye contact with the defendant while testifying.

Obviously closed-circuit television was not contemplated or even imagined in 1789. Testimony had to be taken live and in the courtroom. In 1990, in countless courts throughout the country, much of the testimony in trials is presented on video screens. To accommodate the schedules of busy doctors who are expert witnesses and persons who are ill or unable to be present, testimony is taken in advance of trial, recorded on video cassettes, and played at the trial. With proper safe-guards, this recorded testimony is as reliable and effective as live testimony. The American Bar Association Criminal Justice Section report to the House of Delegates in May 1985 recommended the use of closed-circuit television or one-way mirrors for testimony of child witnesses.

Within two years the Supreme Court retreated a little from its holding that the confrontation clause requires a face-to-face confrontation between a defendant and a complaining child witness. On June 27, 1990, the Court decided two cases involving criminal prosecutions for child sexual abuse. Four justices dissented in each case, suggesting that this area of the law is far from settled. In *Maryland v. Craig*[5] the Court upheld a Maryland statute permitting child victims of sexual abuse to testify by one-way closed-circuit television when the trial court has determined that the "testimony by the child victim in the courtroom will result in the child suffering serious emotional distress such that the child cannot reasonably communicate." The majority opinion stressed the significance of the widespread belief in the importance of a public policy to protect child witnesses from the trauma of testifying, noting that thirty-seven states permit the use of videotaped testimony of sexu-ally abused children, twenty-four states authorize the use of one-way closed-circuit television testimony in such cases, and eight states permit the use of two-way television.

The majority discussed at length cases in which hearsay testimony of adults was admissible under the confrontation clause. Of course, these precedents are significant but shed little light on the special prob-lems that child witnesses face.

The Maryland statute, like a number of others, is applicable only when the trauma to the child confronting her abuser impairs the child's ability to testify. In Mattie's case it was clear that confronting Michael Gardner would have been seriously detrimental to her. Whether it would have prevented her from "reasonably communicating" is far from clear. But harm to the child witness is at this writing insufficient grounds for permitting testimony by videotape or closed-circuit televi-sion.

In the companion case, *Idaho v. Wright,*[6] a majority of the Court concluded that the testimony of a physician as to the statement to him by an allegedly sexually abused child aged three must be excluded as inadmissible hearsay. Again the Court cited as precedent cases involv-ing adult witnesses. With respect to the special needs of young child witnesses the opinion cites with implicit approval the opinion of the Idaho Supreme Court noting that "expert testimony and child psychology text books indicate that children are susceptible to suggestion. . . ." The Court apparently assumed that the testimony of children is less reliable than that of adults, a conclusion for which the Court cited no scientifically verified evidence. Indeed, the Court relied on an apodictic statement in an 1881 British case, *Queen v. Osman,*[7] that "[N]o person, who is immediately going into the presence of his Maker, will do so with a lie upon his lips." The majority also relied on the fact that hearsay evidence with respect to child victims of abuse does not fall within "a firmly rooted hearsay exception." Thus, because the Idaho law of residual hearsay exceptions is not firmly rooted in the common law, it could not prevail.

Whether other state laws that attempt to mitigate the trauma to child abuse victims of testifying in open court will be upheld will depend upon many factors, not least of which is the composition of the fractured Court.

These later decisions limiting *Coy v. Iowa* did not help Mattie or Mary Armont. The week after Michael Gardner was released from prison, Mary Armont was in my chambers. Michael had moved back to his mother's house and was walking back and forth in front of Mary's house, trying to speak to Mattie and attempting to reestablish family ties. She asked me for a protective order. Because his conviction had been wiped out, I had no jurisdiction over Gardner.

Unless he committed another offense, there was nothing that could be done to protect either Mattie or Mary. I suggested, as I often do in cases in which the law provides no protection, that Mary move to another city and not leave a forwarding address. For a thirty-five-year-old woman who has lived in one neighborhood all her life, to move to a strange place is not easy. She has to find another job, an apartment, a school for Mattie, and even baby-sitters. In the old neighborhood she has friends Mattie can be with when Mary has to do night work. The expenses and the problems are formidable. But neither she nor I could find any other option. The law provided every protection for Michael Gardner but none for Mattie or Mary Armont.

Most prosecutions for sexual abuse of little girls do not result in convictions or in therapy for the child.* If the child is forced to testify in the presence of the defendant and the jury, she is usually so intimidated that she cannot tell her story clearly or convincingly. In Mattie's case the doctors and the police officers were careful, professional witnesses.

---

*Note that one-third of the victims of child abuse are under the age of six. See the report of the National Center on Child Abuse and Neglect, *Child Sexual Abuse: Incest, Assault and Sexual Exploitation* (Washington, D.C.: Government Printing Office, 1981).

The physical evidence of the bloodstained dollar bill and the stains on the defendant's bedding *was* presented. When the incident is not promptly reported and the police do not take immediate action, physical evidence is lost and the trier of fact must decide solely on the uncorroborated testimony of a frightened child. Mattie's mother believed her and was supportive. Often that is not so, particularly if the alleged abuser is the mother's husband or paramour. Mattie did not have to live in the same house as Michael Gardner during the months between the incident and the trial, subject to pressure from him to recant. And most important, Mattie did not have to testify in the presence of her abuser.

Heather was sexually molested by her uncle. She was ten years old. Her parents, like Mrs. Armont, were supportive. The child had told her story to the doctor, the police, and the prosecutor. I did not anticipate any difficulties because she was an intelligent child and neither her parents nor the prosecuting attorney had requested closed-circuit television. When Heather took the stand and saw her uncle seated a few feet from her at counsel table, she was unable to say more than her name and her age. When asked, "Did anything happen to you that brings you to court today?" Heather remained mute. We took a recess. Her mother and father and the attorney spoke to her. She adamantly refused to return to court. Defense counsel moved for a directed verdict of not guilty. I denied the motion. The prosecutor withdrew the charges. This unfortunate scenario is played again and again in American courts.[8]

Mattie is one of the more than 2,200,000 children who are the subjects of child abuse reports each year. Many of these girls and boys are allegedly sexually abused. Others are beaten, tortured, starved, and subjected to other cruel mistreatment. Probably more than ten times that number of instances occur. Most of these children were abused by members of their families.[9] In 1986 at least thirteen hundred children in the United States died of abuse. Since the early 1970s every state has enacted child abuse reporting laws. They relieve from liability those who in good faith report cases of suspected child abuse. The laws also mandate state officials to make immediate investigations and take suitable actions to protect children when abuse is confirmed. These laws are a necessary first step, but despite their laudable aims, they have not protected most children who are at risk.

The majority of obvious cases of abuse are not reported because there are no sanctions for failure to report. While many doctors in clinics do report the cases they see, few pediatricians in private practice report suspected abuse of their patients. Many schoolteachers, neighbors, friends, and relatives ignore the plight of abused children through ignorance or because they do not want to get involved.

Even when abuse reports are filed, often public officials fail to take necessary action. And the United States Supreme Court has held that there is no civil liability owed to the injured children even for the grossest negligence in failing to take the required protective measures.[10]

When criminal charges are brought against child abusers, all too often there can be no conviction because the rules of evidence and procedure in adult criminal court impose formidable obstacles for the child witness.* Had Mattie been required to testify in open court in the presence of the man she hated and feared, she would probably not have been able to tell her story and he would have been acquitted.

Under the old common law, children were rarely complaining witnesses. When children did testify, the law was clear that their testimony was not to be accorded the same weight as that of an adult. And children, like women and the elderly, simply did not have the right not to be abused.

Contemporary American law provides statutory remedies for child abuse: reporting statutes, the right to testify in court, and placement somewhere other than the abusive home. The criminal law in every state makes sexual intercourse with a minor (usually under the age of sixteen) a crime. But when the state attempts to prosecute rapists, children are compelled to testify under rules of evidence and procedure that seriously handicap their ability to receive equal justice. The Supreme Court of the United States has held unconstitutional laws and practices designed to adapt the testimonial rules and practices designed for adult witnesses to the needs of children.[11] The Court has also refused to permit the interpretation of child abuse reporting laws to require the protections intended for children. But the child is treated like an adult when he or she testifies. This refusal to recognize the difference between a child's capacity as a witness and that of an adult denies children the equal protection of the laws.

*In the notorious McMartin case, in which Peggy McMartin Buckey and her son, Raymond, were accused of molesting children in their California day care center, both defendants were acquitted, but the jurors told reporters that they believed that the children were abused. However, they found that the prosecution had not proved the charges. The alleged incidents occurred in 1983. The case did not come to trial until 1987. The trial lasted two and a half years.

Obviously a trial of such inordinate length is unfair not only to the jurors and the taxpayers but also to the prosecution witnesses and the defendants. The prosecutor intends to return Raymond Buckey on the thirteen counts in which there was a mistrial (*Philadelphia Inquirer*, February 1, 1990). Michael Gardner was not retried because Mattie's mother refused to permit Mattie to undergo the ordeal of another trial.

9

All in the Family

*I believe that more unhappiness comes from this source
than from any other—I mean from the attempt to prolong family
connection unduly and to make people hang together artificially
who would never naturally do so.*

—SAMUEL BUTLER

APRIL, LIKE MATTIE, was a victim of sexual abuse. In both cases the abuser was a member of the family or household. This is the common pattern in child abuse. The stranger who lurks by the playground to entice children, the seductive baby-sitter, and the hardened rapist do occasionally abuse children. But the vast majority of child abusers, both physical and sexual, are members of the family household.

When I saw April in court, she was eleven years old. Her stepfather had subjected her to bizarre and indecent activities for three years. Unlike little Mattie, April wanted to testify. She was angry not only because of what had happened to her but also because of the abuse inflicted on her helpless mother.

April was a remarkable witness. She was a remarkable child to have survived the first eleven years of her life. Although her experiences seem to be peculiarly bizarre, countless other children in slums, in modest houses, and in the mansions of the rich have undergone similar mistreatment. April looked younger than her eleven years as she sat on the witness chair clutching a Cabbage Patch Doll. She was a very pretty girl with large violet eyes, soft brown curls, and a winsome dimple. There was no question of her competence to testify. She has an IQ of 146.

Arthur, the defendant, looked like a lawyer in his neat charcoal gray suit and college tie. Evelyn, April's mother, is an average-looking thirty-year-old woman. Although she has a bad scar on her face, she is attractive. She has an IQ of 72. No one knows who April's biological father is.

When court opened, the room was filled with people: lawyers and litigants involved in other matters listed before me, the witnesses in Arthur's trial, the usual assemblage of people who have nothing to do and find trials a cheap form of amusement, and three good citizens from a court watchers' committee who are supposed to observe trials and report any misconduct on the part of the judge. This is a good idea, and I welcome the presence of these people even though they seldom understand the procedures and rarely recognize improper rulings and overreaching by a presiding judge. In this case I knew that the testimony would be shocking, and I did not want any outbursts in the courtroom. Also, I did not want April to have to testify before a roomful of strangers, whose presence would add to her discomfort.

I announced to the persons in the room that this was a public trial, that they had every right to be there, and that no one would remove them. Then I explained that this case involved a charge of abuse of a child who would have to testify, and I asked them out of consideration for her to leave. Everyone quietly left the courtroom.

After preliminary motions and the colloquy with Arthur to make sure that he understood his legal rights, April took the stand. Arthur had attended an Ivy League university for three years. He was represented by an able and well-paid attorney. I was confident that his rights would be protected. I was not so sure that April would be protected even though the prosecutor and I would do our best within the limits of the law.

The prosecutor qualified April to testify. Defense counsel asked her only a few perfunctory questions about her understanding of the nature of the oath and her promise to tell the truth. Then he attempted to establish rapport with this adorable-looking but obviously hostile child.

"April, do you know who I am?"

"Yes, you're Arthur's lawyer."

"I'm going to ask you some questions. Will you promise to tell the truth?"

"Yes. I said I would and I will."

She glared at the lawyer, her eyes blazing with anger.

"You don't like me, do you?"

"No, I don't."

"I like you. I think you're a very pretty, smart little girl. Why don't you like me?"

"Because you're going to try to make me look like I'm lying."

The discomfited lawyer said, "No more questions on qualifications," and sat down.

The prosecuting attorney began with unthreatening questions: April's age, her school, her address, the persons who lived in her home. They were her mom, her grandpop, and Arthur "before he was arrested."

"When did you first meet Arthur?"

"He rang the doorbell. He was looking for my mom. He had an ad from a magazine."

I subsequently learned that the ad published in an X-rated magazine read: "Woman with daughter looking for fun."

"What did you think of him when you first got to know him?"

"He seemed to be all right. He was nice to my mom, brought her presents. He took us out to dinner and to the movies."

"Did there come a time when he married your mom?"

"Yes. Thirty-four days after they met." She gave the date and time. April was absolutely precise about all details.

"After the marriage did anything change?"

"He moved into our house. At first I liked that because he cleaned up a little."

"What is your house like?"

"It's dirty, yucky. I don't like it. But I keep my own room clean." April described the aging row house they lived in, the leaking roof, and disrepair.

Within a few days after the wedding Arthur began his sexual abuse of April. He forced her to get in bed with him and her mom when they were nude. He removed the bottom of April's pajamas. They watched "dirty movies" on the VCR. In precise language April described the various deviant acts that he forced her and her mom to perform. If her mom protested, Arthur hit her. He never struck April. At one point the grandfather took his rifle and shot at Arthur but failed to hit him.

April, who had always been an exemplary student, began to misbehave in school. The teacher testified that April was her special delight, the one bright child in her sixth-grade class, many of whom could not read or write. When she noticed that April was withdrawn and sullen and refused to do her homework, the teacher was alarmed and wrote a note to April's mother. In response Arthur and Evelyn came to the school. The teacher was impressed with Arthur. He wasn't like the other fathers. He was a well-dressed gentleman who took a great interest in April. The teacher said she thought April was probably having difficulty adjusting to the new demands made upon her. Arthur said he insisted on April's helping with the housework and doing other chores. The teacher suggested that they seek professional help and recommended a child psychiatric clinic in a leading hospital. Arthur seemed very grateful. April told her teacher that she, Arthur, and her mom went to the clinic once a month.

The psychiatrist at the clinic testified. He was a family therapist, and he saw the three of them intermittently for a period of a year and a half. He never saw April alone and had no idea what was going on in the household. His notes, however, contained an interesting comment. "Wonder what Arthur gets out of marriage with this retarded woman."

April's mother's testimony was of little help. She could respond to questions only with a "yeah" or "nope" or "I dunno." The grandfather, an old wino who earned money by picking through trash cans and selling any usable items, was also unable to say more than he wanted Arthur out of the house and was sorry that he had missed when he shot at Arthur. The police officer was more informative. He testified that in response to a call, "woman being beaten," he went to the house and saw April's mother lying on the floor, screaming. Her face was bloodied; chunks of hair had been pulled out of her head. He immediately sent for an ambulance to take her to the hospital. Arthur gave some account of an intruder whom he had surprised attacking his wife. The mysterious intruder had vanished. The officer did not believe the story and started back to the police station to make out a report and request a warrant for Arthur's arrest.

The officer testified that after he got in his patrol car, he remembered seeing a little girl in the house. "I've got four kids of my own," he said. "I wasn't going to leave a child there with that man, so I went back and got her. I knew I didn't have any authority. The man protested, but the kid came over to me and took my hand, so I just picked her up and left. I took her to a shelter for abused women." There is no shelter for abused children. In most communities, unless a child is so badly injured as to require hospitalization, there is no place he or she can be received without a court order.

A volunteer at the shelter testified that within ten minutes after April's arrival she had told the people there what had happened to her mother and to herself. The volunteer filed assault charges on behalf of the mother and child abuse charges on behalf of April.

When April was asked why she consented to doing the things Arthur asked of her, she replied, "The teacher told me to obey my father, that he knew best. The psychiatrist and all the people at the clinic kept telling me to obey him. I hated it, and I hated him. But I thought I must be wrong because they all told me to obey Arthur."

Arthur took the stand. He testified that he wanted to be a good father to April, that he tried to help her, that he loved her. I wondered if he had read *Lolita*. Here was a man who actually lived out Humbert Humbert's fantasies. I could only speculate that at some point even the passive, retarded mother protested and Arthur became enraged and beat her.

Only two lawyers were needed for this trial, the able prosecutor and the excellent defense attorney. But a half dozen other lawyers were there representing women's organizations, the hospital, the welfare department, the human services department of the city, and a child advocates' society. After I had convicted Arthur and imposed a stiff sentence, I called in these lawyers and social workers for their help.

The real problem was the protection of April. It was obvious to me, as it should have been to them, that this eleven-year-old child would be at risk of abuse if she continued to live with her retarded mother and drunken grandfather. April needed a secure place to live. She also needed psychotherapy. Bright as she was, this child had suffered terrible mistreatment. She had lost faith in the professionals whose advice she'd taken. She was nearing adolescence, when she would need strong adult guidance. For years April had been protecting her mother. She still saw that as her role. But there was no competent adult to protect her.

I was met with a barrage of objections. The mother had parental rights. She had not been convicted of any crime. She had not been declared an unfit mother. It was the policy of all these agencies to keep the family together. What was the problem? Arthur was out of the house, safely locked in prison for a long period of time.

I didn't know how safe Arthur would be. During the course of the trial he appeared in court with his arm in a cast. He had been in custody from the time of his arrest. The other inmates had through the grapevine learned of the testimony and taken the law into their own hands. In a world of thieves, rapists, robbers, and murderers, child abusers are pariahs. Protection of Arthur was the responsibility of the prison authorities. I thought that protection of April was the responsibility of the legal system. I was soon disabused of that notion.

If anything were to be done for April, she would have to be treated as a neglected child, and a petition to that effect filed with the family court. I had been sitting in criminal court and had convicted and imprisoned Arthur. My duties were over. I had no jurisdiction over April, who was treated like any other witness. She was subpoenaed to appear in court and paid a witness fee of seven dollars a day plus carfare. After the trial was over, the legal system was no longer concerned with her, even though she was only eleven years old.

When I pointed out that the mother could have been convicted of contributing to the delinquency of a minor if the prosecutor had chosen to do so, that was deemed irrelevant. April should live with her mother. I need not worry, I was assured, because social workers would counsel the mother.

All the counseling in the world could not raise the intelligence of this unfortunate woman, nor could it stop her sexual activities. There had been many men before Arthur; there would be many after him. And how would April protect herself? I was also given the comforting information that April was receiving cultural enrichment. At the expense of the taxpayers she was getting dancing lessons.

"Why were all you lawyers and social workers here in court if you are not going to protect April?" I asked. "You sat through a week of testimony and a day of oral argument. All this time has cost your agencies a great deal of money. What was the purpose?"

"We were here to see that you convicted Arthur and imposed a long prison sentence," was the answer.

"That is my function," I reminded them. "But whose responsibility is it to protect April?"

To this there was no answer. April went home with her mother.

Tyrone Brown was ten years old when I saw him. The doctor who had treated his wounds presented two little outline drawings, front and back views of Tyrone. There were more than seventy marks showing new and old fracture sites and scars. This child had been beaten by his father most of his life. I marveled that he, too, had managed to survive. That was my reaction in most child abuse cases. Somehow these small youngsters lived through beatings, torture, sexual abuse, and mental cruelty. Often their lives are saved by heroic and dedicated medical treatment and devoted nursing care in hospitals. The public pays more than a hundred thousand dollars on the average to save the life of an abused child. And then the law returns the child to the abusive family, where the mistreatment is repeated. A pediatrician told me that if the doctors see an abused infant three times, they know they will not treat the child again. The next time it will be dead.

Tyrone's father is a big, husky man, a prizefighter trainer. His mother is also a big person. She works in a factory. They have four children; Tyrone is the third. Unlike his siblings, Tyrone is small and slender. The other children testified confidently. They told me their home was fine and their parents were loving but strict. The presentence investigator reported that the home was neat and clean. The family had never been on welfare. The children had had no police contacts. In the neighborhood in which they lived, that was an achievement.

The incident that brought the Brown family to court was noted by an alert schoolteacher. One wonders what happens to abused children whose teachers are bored, uninterested, or simply overwhelmed with the problems of trying to maintain order and teach thirty noisy youngsters.

On a stiflingly hot day when all the other kids were wearing shorts and T-shirts, the teacher noticed that Tyrone was wearing long pants and a turtleneck sweater. The schoolroom was sweltering. Tyrone had his head on his desk. She went over to him to see what was the matter and saw blood oozing through his sweater. When she had him remove the sweater, she saw a raw red wound around his neck. She sent him to the school nurse, who discovered several more wounds on his back and legs. Tyrone told the nurse his father had beaten him with a doubled-over cord from the electric iron.

The police were called, and Tyrone was taken to the hospital. A warrant was issued for the arrest of Mr. Brown. With the help of his wife and the other children Mr. Brown managed to elude the police for three months. By the time we came to trial more than nine months had elapsed. Tyrone was wearing a shirt and tie. The prosecutor asked him to remove them, and I clearly saw a thick ropelike scar around his neck and other smaller scars.

Mr. Brown testified that he "disciplined" all his children. But Tyrone was the one who caused the most trouble. The most trouble was that Tyrone still wet his bed. Mr. Brown had not intended to strike Tyrone's neck. He had ordered the boy to take down his pants and bend over the bed for his "whupping." Mrs. Brown was holding him, but somehow the boy wriggled out of her grasp and was accidentally struck on the neck by the cord.

Mrs. Brown corroborated the testimony and added other details as to the "bad" things Tyrone had done. He had broken one of the good dishes; he had spilled a Coke on the TV set, and they'd had to pay to have it repaired; and, of course, the continued bed-wetting. They had tried everything: keeping him up all night, making him wear diapers. But Tyrone, she said, willfully persisted in wetting his bed.

Both grandmothers testified that Mr. Brown was a good father. They approved of his discipline. They had "whupped" their children. That was the way to bring them up.

A police officer testified as a character witness for Mr. Brown. They had been friends for years. The officer had visited the Brown home many times and considered Mr. Brown a good father.

"Did you ever observe Mr. Brown discipline Tyrone?" I asked.

"No," the officer replied. His dark face turned ashen. "If I had known that he beat the boy, I would have stopped it."

Mrs. Brown argued strenuously that her husband shouldn't go to jail. Disciplining a child was not a crime. Besides, how would they live without his income? On her salary she couldn't pay the mortgage and feed the family. Even the prosecutor suggested family counseling and probation.

But what would happen to Tyrone in this family in which he was blamed for all their problems? The child obviously couldn't stop wetting the bed. Even in the courtroom his hands shook. No wonder he dropped things. He never looked at anyone. He sat silent and withdrawn, his head down, looking at the floor.

I had a conference with the court psychiatrist, the prosecutor, and defense counsel as well as the social worker from the child protective services. The aim of all these good people was to keep the family together and off welfare. We explored the possibilities of finding a relative or friend with whom Tyrone could live. That was fruitless. Neither grandmother wanted him. Nor did any of the other relatives. Mrs. Brown could not be charged with neglect. There was no authority to place the boy in a city shelter, which would be only a very temporary stay. There was no authority to put him in a foster home, which might be no better than his own home. I imposed a prison sentence on Mr. Brown but specified that he be placed on work release. He could go to his job each day and earn money for his family. But he would have to spend the nights and weekends in prison.

Mr. Brown was taken from the courtroom and handcuffed. Mrs. Brown and the three other children walked out talking to one another. Tyrone silently walked behind them.

I have never seen Tyrone since that one day in court. The reports I received from the prison about Mr. Brown were reasonably satisfactory. He goes to work each day, and his paycheck is turned over to Mrs.

Brown, who visits him regularly. Mr. Brown has had one infraction, a fight with another prisoner, whom he beat so badly that the man was hospitalized. No criminal charges were filed against Mr. Brown. What will happen to Tyrone when his brutal father is released from prison? What is happening to him in a home where his mother and brothers blame him for their father's incarceration and the substantial drop in the family income?

I also worry about Arnetta Wilkes. Her parents are not deprived slum dwellers. They are members of the working class. They own their own house in a nice neighborhood. Mr. Wilkes retained private counsel, but the fees were a severe strain on the family budget. Arnetta is also a silent, withdrawn child. Her vocabulary is limited. Questioning her is difficult because she lacks the words to tell her story and she is unable to express feelings. She can only respond to questions with a yes or no answer. When asked, "Did you like what your father did to you?" she replied, "No."

Although Mr. and Mrs. Wilkes are nice-looking, Arnetta is an ugly little girl. She is not a good student. Each year she barely manages to pass. She was in the sixth grade when I saw her. She came to court with her mother and her father. If I had seen the three of them walking down the street, father and mother gently holding Arnetta's hands, as I saw them walking into the courtroom, my reaction would have been that they were a good, loving family. Mr. and Mrs. Wilkes are in their early thirties. Both are employed. Arnetta is their only child. They obviously provide good physical care. She has not only eyeglasses but also braces on her teeth.

The charge against Mr. Wilkes was statutory rape of Arnetta, his own daughter. A few months before I saw them Mrs. Wilkes had noticed that Arnetta appeared to have a vaginal itch. She took her to a doctor, who discovered that she had a bad case of gonorrhea. When the doctor, who questioned Arnetta in the presence of Mrs. Wilkes, asked who had touched her there, she told him it was her father. Mrs. Wilkes was aghast. She asked the doctor what she should do. He told her that under the law he was obliged to file a child abuse report. And he did so. He also suggested counseling.

Mrs. Wilkes knew that her husband had gonorrhea. She had seen lesions, and he had admitted it. He was very protective toward her and took precautions that she not become infected. All the circumstances seemed to point to her husband's guilt. Arnetta had never spent a night away from home; she did not spend much time at the homes of her classmates. After school she came home. Try as she did, Mrs. Wilkes could find no other explanation. She cooperated with the prosecutor.

Mr. Wilkes protested his innocence and his love for his wife and child. He told Mrs. Wilkes he would prove that he did not do it. The three continued to live together. They visited a family counselor regularly. With their permission and the consent of Mr. Wilkes's attorney, the counselor's reports had been forwarded to me. The therapist, who was not a psychiatrist, reported that both parents were very cooperative but that Arnetta was silent and hostile. The therapist saw the family more than a half dozen times but never spoke to any of them alone. Her conclusion was that if Mr. Wilkes had had a problem, he was now cured.

At the first hearing Arnetta had testified that her father came into her room while her mother was out shopping and that he had removed her panties and "done things" to her. Mrs. Wilkes testified that she had gone shopping on a number of occasions and left her husband and daughter home. Mr. Wilkes said that he had gone to Arnetta's room to help her with her homework and that he had not had any improper relations with her. He said Arnetta was angry at him because he scolded her about her poor schoolwork.

Defense counsel requested ten days to file a brief. This reasonable request was not opposed by the prosecution. I scheduled oral argument for two weeks later.

When the Wilkes family returned to court, Mr. Wilkes's attorney asked to recall Arnetta to the stand. The child then recanted her story and said that she had made up the whole thing because her father punished her for not doing her schoolwork. There was no explanation for how she had contracted gonorrhea.

As everyone knows, rape is a charge that is difficult to prove because there seldom are eyewitnesses. As was pointed out in the chapter "Gender and the Criminal Law," Anglo-American law accorded less weight to the testimony of a woman than to that of a man. That rule has been abolished in most jurisdictions. But little has been done to accord a complaining child witness equal credibility with the defendant before the law. Consequently, even though a child is qualified to testify by establishing that he or she understands the nature of an oath and knows the difference between truth and falsehood, the child's testimony is often accorded less credence than that of an adult. In this unequal contest it has become exceedingly difficult to convict a child abuser. Consequently, the child is denied the constitutional right to equal protection of the laws.

Many judges and jurors find the concept of incest so abhorrent that they look for rationalizations to deny the truth of the testimony they hear. Able defense counsel supply them with many reasons: fanciful motives of vengeance attributed to the child and to the mother if she supports the child's complaint; Wigmore's text on evidence stating that children do not distinguish between fantasy and fact; and Freud's seduction theory that a girl who alleges her father raped her is projecting her subconscious wish and imagining an incident that never occurred.

Incest, like other forms of child abuse, is not a novel occurrence. Such acts are recorded at least as far back as biblical times. Incest was not treated as a serious crime under the common law. Nor is it today. The National Index of Crimes does not include incest among major crimes. It is included in the category of child abuse among less serious offenses. In the crime codes of many jurisdictions incest and child abuse are only third-class felonies or misdemeanors. Auto theft in some states is subject to more severe penalties than incest.

In the two weeks since her previous court appearance, Mrs. Wilkes had probably been educated as to all the theories used to rebut the truth of child abuse charges. When she testified this time, Mrs. Wilkes said that Arnetta often told lies, that she lived in a fantasy world, that probably she had seen something on TV about child abuse and made up the whole story. She also said that Mr. Wilkes and Arnetta had a warm, loving relationship.

Whether Mr. Wilkes was convicted and imprisoned or acquitted, Arnetta would have to live with her mother, who had declared that Arnetta had fabricated the charges. Inevitably Mrs. Wilkes would hold her daughter responsible for the family problems and expenses. I asked Arnetta if she wanted to say anything either in the courtroom or to me in chambers out of the presence of her parents. She whispered, "No."

Melinda Tremont is everything that Arnetta is not. Melinda is extraordinarly beautiful. She is very bright and does well in school. She is articulate and determined. She testified forthrightly that her father had raped her not once but many times over the past few years.

"Why did you suddenly decide to report this?" I asked her.

"I saw a TV program called 'Something about Amelia.' In that show the judge believed Amelia, and she didn't have to submit to her father anymore. I thought if people believed her, they would believe me."

I did believe Melinda. But I was unable to protect her. Like many other child abuse victims, the trial may have irreparably harmed her.

After I convicted Mr. Tremont, Mrs. Tremont asked to address the court. She was seven months pregnant. Melinda looks just like her. Even though Mrs. Tremont was grossly overweight and obviously uncomfortable, she was also beautiful. Her pretty features were distorted with rage. Her hair was disheveled. She trembled with fury. Her husband, looking slim and young, crossed his legs and sat back calmly as if none of this passion and anger concerned him.

"What is going to happen to me?" Mrs. Tremont shouted. "How am I going to give birth again and take care of three other children without a man? Send him home to me."

"What about Melinda? Aren't you concerned about her?" I asked.

"Melinda can take care of herself. She's a little bitch taking advantage of me when I'm pregnant."

Again I sought in vain to find a home for Melinda. Neither public nor private social service organizations were interested. The father was in jail. Melinda belonged with her mother. A few weeks later Mrs. Tremont reported Melinda as a runaway. The police put out a flyer. Without help from the family, it is difficult for the police to locate a child who does not want to be found. Neither Mr. nor Mrs. Tremont made any effort to locate her. At the end of the year the school dropped her from its rolls even though she was only fifteen. She is but one of the thousands of missing children in America whom no one tries to find.

Mr. Tremont claimed he was unjustly convicted. "It wasn't a crime. It was only my daughter," he said.

The belief that a man's wife and children are his possessions to do with as he pleases is embedded in the common law. For many years police refused to make arrests on the ground that the complaints were only family disputes, not crimes. A police officer who broke his wife's jaw said to me after a jury had convicted him of aggravated assault, "Judge, I'm not a criminal. I don't rob and rape and murder. I go out and arrest criminals."

"You assaulted this woman," I replied. "You know assault is a crime."

"No," he maintained. "It wasn't a crime. It was only my wife."

Mr. Brown claimed that he had not committed a crime when he beat Tyrone. "He's my kid," Mr. Brown declared. "I have a right to 'discipline' him."

Under the common law a man had the right to beat his wife and children. Although wife beating is no longer legally countenanced, child beating is. It has been approved by the United States Supreme Court.[1] In a case brought against school authorities by parents whose children had been beaten, the Court sustained the actions of the school personnel. Like Mr. Brown, the Court used the euphemism "discipline" instead of the forthrightly accurate word, "beating." According to the opinion of the Supreme Court, several children required medical treatment after the "discipline." Another suffered the loss of the full use of his arm for a week. The Court also employed a legal fiction to give school personnel the same rights as parents. The Court did not doubt that parents had the right to beat their children.

Justice Lewis Powell dismissed these undisputed acts by stating that such "mistreatment is an aberration." So are all crimes. If criminal acts were the norm of behavior, they would not be outlawed. The Supreme Court in its opinion acknowledged the anomaly of prohibiting corporal punishment when inflicted on adult criminals in prison but sustaining such acts when inflicted on innocent children. The Court again explicitly relied on history, citing the ubiquitous Blackstone, who declared more than two centuries ago that teachers have the right to use corporal punishment with force "necessary to answer the purpose." There was no evidence that this degree of force or any force at all was required to maintain order.

Most of the abusers I saw in court had long histories of abusive behavior. Tyrone had physical evidence of repeated beatings—perhaps as many as seventy. After Arthur was convicted of abusing April, I was furnished with his criminal record, a routine practice. I then learned that he had abused the child of his former wife, who had divorced him. Mr. Tremont had been twice arrested for contributing to the delinquency of a minor but never convicted until he was tried before me for statutory rape of Melinda.

I have found that when an abuser discovers that the mistreatment of a spouse or child is not just a family matter but a crime for which the penalty is imprisonment, that acts as a strong deterrent. Whether it is therapeutic or not, I cannot say. But at least further abuse by that individual is prevented. Recent studies show that prosecution of abusers is effective.[2] Such prevention of repeated abuses does not entail large organizations and expensive educational and publicity campaigns. It requires only determination on the part of law enforcement authorities and changes in court procedures that make it easier and fairer for child victims to testify.

Child protection is different from abuse prevention. It involves care of children after they have been abused to protect them from further abuse. Most lawyers and child care agencies have concentrated on prosecution of abusers. Little attention has been paid to the child after the abuser has been prosecuted and sentenced. A trial is a dramatic episode. It has a decisive result: success or failure, conviction or acquittal.

Protecting the abused child victim does not garner headlines or publicity. It requires painstaking, continuing efforts to find a suitable home for the child. There are very few successes.

Whenever I presided over the trial of an adult accused of mistreating a child, I had the uneasy feeling that the legal system was not concerned with the child as a person but was using him or her as a means to a societal end, albeit a desirable end. The morality of using one person for the benefit of another has been questioned by philosophers.[3] There are conflicting viewpoints on this issue. But I doubt that anyone would suggest that it is appropriate or justifiable to subject an abused child to the ordeal of a trial simply for the purpose of law enforcement in order to convict the abuser without providing some corresponding benefit in the form of protection for the child victim.

Most of the children who testified before me suffered as a result of their court appearances although I cannot document the harm done to them. In one case the harm was tragic, indisputable, and irreparable. Jerry, a ten-year-old boy, had the misfortune to be an eyewitness to a gang killing. During the course of a police investigation of the murder it was learned that a number of neighborhood youngsters had been in the playground across the street from the scene of the incident. Many children were questioned. They gave the names of their companions, but all except Jerry, the youngest, claimed not to have seen what happened. He told the truth. He was then subpoenaed by the prosecutor to testify at the trial. He appeared in court, missing school to do so. I was the presiding judge.

This small child sat on the witness chair and looked at the defendant, who was seated at defense table about three feet from the witness stand. The courtroom was filled with adults whom Jerry recognized as members of the defendant's gang. Jerry was terrified. No one had told him that these people would be present. He knew that if he told the truth, he would not live very long.

When questioned by the prosecutor, Jerry replied that he was present but that he had not seen anything. When he heard the shot, he was chasing a ball.

The prosecutor pleaded surprise and under the rules of evidence was permitted to cross-examine his own witness. He did so. He read aloud Jerry's statement given to the police that identified the defendant as the killer.

The next day Jerry came to my chambers with his parents and an attorney. The trial was still in progress. I called in the prosecutor and defense counsel. Jerry said he wanted to recant and tell the truth. He was more afraid of what would happen to him if the defendant was acquitted than what would happen if the defendant was convicted. But the harm was already done. The defendant and his cohorts knew that Jerry had seen the murder. Whether or not he testified in this trial, he was a danger to them. If I permitted Jerry to take the stand and have a sudden resurgence of memory, all his testimony would be suspect. Even if the jury brought in a verdict of guilty, it might be set aside by the appellate court.

I called the chief of police, the chief inspector of police, and all the top brass and explained the peril little Jerry was in. Everyone promised to protect him. The next morning I received a call from the prosecuting attorney. Jerry's body had been found in an alley with a bullet through the heart. No one was ever arrested for the slaying of Jerry. The man accused of the gang murder was acquitted.

Children who are prosecution witnesses, whether in cases of child abuse or other crimes, should, I believe, be given protection from the time they are identified as witnesses until all risk of danger is over. Adult prosecution witnesses in racketeering cases, drug crimes, espionage trials, and other important criminal matters are routinely given elaborate and expensive protection by the government. They are provided with substantial funds, new homes, and new identities in order to enable the government to convict the alleged felons without endangering the witnesses and their families. This protection begins before the arrest of a suspect and continues long after a conviction. Such witnesses are usually criminals themselves with long records of lying, duplicity, and illegal activities. Prosecutors and courts recognize that even the cleverest and most sophisticated persons will be at risk if they testify against Mafia bosses, drug lords, and other people who wield considerable power.

The law has not recognized the risks to which child victims are inevitably exposed when they testify against household members who have illegally abused them. Nothing is done to protect them before, during, or after the trial.

Tyrone and Arnetta probably suffered more as a consequence of their testimony than if they had not come to court. No matter what Arnetta's father does to her in the future, she will never be believed. Unless Tyrone is hospitalized again, he will have no opportunity of stopping the physical and mental mistreatment that he was subjected to by his mother and siblings and is probably still undergoing. One fears to contemplate the life that Melinda is living on the streets. Is she better off being subject to the demands of strangers than of her father? It is not a choice that those engaged in child protection work like to contemplate. April was able to bring Arthur's abuse to an end by her testimony. But one wonders what his successors to her mother's favors are doing to April and how she is surviving with a retarded mother and an aged, drunken grandfather.

The plight of these children and thousands like them can be attributed to old legal doctrines and modern theories. Neither accord personhood to a child. Under British law a man's home was his castle. Whether that home was a slum or a lordly manor, the state could not intrude. What went on behind the closed doors was sacrosanct, whether it was wife beating or child abuse. This notion of the sanctity of the home still dominates American law.[4] It is reinforced by the contemporary emphasis on the family. Every political candidate appeals to family values, ignoring the fact that almost half of America's children do not live in a nuclear family consisting of mother, father, and children. And many of those who do are endangered by their families.

The concept of keeping the family together has become a shibboleth defying fact and reason. I convicted Willard Everett of two counts of child abuse: the rape of his ten-year-old daughter, Debby, and the beating of his fourteen-year-old son, Willard, Jr., who attempted to protect Debby. The therapist who had been treating the Everetts for three years protested when I sentenced Mr. Everett to prison. The family must be kept together at all costs, he argued. But the costs were borne by the children.

As I discovered, a judge in criminal court has no authority to protect child victims who are abused. Family court judges have few options: (1) return the child to the family where he or she has been abused and is still at risk; (2) if the child refuses to go home, commit him or her to a correctional institution as an incorrigible; and (3) hold the child for foster placement.

The first choice is most commonly exercised because it is the easiest and it keeps the family together and costs the public nothing. The second choice is costly to the state and the child, who is victimized a second time. Many teenagers who refuse to go back to abusive homes acquire records of delinquency as incorrigibles or runaways and find themselves in jaillike institutions.

The third option, foster home, is society's choice for a half million American children each year. Some are actual orphans—that is, both parents are dead. Many more are what I call de facto orphans, children whose parents have abandoned them, have abused them, or are incapable of caring for them.

Foster parents are supposed to be a substitute family. The literature urging the public to become foster parents describes the joys of giving a home to a delightful, loving child. Few of these children are pleasant or loving. They are physically and psychically scarred. They are mistrustful and often hostile. They need skilled care.

Many kindly couples have given love, guidance, and homes to strange children. But a judge rarely, if ever, sees them. In court we see countless children who have been abused by their foster parents.[5] Some have been killed. We see troubled children who have been rejected by one foster parent after another and have been moved from home to home, from school to school every few months. I have seen in criminal court foster mothers who have cheated and stolen and engaged in prostitution. I have seen foster fathers with serious criminal records who have beaten their foster children and introduced them to lives of crime.

Even foster parents who are not abusive or unkind are all too often inadequate to care for the difficult children who are entrusted to them. Most foster mothers I have seen are decent, kindly souls who find being a foster parent an easier way of making a living than working in a factory or as a domestic employee. They are seldom adequate child care givers. Few sensible persons who can earn even modest livings will agree to care for a strange child twenty-four hours a day, 365 days a year for compensation of about twenty-five hundred dollars a year, out of which they must buy food and other necessities for the child. They get no vacations, no pensions, or other fringe benefits. But they are expected to take the child to the doctor, to meet with the schoolteacher, and do all the other tasks of a parent for a child who may be hostile, ill, or emotionally disturbed.

Although there is supposed to be investigation of foster homes before a child is placed and supervision thereafter, in fact, most social workers are so busy looking for a home, any home, to place a child that they have little time to investigate or supervise. Each year there is a quantum increase in the demand for foster homes. But the number of licensed homes steadily drops. In 1990 more than one thousand babies from newborns to two-year-olds are in hospitals in New York City as boarder babies because there are no homes for them. In the state of Washington some five thousand children were removed from foster placement after Matthew Eli Creekmore was kicked to death. But the authorities could find only thirty-eight hundred foster homes. In Pennsylvania two-year-old Joseph Huot died of brain injuries inflicted by his foster father two months after being placed with the family. The foster father had a criminal record of rape, aggravated assault, and burglary. In New Jersey a five-year-old girl was beaten to death by her foster parents, both of whom had criminal records.

In 1987 in Pennsylvania alone forty children died from child abuse. Two hundred fourteen cases of abuse occurred in a "child care setting," most in foster care. The sad toll goes on. Social workers are "disciplined" when children die, but few persons engaged in private and government child care agencies question the desirability of relying on foster care for helpless children even though all the people involved in the system know how unsatisfactory it is.

I sympathize with Judge Daniel D. Leddy of New York Family Court, who told the *New York Times,* "It's gotten to the point where we're sending kids home to bad circumstances because foster care is such a terrible alternative."

Government should provide safe permanent homes for all these countless children who are living at risk. Such homes must be staffed by trained, qualified, adequately paid professionals. They must be open to inspection and regularly monitored.

When doctors and judges see children who have been beaten and abused, they should not have to return them to the care of the abusers. Had a group home or orphanage been available, Melinda would have been able to finish high school and lead a safe and satisfying life. April would not have been returned to her retarded mother, and Tyrone to his abusive family.

Edward Lozano, a former professor of urban planning at Harvard University, drafted a plan for Leninakan, one of the Armenian cities leveled by a severe earthquake in December 1988. It includes dozens of small group homes linked to schools. He commented, "Those kids [orphans as a result of the quake] should not be in an institution and they should not be torn from their roots and sent to other cities."[6] I, too, believe that children should not be torn from their roots and sent to live with strangers. For a child to go from his own neighborhood to another neighborhood miles distant and with different mores and loyalties is needlessly uprooting. Many American children are sent to other communities and other states. They are contemporary migrants, moved from place to place with little consideration for their rights and needs.

The common law denied children rights. Contemporary law subsumes the rights of the child to those of the family. Neither affords children equal protection of the laws.

10

Children and Equal Protection of the Laws

The child receives the worst of both worlds.

—UNITED STATES V. KENT, 383 U.S. 541, 556 (1966)

EXCLUSION OF CHILDREN from the legal rights accorded adult males of sound mind, like the discriminatory treatment of women, is part of the heritage of the common law. It reflects and reinforces the historic status of children in the Western world. From the intended sacrifice of Isaac in the Bible and that of Iphigenia in Greek mythology, it was assumed that fathers had absolute control over the lives of their children. They could sell them, apprentice them to labor at an early age, control their property, their right to work at employment of their own choice, and their right to marry. As late as the nineteenth century there were few legal limitations on the authority of parents to control their children's lives and few legal responsibilities placed on parents to provide for them.

In eighteenth- and nineteenth-century Britain children were valuable commodities.[1] They were sold for adoption, to be beggars, chimney sweeps, and prostitutes. Often they were blinded to make them more effective beggars. Children were often stolen for these purposes. It was not until 1814 that Parliament enacted a law prohibiting the stealing of children.

Children of the well-to-do were often given up as foundlings by parents who wanted to limit the size of their families to preserve their property or who simply did not want the responsibilities of parenthood.[2]* There were no laws prohibiting this common practice. Baby farming was a profitable occupation. Women who advertised to adopt children were paid by the parents, then pawned the babies' clothes and let the infants die of neglect. The first statute requiring registration of those who cared for children under the age of two was enacted in 1872.

In the latter part of the eighteenth century in Britain homes for poor, abandoned children were established. No schooling was provided. These unfortunates were compelled to labor long hours. Children in workhouses soon graduated to lives of crime, the girls as prostitutes, the boys as thieves and robbers.

The British Factory Act prohibiting the employment of children under the age of nine was enacted in 1833 over the strong opposition of those who saw child labor as a desirable means of providing for children whose mothers were working and unable to care for them. Throughout the nineteenth century in Britain there were parliamentary committees on crime and delinquency that proposed such remedies as whipping and solitary confinement. The first prevention of cruelty to children act was not adopted until 1889, the same year that the National Society for Prevention of Cruelty to Children was formed in Britain, three-quarters of a century after the establishment of the Society for Prevention of Cruelty to Animals. Children as young as eight or nine were transported to Australia,[3] a legal penalty imposed for such trivial offenses as stealing a handkerchief.

Conditions in the United States, while not so brutal, were not dissimilar. Between 1854 and 1929 more than 150,000 children in the eastern part of the United States were put on trains and shipped west. These abandoned and orphaned children were supposed to be taken in as unpaid labor by farmers and ranchers. Survivors of those train trips describe the procedure at each stop on the way as a slave market at which the strong and healthy were selected. There was no supervision of these "adopting families" and no follow-up to learn what became of the children.

The treatment of children described above appears to most people to be unthinkable. But conditions today have striking similarities. There is no registration for foster parents who are paid for caring for unwanted and abandoned children. Many such children are abused, and some are killed. Beating of children by parents and teachers is legal.

*Jean Jacques Rousseau gave up his five children as foundlings, a practice he defended as being in their best interests.

In many juvenile detention centers and correctional institutions there is little schooling. Despite countless organizations for prevention of cruelty to children, child abuse is a major, pervasive problem for which the law has found no adequate remedy or protection. Poor, troublesome children are turned over to the custody of the juvenile court. And troublesome children of the middle class and wealthy are often placed in mental institutions with none of the safeguards applicable to adults.[4]

The problems of the daily lives of American children in 1990 are well known. Children are the fastest-growing segment of the population living in poverty. Thirty-nine percent of the poor are under the age of eighteen.[5] The trend has continued at an alarming rate. Child abuse is a problem that has overwhelmed the courts and social agencies. According to a Gallup poll, 15 percent of American adults claim to know children they suspect have been physically or sexually abused, a much larger number than is actually reported. Moreover, 5 percent of men and 10 percent of women say they themselves were abused as children. Child abuse deaths in the United States rose 5 percent in 1988 over 1987.[6] There is every indication that serious abuse and deaths of children will continue to rise. Lack of health care for enormous numbers of American children[7] and the deterioration of the educational system are well known.* Undereducated children in a high technology society are at risk of failure, crime, drugs, and teenage parenthood.

Politicians decry and deplore. Leaders of the legal profession place the problems of children high on the agenda for reform. But to date little has been done by government, social agencies, or the law to bring children within the protections of the Constitution or give them benefits comparable with those accorded to the elderly.

These severe social problems have many causes. Children do not vote and cannot lobby for protective legislation. They do not operate or control the social institutions that affect them, such as schools, hospitals, and facilities for abused, abandoned, and delinquent children. Nor do they have any input in the legal system. In the day-to-day operations of the courts children are consistently denied the legal rights and protections accorded to adults. This discriminatory treatment permits many of the problems that beset children to continue unchecked whereas similar conditions affecting adults have been rectified by court decisions.

When the Supreme Court has decided cases involving the rights of children, it has vacillated between denying children legal rights under

---

*Pediatricians are the lowest paid of all physicians.

Anglo-American common law and treating them exactly the same as adults. In most instances, when children claim First Amendment rights or due process rights, the Court has held that children are not entitled to the rights accorded adults. But when children appear in adult court as witnesses or defendants, they are treated as if they were adults, required to testify under the same rules and punished as severely as adults.* Neither course, in my opinion, is appropriate or justifiable. Children need special protections because of their youth and vulnerability. But that is no reason to deny them fundamental constitutional rights.

At the turn of the century social reformers pressed for legislation to protect women and children. As was pointed out in Chapter 5, on gender and equal rights, many of these statutes were bitterly opposed. And many were declared unconstitutional by the United States Supreme Court. Protective legislation for children was also held unconstitutional.[8] Recently the United States opposed a resolution by the United Nations to prohibit children under the age of eighteen from serving in the armed forces.

The most significant change in American law with respect to children occurred by statute in 1899 with the establishment of the first juvenile court in Illinois. Shortly thereafter juvenile courts were created in every state. Britain followed suit. It is in these courts that on a day-to-day basis serious deprivations of rights of children occur. Juvenile court (either a special court or a division of family court where divorce, custody, support matters, and delinquency charges are heard) is a special court for children.† Unless juvenile court relinquishes its jurisdiction over the child to adult criminal court, a child has no right to be heard in the general courts available to all other persons in the United States. If blacks, Hispanics, or any other segment of the population were required to be tried in a separate judicial system that denied them the legal rights afforded to all other Americans, undoubtedly that

---

*Note that a sixteen-year-old whose death sentence was upheld by the United States Supreme Court was tried as an adult (*Eddings v. Oklahoma,* 455 U.S. 104 [1982]), as was a boy who was fifteen when he committed the crime for which he was sentenced to death. In the latter case the Supreme Court set aside the death sentence, holding that it was cruel and unusual punishment to execute a child that young (*Thompson v. Oklahoma,* 108 Sup. Ct. 2687 [1989]). The obvious solution to this hairsplitting reading of the Constitution is the abolition of the death penalty.

†When a child is injured in an accident and asserts a civil claim by an adult because the child has no standing to sue, the case is heard in adult court. Also, a child's claims to property asserted on his or her behalf by an adult friend are heard in adult civil court. Some jurisdictions have special youth courts for older juvenile offenders. Significantly, a committee of distinguished citizens appointed to appraise the operations of the New York Youth Court complained that fewer children were committed to correctional institutions by that court than by the juvenile court. See "The Experiment That Failed: The New York State Juvenile Offender Law," a report by Citizens' Committee for Children, New York, Inc., December 1984.

would be held to be unconstitutional. But the long history of Anglo-American law has consistently denied children the rights and privileges accorded to adult males of sound mind.

When adults are accused of crimes, they are entitled to procedural protections in every step of the prosecution from arrest to imprisonment and release from custody. Few of these safeguards are extended to children. Children can be arrested without a warrant. They have no right to bail, no right to a jury trial, few appellate rights, and few rights while in custody. Children can be arrested and held in custody for acts that if committed by adults would not be crimes. Many juvenile courts do not even have rules of procedure. Neither the rules of evidence nor the constitutional protections accorded to adults are observed in most juvenile courts.

Juvenile court is not a place where a child goes to assert rights or obtain redress for wrongs.* It is the place where children are taken to be punished or otherwise disposed of.† In these courts the child either is a defendant accused of crime or other misconduct or is alleged to be in need of care. Children are haled into court to be placed, without their consent, in some place other than their homes. A child is treated as an object to be transferred, punished, or treated—often all three at the same time.

This was not the intent of the well-meaning reformers who designed the juvenile court system. They were rightly shocked at the spectacle of little children being tried as criminals in adult courts. They envisioned a friendly atmosphere where a kindly, paternalistic judge would place his arm around the shoulders of an errant lad and gently lead him into paths of righteousness.

In the nineteenth century criminal courts were brutal and punitive institutions where defendants had few rights and were subject to cruel penalties. Then, as now, most of the defendants in criminal courts in both Britain and the United States were poor, deprived persons.[9] They had no right to free counsel. If they could not make bail, they spent many months in custody awaiting trial. A defendant had no right to be informed of the evidence against him until it was presented at trial, nor did the prosecutor have an obligation to inform the accused of exculpatory evidence. Sentences were severe. The death penalty was imposed for many crimes other than murder. In Britain people were hanged for

---

*Some child abuse matters are heard in family court. Serious cases of abuse are prosecuted in adult criminal court, where the alleged abuser receives all the protections provided by law and guaranteed by the Constitution but the child receives little, if any, protection.

†In custody proceedings the child is accorded no rights, receives few protections, and is often brutalized in the process.

theft. Prisoners were required to work long hours under frightful conditions. As recently as 1910 Mr. Justice Holmes held that the Eighth Amendment's prohibition against cruel and unusual punishment did not bar the manacling of convicts.[10]

Under the common law a child under the age of seven was presumed to lack the mental and moral capacity to commit a crime—that is, he could not form the evil intent required under criminal law. From the age of seven to the age of fourteen, this presumption steadily weakened. At age fourteen a child was tried and punished under the same laws and procedures as an adult accused of crime.

For the child faced with such a criminal justice system, any change could only have been for the better. Again reform came not from the courts but from the state legislatures at the insistence of men and women sincerely concerned with the welfare of children.

The hopes of the reformers were never realized. From its inception the juvenile court became the dumping ground for poor children who were troublesome.[11] In an effort to mitigate the harshness of the criminal law, many legal fictions were employed. The child was to be charged not with a crime but an act of delinquency. He or she was not being punished but protected. The judge decided not guilt or innocence but what disposition was best for the child under the circumstances. Consequently juvenile courts operated without rules of law or procedure.* Many juvenile courts still have no rules of procedure.

The concept of delinquency was broadened to include not only violations of criminal law but also what are euphemistically known as status offenses, acts that if committed by an adult would not be crimes but that when committed by a child constitute delinquency and invoke the enormous all-encompassing powers of the court. These include runaway, truancy, and incorrigibility. Because the child is not charged with a crime, there is no legal limit to the length of sentence. Even though children are sent to a correctional institution with bars and walls, a place that they are forbidden to leave and where there is little, if any, contact with family members, this is not considered imprisonment or punishment.

---

*For descriptions of the actual operations of the juvenile court, see Howard James, *The Littlest Victims* (New York: David McKay, 1970), Lois G. Forer, *No One Will Lissen* (New York: John Day Co., 1970), and Peter Prescott, *The Child Savers* (Alfred A. Knopf, 1981). Both James and Prescott are journalists who observed the operations of juvenile courts. Significantly there has been little, if any, change in according children minimal due process rights since the landmark decision *In re Gault* in 1967 (387 U.S. 28). Children are now represented by counsel, but the hasty, irregular procedures and punitivie dispositions continue. See also "In re *Gault* Now 20, but . . .," *ABA Journal* (June 1, 1987), p. 29, reporting that 5 percent of counsel in New York had done no preparation, half the transcripts disclosed appealable errors that were not challenged, and fewer than 15 percent of the lawyers viewed their role as analogous to defense counsel.

All through the twentieth century, while juvenile courts were disposing of the lives of hundred of thousands of children each year without lawyers and without observing constitutional standards of due process, the criminal law applicable to adults was being reformed and transformed. The Supreme Court held in 1932[12] that indigent accused adults in federal court were entitled to counsel at public expense. That right was extended to all adult defendants in 1963.[13] The constitutional right to bail that is not excessive began to be enforced. Throughout the nation projects were instituted to make bail available to poor persons accused of crime. The right to a speedy and public trial was enforced by judicial decisions. By 1980 in most states an adult was entitled to be tried within 180 days of arrest. Coerced confessions were held to be inadmissible.[14] At arrest the accused had to be informed of his or her right to counsel and to remain silent. Racial discrimination of jury selection was outlawed. Prison conditions were improved. Prisoners were held to be entitled to medical care, access to law libraries and lawyers, regular outdoor exercise, and decent meals.

The revolution in the treatment of those accused and convicted of crime occurred within a relatively short time.* It was the result of aggressive litigation brought on behalf of adult male suspects and prisoners. There was no analogous reform of juvenile court law and procedures. Without attorneys children were unable to raise these serious constitutional issues. It was not until 1966 that the United States Supreme Court took jurisdiction of a case involving the rights of children.[15] The following year the Court issued the landmark decision *In re Gault*[16] in which Justice Fortas declared that "the state of being a boy does not justify a kangaroo court." The decision established several significant rights, the most important of which is the right to counsel in matters that would be crimes if adults were involved. But many of the fundamental rights of adults accused of crime are still denied children. They have no right to bail,[17] to a speedy public trial, or to trial by jury.[18] Juries are the citizens' protection against arbitrary and corrupt judges.

While there is little opportunity for corruption in juvenile court, there is practically no check on the arbitrariness of the judge. In small communities where only one judge sits in juvenile court, that individual exercises absolutely unlimited authority except in rare cases that are appealed or collaterally attacked.

In many juvenile courts evidence against children is often presented in the form of reports and documents furnished to the court. School records and reports from institutions are commonly received in evi-

---

*In the 1950s, for example, I represented a fugitive from a Georgia chain gang. This man bore permanent and terrible scars from carrying heavy shackles on his legs for twenty years.

dence. The child rarely has an opportunity to confront his or her accusers and to cross-examine them. A child defendant has no right to remain silent. Because confession is believe to be good for the soul of an evil child, children are often urged to testify against themselves. In many respects juvenile courts function in 1990 much like the infamous proceedings of the Star Chamber in England, which was abolished by an act of Parliament in 1641.

The Supreme Court has held that delinquency must be established by proof beyond a reasonable doubt.[19] But few of the other rights and procedures accorded to adults are observed in most juvenile courts. Children are still held in detention for long periods awaiting trial. They seldom obtain discovery of the evidence against them. Rarely does counsel in juvenile court demand the right to examine teachers, guidance counselors, and court employees who present reports that are read by the judge. Rank hearsay is frequently received as evidence. Most significantly, many juvenile court judges still see their role as that of a social worker making dispositions of a child for his or her "benefit," rather than deciding guilt or innocence and enforcing legal rights. Many lawyers representing children also view their role as helping rather than defending their clients. These judges and defense counsel often have social work backgrounds and little experience as trial lawyers. They are unaware of the vast disparity between the rights of adults and the treatment of children in family court. In Britain the use of lay magistrates in juvenile court is widespread. These magistrates are often well-meaning upper-class ladies who look at the problems of the young defendants not as judges deciding rights but rather as good, caring parents. Most American family courts are staffed with judges and lawyers, but their procedures and the attitudes of many judges are similar.

Under these conditions it is understandable that not many experienced lawyers and judges seek assignment in juvenile court. Chief Judge Sol Wachter of New York calls family court the stepchild of the state justice system.[20] In most jurisdictions abler judges are assigned to complicated civil cases involving large sums of money or to criminal court, where they preside over trials of major felonies and homicides. Ambitious members of public defender's and prosecutor's offices look upon assignment in family court as an unpleasant, unchallenging duty and eagerly await the end of their services there so that they can try real cases and advance in the profession.

In my court, when a sufficient number of lawyers protested that a judge was so ignorant of the law or so corrupt that they refused to try cases before him or her, that judge was transferred from civil or criminal court to family court. The overworked public defenders who represent the vast majority of children do not protest. Both prosecutors and defenders simply try to get along with the judges to whom they are assigned until they can get transferred to adult criminal court.

Attorneys in private practice rarely appear in juvenile court to represent children accused of delinquency. When they do, it is often as a favor to a client whose child has been arrested or who is interested in the child of a friend or employee. If this affluent parent or protector proposes a disposition to the court, such as boarding school, counseling, or even a promise to supervise the youngster, that disposition will be gratefully acceded to by the prosecutor and the judge. It is one fewer child to deal with, one fewer youngster for whom they must try to find a suitable place that probably does not exist.

Any notion of equal justice for rich and poor, children and adults is soon dispelled by spending a day in any juvenile court. The children are predominantly poor; in most cities they are disproportionately non-white. The goal of the court is to make a disposition—that is, to put the child someplace, not a determination of guilt or innocence. As the Queen of Hearts ordered, "Sentence first—verdict afterwards." In many juvenile courts sentence is imposed without a verdict ever being rendered.

In the 1960s one juvenile judge disposed of some eighty cases a day without defense lawyers. In 1990 in many a juvenile court one judge disposes of fifteen to twenty cases a day with lawyers. With an hour for lunch and two fifteen-minute breaks and if court opens at 9:30 A.M. (as it seldom does) and if the judge sits until 5:00 P.M. (a rarity in most courts), that allows an average of twenty-four minutes per case if there are only fifteen cases. In fact, the child's day in court was aptly termed by the President's Commission on Law Enforcement and Administration of Justice the "Five Minute Children's Hour."[21] In 1990 juvenile court could be called the Ten-Minute Children's Hour.

Family court is an anathema to judges who as practicing attorneys were accustomed to dealing with legal rights, trials that are conducted with proper introduction of evidence, lawyers who are prepared and present written and oral motions and who make legal arguments. The problems presented do not yield to legal solutions. The judge finds him or herself entering orders that have no legal justification but that are required by the system and the pressure of difficult societal problems.

Juvenile court judges frequently place children in custody even though they are not accused of any crime simply because the parents don't want them at home. This is done under the rubric of incorrigibility.*

Following common law tradition, juvenile courts rarely, if ever, order parents to care for their children. Juvenile court has become the foundling home and orphanage for tens of thousands of children whose parents simply abandon them to the custody of the legal system.

When a child seeks to assert rights as a person, rights that an adult would unquestionably be able to enforce, courts frequently rely on ancient doctrines to justify the denial of these rights to children without considering the applicability of the Fourteenth Amendment. Not many such cases have been litigated. The majority of them have been brought in federal court. A state judge sees comparatively few cases explicitly raising constitutional rights of children although such issues are implicit in countless run-of-the-mill cases involving child abuse, discriminatory school practices, and treatment of children in institutions. Because lawyers recognize that ultimately these constitutional questions may have to be decided by the United States Supreme Court, these actions are usually brought in federal court.

During my sixteen years on the state court bench, I presided over only one case brought on behalf of children that explicitly raised an issue of deprivation of the child's constitutional rights. This was a class action against a school district. Plaintiffs were schoolchildren who had been suspended for long periods of time without hearings. The school district and the association of school principals bitterly opposed the action and asked that the case be summarily dismissed. I held that under the due process clause a child could not be suspended for more than five days without a hearing at which the child would have the right to be represented by counsel, to cross-examine the witnesses against him or her, and to present witnesses and testify. In order to find that the child was entitled to a due process hearing, I held that the right to attend school was a property right of which the child could not be deprived without constitutionally required procedures.

Dire disruption of school discipline was predicted. It was alleged that teachers, principals, and counselors would be spending all their time at hearings to the detriment of their regular duties and that children would take advantage of these rights and be more disruptive than ever. None of these prophecies eventuated. Very few hearings were held. The school administration found that a five-day suspension had as

---

*See the account of a sixteen-year-old boy in the Manhattan family court. When his parent begged, "Place him somewhere—I can't have him home," the judge ordered the boy who had committed no crime to be held in custody (*New York Times*, December 15, 1987, pp. B1, B10).

much effectiveness as a two- or three-month suspension. Children no longer had to miss extended periods of schooling that led to their being left back a year or dropping out of school. Discipline was no worse and no better than before my decision. Several years later in a similar case the United States Supreme Court upheld the rights of children to a due process hearing before suspension.[22]

During the turbulent era of the 1960s, college campuses became centers of protest. Young people dissatisfied not only with the Vietnam War but also with a society they perceived as rigid, anachronistic, and hostile to their wishes engaged in protest and litigation. Their younger brothers and sisters in high school were also moved to protest and litigate.

A signal victory for the First Amendment rights of children was won in 1969,[23] when the United States Supreme Court held that high school students protesting the Vietnam War could not be suspended for wearing black armbands in school. The Court held that this was symbolic speech protected by the First Amendment. It is interesting to note the opinions expressed by three of the justices. Justice Potter Stewart in a concurring opinion declared that the rights of children are not coextensive with those of adults. Justice Hugo Black, the great civil libertarian who frequently took an absolutist position in defense of First Amendment rights, flatly declared that children do not have the right to speak in school. Justice John Harlan also dissented, finding that the suspension of the students was a reasonable measure to preserve school discipline. There was no evidence in the record that wearing armbands had caused disruption or that this was the "least restrictive" means to maintain discipline.

The court has since retreated from the recognition of children's rights under the First Amendment. In 1988[24] the Supreme Court upheld the right of school authorities to delete articles from a high school newspaper written and edited by the students. The deleted articles dealt with problems of pregnant high school students and of children of divorced parents. There were several pregnant girls in the school. Many students had divorced parents. Certainly these were topics of interest to the student body. There was no suggestion that there was anything lewd, obscene, or offensive in the articles. The majority of the Court flatly declared that the "rights to freedom of speech end at the school house gate." The dissenting opinion pointed out that there was no disruption of classwork and that the articles did not invade the rights of others.

Public schools have long been considered the bulwark of American democracy and the training ground for citizenship. If the Battle of Waterloo was won on the playing fields of Eton, as the Duke of Wellington eloquently declared, the battles of the United States were won in the classrooms of the American public schools. Censorship of inoffensive speech scarcely promotes training for responsible citizenship. Had the same articles been written by adults in a publication of the parent-teacher association that was read by the students, no court would have countenanced such censorship.

The Court also upheld discipline imposed on a high school student who, while making a nominating speech in a school assembly, used a popular obscene gesture. Chief Justice Warren Burger justified the action of the school authorities on the ground of protecting minors from exposure to vulgar language.[25] Apparently within the marble cloister of the Supreme Court, the justices do not look at television. I recall that Governor Nelson Rockefeller made the same allegedly offensive gesture on television during his presidential campaign.

When the religious beliefs of the child and parents are consonant, the Supreme Court has upheld those rights against the claims of the school that prayers are an appropriate public school activity.[26] More difficult questions are raised with respect to the deference to be accorded parents' religious beliefs in the foster placement of children, awarding of custody, and adoption.[27] In these cases, in which the child is too young to have a religious preference, courts are faced with deciding which rights shall be given priority: the religious beliefs of the parents or the best interests of the child.

Following the popular legal trend that prefers the rights of the family to those of the individual, the Supreme Court upheld parental First Amendment claims in utter disregard of the rights of the children.[28] Amish parents asserted their opposition to high school education for their children on religious grounds. The Court held that the parents had the right to withdraw their children from school in violation of compulsory school attendance laws. Certainly no one should be coerced into taking actions offensive to that person's religious beliefs. In this case the parents were not compelled to espouse religious tenets. They were by statute prohibited from preventing their children from attending school.

As Justice William O. Douglas observed, the rights of the children to a high school education were violated. It requires no citation of authority for the proposition that in our contemporary technological society a person with only an eighth-grade education is seriously disadvantaged. The loss of this essential education and training during the teenage years can scarcely be compensated for in later life, when adults must engage in productive labor to support themselves. The majority of the Court, probably influenced by centuries of common law under which children had no rights and were the property of their parents, refused to grant these children the rights of persons under the Constitution.

Parents who assert their First and Fourteenth Amendment rights are given serious consideration, and often these rights are sustained. But when children raise such issues, they are given short shrift even when their claims are not in the context of school or family. For example, in 1989, the Supreme Court denied recovery of damages to a child in Wisconsin who was so severely beaten that he was in a life-threatening coma and suffered profound and permanent retardation.[29] He asserted an interest in his life and liberty under the Fifth and Fourteenth amendments. The facts were undisputed. The majority opinion of the Court recited the brief and tragic history of the child plaintiff. He was one year old when his parents were divorced. Custody was awarded to the father. In January 1983 the child was admitted to the hospital. Suspected child abuse was reported to the proper governmental authorities, and the child was placed in temporary custody. The investigating team found insufficient evidence to charge the father, and the child was returned to him. A month later the child was taken to the emergency room with suspicious injuries. Again the authorities were notified. In November the child was again hospitalized, and the authorities were again notified. In March 1984 the beating that prompted the lawsuit was inflicted. The father was prosecuted and convicted of child abuse. The child's mother filed suit against the Winnebago County Department of Social Services seeking damages on behalf of the child.

The Court held that nothing in the law "requires the state to protect the life, liberty and property of its citizens against invasions by private actors." The majority opinion, while expressing sympathy for the child, treated the case exactly as it would have if an adult had been beaten by another adult.

The fact that child abuse, as required by state law, had been reported to the defendant, the County Department of Social Services, which was mandated to assume responsibility for abused children, was deemed to be irrelevant. Justices William Brennan, Thurgood Marshall, and Harry Blackmun dissented, pointing out that when the defendant "cuts off private sources of aid then refuses aid itself it cannot wash its hands of the harm that results from inaction." The abuse of this child was reported by neighbors, the hospital, and the natural mother. They had a right to assume that protective action would be taken. Obviously these persons would have pursued other remedies had they known that the defendant would not act.

The cavalier and narrow reading of the Constitution when a helpless abused child attempts to assert his rights must be contrasted with the protection given to adults. The Supreme Court in 1962 held that when a prisoner "by reason of deprivation of his liberty is unable to care for himself, it is only 'just' that the state be required to care for him."[30] The felon was held to be entitled to appropriate medical care. Suspects in police custody who are injured while arrested are entitled to medical care, as are involuntarily committed mental patients.[31] Such protections for vulnerable adults are right and appropriate. But one must certainly question why similar rights are not recognized for children, who by reason of their immaturity are especially vulnerable, particularly when the state has assumed responsibility for their safety after suspected abuse is reported.

The Supreme Court has also denied that children have a right not to be beaten[32] even though adult prisoners convicted of crime may not be "paddled."[33] The Court again relied on Blackstone, holding that corporal punishment of children is justifiable and lawful.

One of the most blatant judicially sanctioned discriminatory treatment of children occurs with respect to pregnant, unmarried minors. While the majority of the Supreme Court recognizes that under *Roe v. Wade* a pregnant adult's right to an abortion may not be obstructed by the state, when the pregnant female is a minor, that right is circumscribed by the paramount interest of the state in preserving parental and family interests. Justice Stevens writing for a majority of the Court held: "Three separate but related interests—the interest in the welfare of the pregnant minor, the interest of the parent, and the interest of the family unit—are relevant to our consideration of the 48 hour waiting period and the two-parent notification requirement."[34] The Court held that the judicial bypass provision permitting a pregnant minor to obtain a court-ordered abortion obviated the burden of two-parent notification and upheld the statute. Similar restrictions of notification to an adult woman's male partner and a waiting requirement would violate the Court's ruling in *Roe v. Wade.* Again it must be noted that the Constitution does not guarantee any rights to the family but only to persons.

Not only has the Supreme Court repeatedly denied children the rights accorded to adults, but it has also denied them the benefits of state legislation enacted to provide for their needs. Every state has compulsory school attendance laws because the legislatures recognize that without adequate education children are severely handicapped. Children are prosecuted and imprisoned when they fail to attend school. When children sued to compel their admission to public schools, the Supreme Court flatly ruled that there is no constitutional right to an education.[35]*

When children are placed in foster homes† and given (or sold) in adoption, they are denied all the rights accorded adults. Although the theory is that these placements are in the best interests of the child, the child is not represented in court with respect to the placement or adoption. The child has no right to appeal the order. And the court does not retain jurisdiction to monitor the safety and welfare of the child.

The failure to recognize and enforce rights of children can be attributed, I believe, to two legal doctrines. First is the failure to read the plain language of the Fourteenth Amendment, which speaks of "persons" as being applicable to children. Children are human beings. Children are also citizens. Children may obtain passports. They cannot be denied readmission to the United States if they leave and seek to return. Children are not in a limbo of stateless persons until they reach their majorities. Nor should they be treated as a form of second-class beings.

The second barrier to the recognition of children's rights is the recent judicially created doctrine of strict scrutiny. In cases of alleged discrimination the Supreme Court has promulgated categories of degrees of scrutiny of these claims. Courts are now required to scrutinize strictly allegations that statutes or practices discriminate against a "suspect class" or interfere with a "fundamental right." Race is a suspect class. To date neither youth nor gender has been held to be a suspect class. Nor has the Court examined vulnerability‡ as a suspect class.

Education, bodily integrity, and protection from abuse have not been held to be fundamental rights. The definitions of these categories and classes have been judicially declared without reference to precedent, societal conditions, or popular perceptions[36] and beliefs as to

---

*In 1983, 1,800,000 schoolchildren were labeled "learning-disabled" and denied regular schooling. Whether all these children who were not accorded legal rights before being so classified were correctly diagnosed is highly questionable. See Gerald Coles, *The Learning Mystique: A Critical Look at Learning Disabilities* (New York: Pantheon Books, 1987).
†More than a million children are in foster placement.
‡The elderly and mentally handicapped as well as children should be recognized as vulnerable persons and treated as suspect classes.

which rights the public considers fundamental. Neither "suspect classi-fication" nor "fundamental right" as defined by the Supreme Court is sanctified by history or legislation. In contemporary America, as in nineteenth-century Britain, there are countless committees and com-missions studying the problems of children and innumerable remedies proposed to deal with teenage pregnancy, drugs, illiteracy, and juvenile crime. But few suggest that children be accorded the constitutional rights of due process of law and equal protection of the laws.[37]

11

The Elderly in Court

They say an old man is twice a child.

— WILLIAM SHAKESPEARE

EVERY MAN AND WOMAN, no matter how old, who is not incompetent or insane is entitled to sue and can be sued, and can testify in court to assert all the legal rights and protections of any other adult. All too often, however, the legal rights of older people who are competent, intelligent, and capable but ill or feeble are disregarded under the ostensibly benign camouflage of protection. These older persons are treated like children by younger adults who presume to make decisions for them and in their best interests. As in the case of children, the caretakers sometimes do not act in the best interests of the elderly but rather in their own self-interests.

The difficulties many elderly people face in attempting to use the law to protect their rights are also similar to those faced by children. Although parents were never considered the chattels of their adult children, history and literature are replete with tales of greedy, ungrateful offspring and mistreated aged parents. I have seen countless King Lears in my courtroom, loving parents who turned over their assets to their children and lived to regret it.

A gift is legally completed when there is a donative intent and an actual transfer of the property or the documents signifying ownership. To retract or nullify such a gift is extremely difficult unless the elderly donor at the time of the transfer was insane, incompetent, or subject to undue influence. Just as the criminal law divides accused persons into two categories—sane and insane—so the civil law divides litigants and witnesses into two categories: competent and incompetent. Unless the individual is incompetent, he or she must submit to the same rules of procedure and evidence applicable to all persons but designed for the hypothetical reasonable man, a male in the prime of life. These rules are carefully structured to screen out lies and half-truths perpetrated by canny, conniving persons. They also often bar the truthful testimony of sentient but distraught elderly persons.

As has been shown in the chapters on children, the law fails to acknowledge the differences in the testimonial capacities of a sentient, intelligent five-year-old and an adult. Similarly it does not acknowledge the differences between a feeble octogenarian and an adult in the prime of life. So long as a person knows the difference between truth and falsity and promises to tell the truth, that individual may testify in court. Regardless of age, all witnesses are subject to the same rules of evidence. Incompetent older persons rarely are called as witnesses. If they are senile, they are disqualified from testifying. Elderly people who do testify know the facts they wish to describe; they have the necessary vocabularies even though they occasionally grope for words. Their reasoning is not impaired. But the rigid question and answer format required often interrupts their train of thought. Many have a tendency to ramble or speak of matters that are legally irrelevant. Counsel sometimes have great difficulty in directing the attention of elderly witnesses to the specifics at hand.

Most witnesses of any age find testifying in court an ordeal. For the elderly it is especially frustrating because they are not permitted to tell their stories in their own way. And the rules of evidence often prevent their attorneys from giving them the assistance required. A judge agonizes during these trials when the law bars counsel from asking the very questions that will elicit the crucial testimony. Such situations occur in many contexts: accident claims, contract actions, estate matters, and all kinds of civil suits as well as criminal prosecutions.

Leonard Jordan was such an older litigant-witness. I recount his trial because his difficulties in court are stereotypical. Only the happy ending is unusual.

Mr. Jordan was eighty-two years old when he was wheeled into my courtroom by a nurse. He was accompanied by his seventy-year-old wife. An intravenous tube dripped its life-sustaining fluid into one of Mr. Jordan's arms. A catheter bag dangled embarrassingly from the wheelchair. I wondered whether it was necessary to subject this frail, sick man to the ordeal of testifying. It soon became apparent that his testimony was essential if he was to prevail. If the lawsuit were successful, Mr. and Mrs. Jordan would be able to live out their remaining years without financial problems. If the lawsuit were lost, their situation would be precarious. Their only income would be Social Security, which would put them just above the poverty level, and twenty thousand dollars, which Mrs. Jordan had in her own bank account.

The facts were simple and uncontested. Some eight months before the trial Mr. Jordan suffered a severe heart attack. While he was in the hospital, his wife had a gallbladder attack and underwent surgery. During their illnesses Mr. Jordan's forty-five-year-old son, Elmer, took care of their affairs. He arranged for nurses for his father and stepmother. He went to their apartment and took care of the bills and necessary housekeeping. After two weeks Mrs. Jordan was discharged and returned to their modest apartment, where she managed to care for herself.

Several weeks later Mr. Jordan was discharged from his hospital. Elmer went to the hospital to get his father. On the way home they stopped at Mr. Jordan's broker and at the three banks where Mr. Jordan had accounts. Mr. Jordan transferred all his assets, his entire life savings amounting to a half million dollars, to Elmer. A few days later he told his wife what he had done but said that she was not to worry. Elmer had promised that he would take care of them for the rest of their lives.

Mrs. Jordan testified that for the first month after her husband's return from the hospital she did her minimal shopping by phone, as was her habit. At the end of the month she wrote checks for the rent, the grocer, the utilities, and the department stores on the joint checking account that she and Mr. Jordan had maintained during the thirty years of their marriage. When the bank returned the checks and notified her that the account had been closed, she and Mr. Jordan were shocked. Mr. Jordan promptly called Elmer. When Elmer finally came to see them, he told Mrs. Jordan that he would not pay the bills. She had her own money in the bank and should use that to pay the bills.

"But what will I do when that money is gone?" she asked him.

"I won't let my father starve," Elmer replied.

"What will happen to me?" she asked him.

"You're not my mother, and you're not my problem," was Elmer's response.

Mrs. Jordan talked to her neighbors, and on their advice she consulted a lawyer.

On direct examination Mrs. Jordan was asked:

"Did your husband tell you why he transferred all his money to Elmer?"

"Yes."

"What did he say?"

"Objection—hearsay."

I was obliged to sustain the objection. Whatever Mr. Jordan told his wife that Elmer had promised him was inadmissible to prove the truth of the statement. Mr. Jordan would have to testify as to the promises Elmer made to him.

The broker and the bankers testified that Mr. Jordan and his son had been to their respective offices and that they had made the transfers in accordance with Mr. Jordan's instructions.

Mr. Jordan's lawyer asked each of them if he had known that Mr. Jordan had just been discharged from the hospital. All four witnesses said that they had known it but that Mr. Jordan had been very positive as to what he wanted to do, and they had carried out his orders. The broker said that he had urged Mr. Jordan to wait a few weeks, but Mr. Jordan said he wanted to take care of everything that day so he wouldn't have to come back. The broker further testified that he knew Mr. Jordan had several bank accounts and he had no idea that they would also be transferred to Elmer. "Had I known that was what he was doing, I would have consulted our lawyer," he said. Defense counsel objected. That remark was stricken from the record as irrelevant and prejudicial.

Mr. Jordan had been sitting in his wheelchair for several hours, silently weeping. I called a recess and suggested that he be examined by his physician over the lunch hour to make sure that his health would not be endangered by testifying.

When we reconvened, Mr. Jordan looked a little better. He wanted to get up and take the witness stand, but counsel agreed that he could testify from his wheelchair.

My first impression was that this elderly gentleman was probably senile and incompetent. I asked him a few routine questions. He knew the date, the time of day, where he was, who I was, and that we were hearing his lawsuit against his son for the return of $524,315.76. He was precise and accurate about everything.

Then he burst into tears and said, "Your Honor, I love my son very much. Don't send him to jail. I don't want my son to go to jail no matter what he did."

Mr. Jordan's lawyer quickly led him through the events of that fateful day when he transferred all his assets to Elmer. Then he asked the crucial question: "Why did you give all your property to your son?"

"I love my son, I don't want him to go to jail." He turned to me. "Judge, promise me you won't send my son to jail."

I assured him that this was not a criminal prosecution. We were concerned only with the title to the money and securities.

Counsel again asked Mr. Jordan why he had given the money to his son. Again the old gentleman renewed his pleas that his son not be sent to jail.

Counsel rephrased the question a half dozen times but was unable to get a responsive answer. He then asked, "What, if any, promises did your son make—"

There were immediate cries of "Objection, objection—leading question" from defense counsel. I was obliged to sustain the objection. After several more futile attempts to get Mr. Jordan to tell what arrangements he had made with his son when the money was transferred, counsel sat down in despair.

Had defense counsel done nothing at that point except move for a directed verdict, I should have been required to grant a verdict for the defendant. Mr. Jordan, Sr., was legally sane and competent. A father has a right to give an unrestricted gift to his son, who is, under the law, the natural object of his bounty. The broker and the bankers testified that Mr. Jordan was sentient at the time and knew what he was doing.

Defense counsel wanted to press home the point that Mr. Jordan had freely made a gift of love for his son. He rose and began his cross-examination.

"Mr. Jordan, you love your son, don't you?"

"I love my son very much. Don't let him go to jail."

"You gave your son five hundred thousand dollars, didn't you?"

"Yes, I did."

"You gave your son this money because you love him. Isn't that true?"

"No. I gave him the money because he promised to take care of me for the rest of my life."

At that point the people in the court—witnesses waiting to be called in the next trial, court watchers, and idlers—began to applaud. This was the answer Mr. Jordan's counsel had tried in vain to get. Under the rules he was not permitted to lead his own witness.

Had defense counsel not asked that crucial question, Mr. Jordan would have been deprived of his life's savings. Although Elmer later testified that his father had made an unrestricted gift and that Elmer had made no promises, the jury did not believe him. The testimony of the father had the ring of truth. The jury found that Elmer had breached his contract with his father.

Leonard Jordan's difficulties in court were caused by the rigidity of the rules of evidence that make no allowances for the different testimonial capacities of the elderly as well as the very young.

The elderly appear in criminal court most frequently as victims of crime. They are seldom accused of crime. Even when an elderly person is accused of white-collar crime, he is usually the victim of a younger colleague who seeks to shift the blame to an unsuspecting older associate.

Infirm elderly persons are often victims of robbery because they are unable to offer physical resistance or to chase the robbers. Unless there happens to be an eyewitness to the crime, the testimony of the victim is essential to obtain a conviction because only the victim can make the crucial identification. All too often elderly victims of crime are victimized again by the legal system, which makes it difficult for them to testify effectively.

Knowing the problems of obtaining convictions in such cases, many police departments have "grandpop" and "granny" squads—police officers disguised as elderly persons.

Laura Jenkins was one of countless elderly women whose purses have been snatched by young robbers. Hers was a shoulder-strap bag. When the robber grabbed it, the force of the tug on her shoulder knocked her to the ground, severely injuring her. The robbery occurred in a shopping mall. When Laura fell, she screamed, and other shoppers came to her assistance. She pointed to the fleeing robber, and an alert security guard chased and caught him. The guard, however, had not seen the purse snatch.

The suspect's lawyer demanded a lineup. Because Laura was in the hospital, a lineup could not be held promptly. When she was discharged a month later, she called the police to inquire about the robbery case. Her pocketbook had been found in the mall and was returned to her. But no lineup was ever scheduled.

When the case came to trial before me some six months later, Laura was asked to identify the accused. She looked at him carefully. Then she took out her eyeglasses, put them on, and peered at him again.

"This is the man you arrested in the mall, isn't it?" she asked.

Defense counsel cross-examined her carefully: "Madam, you took a solemn oath to tell the truth. Can you swear before God that you are certain this is the man who snatched your pocketbook?"

Laura hesitated. "The man the guard arrested was the one who grabbed my bag and knocked me to the ground."

Defense counsel: "Can you swear that this is the man?"

Laura: "Somehow he looks different, but the one they arrested was the thief."

The jury returned a verdict of not guilty.

I then looked at the mug shot of the defendant (the picture taken when he was arrested). In the picture he was clean-shaven. In court he had a beard. No wonder Laura thought he looked different.

Geronimo was the victim of a scam. The day he received his Social Security check he went to the corner bar to cash the check and have a beer. A sexy-looking young girl wearing a tight sweater and dangling earrings sat down beside him and asked him to buy her a beer. According to the bartender, they stayed in the bar for more than an hour while Geronimo had three more beers. They left together. A few seconds later when the bartender heard Geronimo shout, "Stop, thief," he ran out, pursued the female, who had snatched Geronimo's money, and tackled her.

The thief was a young man in drag who made a practice of preying on susceptible elderly men. Because he was wearing high-heeled shoes, he couldn't run very fast. Geronimo saw the arrest and heard the thief give his name, but he did not understand that the person was a man.

Every crime victim who appears as a prosecution witness is asked to identify the accused. The prosecutor says, "Look around the courtroom, and tell us if you see the person who attacked you." As is customary, the defendant was sitting with his attorney at counsel table and obviously was the person on trial.

Geronimo looked around the room and said, "I don't see her." The defendant was wearing jeans and a sweat shirt and looked like any young man. The prosecutor asked the question several times, and Geronimo replied, "She isn't here."

The prosecution had to be withdrawn.

Because Laura and Geronimo were elderly persons who did not understand the legal process, they were defeated by the law. And so was the public.

When elderly persons are plaintiffs in accident cases, they are doubly disadvantaged, first as witnesses and second in the verdict. Even when they win, the amount of damages awarded by a jury is often woefully inadequate.

The jury that heard the accident case of Norman and Helen Anderson and Helen's mother, Cecilia Johnson, consisted of seven women and five men. They ranged in age from a twenty-two-year-old female college student to a sixty-six-year-old male retired executive. Like most juries, they took their task very seriously. They deliberated for an entire day.

The case arose out of an automobile accident, an intersectional collision. Norman Anderson was the driver of the car that was struck by a delivery truck driven by Forrest Hankins. Helen was in the passenger seat. Mrs. Johnson was in the back seat. The accident had occurred more than three years before the case came to trial. Norman and Helen had completely recovered from their injuries. Mrs. Johnson was using a walker. The truck driver was not injured.

Lawyers for the Andersons, the trucking company, and Mrs. Johnson were competent and well prepared. The jury had been carefully selected. The trial took four days. Accident reconstruction specialists were called by both sides. These experts explained from the damages to the vehicles how the accident must have happened. Norman and Forrest each claimed to have had the green light, which was a physical impossibility. Helen testified that they had the green light. Mrs. Johnson said she was not watching the lights. There were no other eyewitnesses.

Under the law of this state, like that of most states, the jury was instructed to find the comparative degree of fault of each driver and reduce the damages by the percentage of fault. Helen and Mrs. Johnson, who were passengers, of course, could not be held responsible in any degree for the accident and therefore, were entitled to full recovery from the drivers.

The jury was not allowed to be informed about insurance coverage. However, the jurors were sensible people who understood that a large trucking company must have had adequate insurance. The Anderson car was a one-year-old Buick in good condition at the time of the accident. The jury found that the truck driver was 80 percent negligent and Norman Anderson 20 percent negligent.

The jurors then had to determine the damages that Helen, Norman, and Cecilia Johnson were entitled to recover. The damages to the car were $2,500. Norman's lawyer presented evidence showing that his income for each of the three preceding years was slightly more than $100,000. He was a salesman for a sophisticated computer company. He was paid on a commission basis. The year of the accident Norman was out of work for more than three months, and his income dropped to $64,000. His medical expenses were $24,000. Although Norman had medical insurance that covered him and his wife, the jury could not be told this fact.

Loss of life's pleasures, as counsel explained to the jury, is a substantial item of damages and must be computed separately. He showed that Norman Anderson was a good skier and an avid tennis player. The accident occurred in December, and Norman missed the entire ski season. Because of his leg injury, he could not play tennis all that summer. Norman was also president of his lodge. He resigned that office because he was unable to get to the meetings.

Norman was also entitled to damages for loss of consortium. Under the old common law "consortium" meant the wife's sexual services to her husband. Under contemporary law it has been broadened to mean the household duties that the wife normally performed. Helen and Norman had two children, aged eight and ten. Although the Andersons had a day worker who did most of the housecleaning and laundry, Helen did the cooking. She also drove the children to their music and dancing lessons and to scout meetings. Norman was entitled to recover the cost of the cook who was hired for a month while Helen was recuperating and the taxi fares for transportation for the children.

Helen's medical expenses were $19,000. She was an active person involved in many community projects. She also worked part-time as a librarian. She earned $60 a week. She was out of work for two months. She was president of the local garden club, program chair of the PTA, and secretary of the League of Women Voters. Helen's passion was gardening. She testified that she had to hire a gardener to do the spring planting that she customarily did. His charges were $700. She testified that she had been unable to go on a two-week tour of flower shows and gardens with the garden club and that she had also missed concerts and plays that she normally attended.

Cecilia Johnson testified for more than two hours and described her life as it had been before the accident and since the accident. She was seventy-two at the time of the accident, in good health. She was living in the house she and her deceased husband had owned for more than forty years. She, too, was an avid gardener. Her small front yard regularly won prizes in the city beautification contest. Her principal pleasures in life were her garden and her grandchildren. She regularly took them to children's concerts and plays. She attended all the school plays and performances. She baked cookies for the school bake sales. She spent most evenings with her neighbors, who had been her friends for many years.

In the accident Cecilia had suffered a broken hip, two fractured vertebrae, and a mild concussion. The femur had been badly shattered, and she could no longer walk unaided. She had continual backaches. "When the weather changes, I have difficulty even getting out of bed," she explained. Cecilia was living in a nursing home. It was a clean, pleasant place, but she had only one room. The home was far from her old neighborhood and not served by public transportation. Her friends could visit her only on the rare occasions when someone would drive them to the nursing home. Cecilia could visit them only when Helen or Norman could take the time to drive her back to her old neighborhood.

The jury found that Norman's out-of-pocket losses for damage to the car, lost earnings, loss of consortium, and medical expenses were $70,000. He was awarded $100,000 for loss of life's pleasures.

Helen was entitled to her medical expenses even though they were covered by insurance, and to loss of consortium, a change in the common law that limited this recovery to the husband. Norman's principal services around the house consisted of taking out the trash and cutting the grass. Helen was awarded $4,800 for loss of wages and $2,000 for loss of consortium. She was awarded $70,000 for loss of life's pleasures.

Cecilia Johnson was retired and had no lost wages. She was awarded only $12,000 for medical expenses because, as the jury later told me, she had Medicare. She was awarded $30,000 for loss of life's pleasures. The doctor for the trucking company's insurance carrier testified that broken hips are common occurrences in elderly females. He implied that if she had not broken her hip in the automobile accident, she would most likely have done so slipping on the ice or tripping on a stair. He also brought in a wealth of evidence about the benefits of living in a life care community and said that this was an appropriate way for elderly persons to live.

Norman's award was reduced by 20 percent to account for his own negligence in partially causing the accident. He recovered $136,000. Helen recovered $76,800. Neither his life-style nor that of Helen had been altered by the accident. They suffered temporary inconveniences. But Cecilia Johnson, whose entire way of life had been irrevocably changed, received $42,000, the smallest recovery.

Aged persons who are mentally competent are also disadvantaged by provisions of substantive law that make good sense when applied to reasonable men in the prime of life but have unfortunate and sometimes appalling consequences when one of the parties is old.

Madeleine Ackerly was an intelligent woman. She was a well-known artist whose paintings had been bought by many museums. No question was raised as to her competence to enter into contracts, to make a will, or to testify in court. But she, like many other older persons, was treated like a child who must be protected rather than as an adult who can use her own judgment.

She went to court to claim distribution of a substantial trust fund of which she was the sole life beneficiary. This was not a spendthrift trust established to deprive the beneficiary of the right to use or waste the assets. Madeleine's husband specifically provided that she should have the right to invade principal. On advice of counsel, he had placed his entire estate in trust to spare her the burden of investing her inheritance from him. This usual provision, designed to ensure the comfort and happiness of a widow in old age, destroyed her comfort, happiness, and good relations with her only son. This is a common scenario played over and over in courts throughout the country.

Male lawyers when drafting wills customarily advise their male clients to leave their property in trust for their wives rather than give it to them outright. The lawyers believe that most women are incapable of handling money, that they may make improvident investments or spend their inheritances foolishly. Most wives outlive their husbands. There is always the possibility that a widow may remarry and her second husband will enjoy the fruits of the first husband's labor. Many husbands believe they are sparing their widows problems and securing their future by the device of a trust. Of course, the attorney, who is usually named a cotrustee, also profits from the arrangement since he receives continuing fees for his services as trustee.

The Ackerly case was assigned to me. Because I was an acquaintance of Mrs. Ackerly, I declined to hear the matter. But I followed the case closely. The judge to whom it was assigned was an able young man who scrupulously followed the law. Later he told me that he was troubled by his decision but felt compelled to adhere to precedent. The appellate court affirmed his decision without opinion.

Some years before his death, when Mr. Ackerly had a serious illness and was hospitalized, his only child, Chris, suggested that both his parents give him powers of attorney, and they did. Chris was a lawyer, a partner in a respected law firm. One of his associates drafted Mr. Ackerley's will. Paul Ackerly left his entire estate to his wife, Madeleine. All the household goods, books, and works of art he left to her outright. The moneys from his investments and his business he placed in trust for Madeleine as sole beneficiary with power to invade the trust to provide for her needs and comfort. The remainder was left to his grandchildren,

Chris's daughters. He left only a few mementos to Chris, stating that Chris was well-to-do and had no need of his money. He named Chris and his bank as trustees. During Paul's final illness Chris had paid all the bills, liquidated the business profitably, and taken care of all his parents' financial problems. Madeleine was grateful that Chris spared her these tasks so that she could devote her time to her husband.

After a lingering illness Paul died. Madeleine was sad. She sorely missed Paul. But she was determined not be a pitiful, complaining widow. She continued her customary activities. She worked on her paintings, entertained friends, and attended concerts and plays as she had done prior to Paul's death. Madeleine told her sister and brother-in-law how fortunate she was that Chris had relieved her of all the burdensome chores that most widows had to take care of.

When Madeleine received a notice from her landlord that the lease on her apartment would expire in ninety days, she told him she would renew the lease. A few days later the landlord phoned her apologetically and explained that he had been instructed by Chris not to renew the lease. He would be sorry to lose her. The Ackerlys were wonderful tenants. He hoped she would be happy wherever she was going. Would she permit him to show the apartment to a nice couple who were eager to rent it?

Madeleine was aghast. She assured the landlord that there was some mistake. She had no intention of moving. As soon as Chris returned from his European vacation, the matter would be explained.

For the next few weeks Madeleine was unable to work. She could not sleep. She walked around her apartment, touching her little treasures: the glass figurines she and Paul had bought in Venice, the Munch lithographs purchased in Oslo on their honeymoon, the jades and cloisonné they had found in the Orient. Every item in the apartment was dear to her and reminded her of the wonderful life she and Paul had shared. She played some of Paul's favorite music on his beloved Steinway grand. The worn rare Persian rugs gleamed softly in the lamplight. How could she leave this home where she had been so happy for almost two decades? She and Paul had sold their house in the suburbs and moved to this big, airy apartment with a view of the river and a lovely terrace shortly after Chris had married.

"This will be our home for the rest of our lives," Paul had assured her. "When I die, you will be able to manage here by yourself."

Madeleine had told Paul he was morbid. They both would live for years. But Paul was ten years older than she and had already had a heart attack. The doctor said he should not walk stairs. Although

Madeleine had loved her house, her garden, and her big studio on the third floor, she had not hesitated to move. They had remodeled two bedrooms into an adequate studio. Paul had a small study. She made the terrace into a garden. They were more than content. They were happy.

When Chris returned from his holiday, Madeleine told him about her conversation with the landlord and said that she had no intention of moving.

"Mother, you must be practical," Chris replied. "This is an expensive apartment. You don't need it. In fact, you shouldn't live alone. I've found a wonderful life care village for you where you can have a nice one-bedroom apartment. All your needs will be provided."

"But that is not what I want," Madeleine protested. "And it's not what your father wanted. You know that. Moreover, I can afford to live this way if I choose."

"Dad did not leave his estate to you outright. All the money is in trust and wisely invested. You can live comfortably but not lavishly on the income. In the event of a serious illness, there will be enough to provide nursing care for you.

"I'm seventy-two years old," Madeleine replied. "How many more years do you think I have? At the most fifteen years. I'll live them as I see fit. If I invade my principal to the extent of one-fifteenth each year, if that is necessary, I can continue to live here."

"Mother, I'm afraid that is not your prerogative. Both the First National Bank and I as trustees under Father's will do not approve. And we have the obligation of conserving your estate."

This was the first time since he was an adult that Madeleine had a dispute with her son. After several sleepless nights she consulted a lawyer.

He advised her immediately to revoke the power of attorney she had given her son. She was then free to renew her lease. But could she afford the apartment, her month in the south of France each year, and her winter vacation in an artist colony in Mexico? That would depend upon her trustees.

Chris and the bank positively declared that they would not invade principal. It would not be prudent. What if Madeleine had a stroke and required around-the-clock nursing care? She might live to be ninety. Madeleine's lawyer told her it was probably too late to contest Paul's will. Besides, Madeleine was adamant that she would not allege that Paul was incompetent or that Chris had exercised undue influence on Paul. Her only recourse was to petition the court to order the trustees to invade principal and allot her a larger annual income.

And so with ambivalence of sorrow and anger Madeleine sued Chris and the bank. The judge patiently heard testimony for two full days. Madeleine discovered that she, not the trustees, was on trial. They were the prudent, reasonable men of affairs who were seeking to conserve her estate and increase its value. She was considered an unreasonable, willful old lady who must be treated like a child and protected from herself. The tables were turned. Mother no longer knew best. She must defer to her son's judgment.

Chris's lawyer cross-examined her with infuriatingly polite condescension. He went through the years of her marriage, making her appear to be an idiot.

"Your husband handled all the money matters. He paid the bills, he earned the money, he made the investments, he supported you, didn't he?"

"Yes, but—"

"Just answer the questions. He gave you a generous allowance for your personal spending money—"

"He did not give me an allowance. I was not a child. We had a joint checking account. We made our purchases together."

"But he supplied the money."

"Young man, my husband ran a successful business. He made a lot of money. I am a successful artist. I also made money, which I put in our joint account."

"Your husband made several hundred thousand a year. How much did you make?"

"My pictures sell for ten thousand dollars apiece. I am not a pauper."

Madeleine's lawyer objected to the entire line of questioning, and the judge sustained the objection.

A long, heated argument by counsel followed.

After briefs were filed and further argument, the judge rendered his decision. The trust was valid. Mrs. Ackerly, the life beneficiary, could not overrule the decisions of the trustees, provided they were prudent, reasonable, and in her best interests. It would be improvident to deplete the estate. Mrs. Ackerly might live to be a hundred and need around-the-clock nursing care and treatment not provided by her insurance and Medicare.

He also held that the trustees' sole duty was to administer the estate. They had no right to decide where Mrs. Ackerly should live. She could live wherever she wanted within her means. The judge advised Chris to terminate the agreement to purchase an apartment in the life care village although he expressed the opinion that this was a wise and prudent choice for Madeleine to make. He also removed Chris as a trustee because his children had a remainder interest in the estate and there was always a possibility of conflict between the life tenant and the remaindermen. The judge appointed as a new trustee a reputable attorney acceptable to Madeleine's lawyer and Chris's lawyer.

After consulting with Madeleine's lawyer, the trustees agreed to pay her the entire income from the trust in quarterly payments. If there was an emergency, she could apply to them for additional moneys. But the income on $850,000 plus Social Security was insufficient for Madeleine to maintain the apartment and her accustomed life-style. Regretfully she sold all her cherished possessions and with the proceeds bought a small house in the south of France near some artist friends.

After the decision in her case Madeleine came to see me. "Why was I treated like a child?" she asked. I assured her that she was not singled out for discriminatory treatment. The judge had simply followed the law.

She wanted to know if it would have made any difference if she had had a woman judge or an older judge who could understand her desire to control her own life. To these questions I gave no answer. However, if the beneficiary of a testamentary trust had been a fifty-year-old man who wanted to invade principal to invest in his growing business, the trustees most probably would have gone to court for an order permitting them to make such a payment without incurring any liability. And most courts would have entered such an order.

Three years after her case was decided, Madeleine became ill. The local doctor in France urged her to fly to the United States, where she could receive more sophisticated treatment, or at least to go to a hospital in Paris. She refused. Madeleine died quietly at her home a few weeks later. The wishes of elderly persons can easily be overridden by fifty-year-old men of affairs.

Madeleine left a letter with her handwritten will. In the letter she wrote that she was seventy-six years old and had had a good life. She did not want to spend her last days in a hospital or nursing home simply being kept alive. She feared that if she returned to the United States, she would not be permitted to refuse unwanted medical treatment.[1] Therefore, even though she knew that surgery might prolong her life for a few years, she chose to die while she could still make her own decisions.

The law prevents many elderly people from making their own decisions.[2] Although they are legally sane and competent, the law treats them like children who are subject to the wishes and judgments of the guardians of their estates.

Almost every time an elderly person comes to court the experience is traumatic and difficult. Because the rules and procedures fail to take into account that individual's condition, the result is often legally sanctioned denial of equal protection of the laws.

12

Law and the Elderly

Every age has its pleasures, its style of wit, and its own ways.
— NICHOLAS BOILEAU-DESPRÉAUX

DURING THE LATTER PART of the twentieth century the problems of the elderly have captured the attention of countless professions and disciplines. Gerontology has become a booming speciality in the fields of medicine, sociology, and social work. City planners, builders, and developers are also concerned with the elderly. They focus on their special needs for housing, life care institutions, and nursing homes. Vendors of all kinds of products and services—health foods, patent medicines, vacation packages, education, magazines, and insurance—perceive the elderly as a growing market. And with good reason.

Persons over the age of sixty-five are the fastest-growing segment of the population in the United States. In 1990 more than twenty-seven million people were in this age-group. They constitute 10 percent of the population. As people continue to live longer, thanks to the progress in medical science, the elderly will increasingly constitute a larger proportion of the population.

But courts and the legal system as a whole have largely ignored the elderly. Although many bar associations have established committees to provide free or low-cost legal services to the needy elderly, little attention has been paid to the impact of substantive law and the litigational process on the rights of elderly people.

Legislatures, on the contrary, have been mindful of their needs and responsive to them. More older people vote proportionately than do other segments of the population. They write frequently to their representatives. The elderly also have energetic and forceful advocacy groups, such as the Gray Panthers and the American Association of Retired Persons, which are effective lobbyists.

Older people are now protected by many statutes—to name only a few: Social Security, Medicare, the Age Discrimination in Employment Act, and pension laws. They also receive many benefits as a result of state and local legislation, including subsidies for public transportation, heating fuel, and other necessities.

Although when first introduced, many of these laws were bitterly opposed as being "socialistic," they are now an integral part of the fabric of contemporary life. Indeed, they are no longer considered benefits but entitlements.

Not only has the demographic place of the elderly in American life changed dramatically, but their problems have also increased and changed. In previous generations most elderly persons lived with their children and were cared for by them, both physically and financially. Although this is still true for many older persons, it is no longer the only or the expected pattern of living arrangements,

As the number of older persons has increased, the number of "frail" or dependent elderly has increased even more sharply. These people require more medical and physical care than do other individuals. Much of this care is both unremitting and sophisticated and beyond the capabilities of many of their offspring. Many of the caretakers of the very old are themselves over the age of sixty-five.[1] This situation cannot continue indefinitely as the caretakers themselves age and require care.

Thoughtful professionals and members of the public are asking many questions. Should the elderly live in special housing? Should they live independently with the help of services furnished in their homes or should they live in institutions?* What fiscal arrangements should be

*The most common types of housing for the elderly are life care retirement complexes, nursing homes, and community care facilities. There is a severe shortage of accommodations in all three types and many serious problems. Life care complexes burgeoned in the 1980s. Although many are church-related, nonprofit institutions, they have experienced severe fiscal difficulties. Older people who have used their life savings to purchase total life care homes find that they have no meaningful redress when the institution curtails services or goes bankrupt.

Both nursing homes and community care facilities are licensed by the states. But in most jurisdictions supervision is lax, and conditions are often deplorable. A California commission found "abusive, unhealthful, unsafe and uncaring conditions" in that state's community care facilities (*New York Times,* January 16, 1984, p. B11). Other states and municipalities throughout the nation have also reported substandard conditions in nursing homes and other residential facilities for the elderly. Because many of the residents are not mobile and lack funds (their Social made? Meanwhile, individuals and families as well as social planners grapple with these problems.

One of the most pressing questions is fiscal. Who shall pay for shelter and services for the elderly? As the cost of medical care continues to rise dramatically and far in excess of the cost of living and indexed pension and Social Security payments, questions are increasingly being raised with respect to the fairness and, as some see it, the special benefits for the elderly. For example, former Governor Richard D. Lamm of Colorado pointedly questions whether funds spent on the care of the elderly would not be better spent on care of infants and children.[2]

Although the United States is now in its third century, the perception persists that this is a young nation, vital and expanding. Youth is considered the optimum period of life. Unlike other cultures, such as the Chinese, that venerate age, Americans have negative feelings toward the elderly. Professor Phyllis Rubenfeld notes that old people are "generally seen as senile, rigid in thought and manner, garrulous and old fashioned. Ageism* . . . leads the young to see their elders as not fully human."[3]

The literature on the elderly and aging in many disciplines uses, subconsciously perhaps, legal concepts of discrimination in describing the problems and treatment of the elderly. But there is little recognition in legal literature of the elderly as a category of persons who are denied equal protection of the laws. Other than in cases of employment discrimination and pensions, the practicing bar and legal philosophers have largely ignored the denial of rights to the elderly.

Professor Rubenfeld, again borrowing legal phraseology, points out that the frail elderly receive the worst of both worlds. Her language, taken from a Supreme Court decision involving the rights of children, is aptly used. Both children and the elderly are denied independence, both are mistreated in the litigational process, and both are considered not entitled to the rights guaranteed to reasonable men.

Despite the legislative protections and benefits granted to the elderly, the law in the day-to-day operations of the courts is bound by old misperceptions and old common law doctrines. These instances of injustice are not treated as illegal or unconstitutional forms of discrimination and are rarely appealed.

Most reported cases involving discrimination against the elderly arise in the context of employment, retirement, and pension benefits.

Security checks are usually made over to the facilities), they lack access to lawyers and legal services agencies that might press their claims.
*A popular sociological neologism.

They involve interpretations of statutes, not common law doctrines. Mandatory retirement, except for elected public officials and jobs requiring special qualifications, is barred by statute. The stated purpose of the federal Age Discrimination in Employment Act is "to promote employment of older persons based on their ability rather than age."[4] This is a laudable goal. Whether the aim of prohibiting mandatory retirement will also be used to deny the right to retire with pension to those older persons who find continuing to work a drain on their energies and a burden presents a danger. To date there has been no legislative move to raise the age of retirement eligibility or the age when pensions and Social Security are payable, although there is much discussion of the deleterious effects of retirement and the need for reliable older workers.[5] The possibility that younger adults will seek to postpone those payments to older persons is a hazard that should not be ignored.

In contexts other than employment, courts have not held that age is a suspect classification, like race, requiring strict scrutiny.[6] Numerous forms of discrimination against the elderly as well as discrimination against women and children have not been treated by the courts as raising significant constitutional questions.

But as the cases described in the preceding chapter reveal, elderly persons are routinely denied equal protection of the laws in countless uncelebrated cases. The elderly are prejudiced when they appear in court as witnesses and litigants because the law unthinkingly applies to them standards and procedures appropriate to a reasonable man in the prime of life. Rectification of these inequities is an uncharted area of the law that requires intensive examination and remedial action.[7]

13

Looking Ahead

> *People could make it against flood and pestilence;*
> *but not against the laws; they went under.*
>
> —JORGE AMADO

ALEXIS DE TOCQUEVILLE with extraordinary pre-
science described not only the America he observed but its fundamental
characteristics. He noted Americans' concern for the future and their
willingness to abandon past customs and practices. "Democratic nations," he wrote, "care but little for what has been, but they are haunted
by visions of what will be. . . ."[1] Congress and the state legislatures face
the problems of the present and attempt to legislate for the future unen-
cumbered by the dogmas of the past. Statutes have rectified many of the
inequities of common law doctrines that denied both equal rights and
personhood to women, children, and the elderly* These statutory abro-
gations of discriminatory laws, significant and essential as they have
been, dealt with discrete, specific problems. Judicial abolition of long-
standing legal doctrines that in operation discriminate against women,
children, and the elderly must be predicated on a broad, coherent philosophical basis for the jurisprudence that will be needed in the future.
This requires a new concept of equality that acknowledges and protects
differences.

A democratic government that derives its authority from the con-

*Legislation has also ameliorated legal discrimination against the mentally and physically handi-
capped.

sent of the governed presupposes a common consensus. In the colonial period, despite the diversity of national origins, bitterly divisive religious differences, the existence of slavery, and the absence of a unified government, there was a common core of values. In a new land to which most settlers had fled from various forms of oppression, within a few generations people had developed a sense of national identity and a proud, fierce loyalty. Economic opportunities appeared to be boundless despite the poverty and hardships endured by many immigrants.

The vision of the melting pot, in which people of many backgrounds, languages, religions, and social patterns would blend into a homogeneous new nationality, obscured many intractable differences. Americanization of these multitudes proceeded steadily despite ethnic and religious struggles that often became pitched street battles. Poor Irish Catholic immigrants fought the dominant Protestant majority in the streets of Philadelphia and Boston. Southern and Eastern Europeans were subject to discrimination in employment and housing. Jews faced rigid quota systems in most institutions of higher learning.* Nonwhites were subject to rigid housing restrictions in the North as well as deprivation of civil and political rights in the South.

But the English language and the public school system enabled many to move into the mainstream of American life. These unifying factors, a prevailing sentiment in favor of individual rights, and a rather touching faith in individual self-sufficiency suffused white male adults and provided the basis for a solidarity of belief that lasted many years.

As the twentieth century draws to a close, differences among our heterogeneous citizenry often seem to loom larger than fundamental similarities. Many pressures from different segments of the population converging at the same time appear to have fractured the consensus that unified the nation for two centuries. Blacks, Hispanics, Asians, women, the young and the old, the physically and mentally handicapped, and the various economic strata all demand recognition for their special interests. A resurgence of religious stridency by many sects, claiming not merely rights and recognition of their own beliefs and practices but dominion over the laws governing the entire population, threatens to burst the barriers of the First Amendment. Abandonment of the use of English as the national language in the public schools and derogation of Euro-centered education, the espousal of ethnicity rather than unity, the widening economic chasm between the rich and the poor, and the diminution of the once-predominant middle class

*In the 1990s Asian-Americans face similar discrimination in admission to colleges and universities.

place extraordinary strains on national unity that sometimes exceed the bounds of civility. This tendency has been accelerated by the collapse of the public school system as well as the limitations on upward mobility imposed by formal educational qualifications for most gainful employment. In a few short decades the notion of a classless society has been supplanted by an educational and oligarchical hierarchy as class-conscious as an hereditary aristocracy.

Many question whether there is a common consensus on which a legal system can be predicated that will recognize the rights of all members of this diverse national community and fairly enforce them. Lord Denning, a retired jurist member of the British law lords, expressed an opinion shocking for its insensitive bluntness. He suggested that recent immigrants to Britain (predominantly nonwhite Pakistanis, Jamaicans, and East Indians) be excluded from serving on British juries because, he opined, they have no understanding of the principles of the common law.[2] In my view, a more appropriate question would have been whether the common law has embraced these new citizens and granted them the rights and protections that should be available to all members of the community.

As the preceding chapters have revealed, American law has not extended those rights and protections to all segments of our population. A number of American legal philosophers, in more delicate and oblique language, have raised the same question as Lord Denning. Professor Frank Michelman of the Harvard Law School, pointing out that republicanism reflected an inclusory plurality of the citizenry, comments: "It is also true that extension of the circle of citizens to encompass genuine diversity greatly complicates republican thinking about the relation between right (or law) and politics."[3] Professor Daniel Bell carries this idea even further. He states: "The opportunity principle has become the crucial one in American life; it's based upon some notion of meritocracy. However, it's quite clear that even though people start out equally, they end up unequally. . . ."[4] This facile statement really begs the question. Professor Bell does not define "equal." Does he mean that most people start out with the same wealth and educational and social opportunities? That is obviously not the fact. He ignores the obvious differences of sex, age, and mental handicaps. Whether one denominates American society as a meritocracy or not, the basic structure of government is a democracy in which each adult has one vote that has roughly the same weight.[5]

If we start with that irreducible base line, it seems to me that the law must accommodate the different needs of all members of the community in such fashion that each does in actuality receive equal legal rights and protections. Such a jurisprudence cannot be based on legal fictions but must reflect biological and social facts. Legal fictions that label proceedings under which a child may be deprived of liberty as not being criminal, that find pregnancy is not gender-related, and that treat frail elderly people under rules designed for reasonable men in the prime of life permit the maintenance of conceptual purity but do little to enforce legal rights or afford needed protections. Ancient doctrines are applied by courts with principled neutrality by refusing to recognize disconcerting facts. Such decisions fail to provide even a minimum degree of fairness, much less equal protection of the laws.

A recent play, by David Henry Hwang, with music by Philip Glass, *1000 Airplanes on the Roof,* describes the torment of an individual forced by society to deny the reality of his/her life experiences. Significantly the protagonist of the play can be either male or female. Many men, women, and children are compelled by social institutions, backed by the force of the law, to deny the obvious facts of difference that they encounter every day in their lives.

Such denial of difference is as dangerous to a society as to an individual. Elizabeth Kristol, director of the Institute for International Health and Development, is one of the new breed of thinkers who call for recognition of differences.[6] She points out that when differences in a pluralistic society are denied, there can be no tolerance and civility is imperiled.

An entire community may for many years delude itself with slogans, big lies, and customary practices into accepting fiction as fact. Eventually people realize that the future that works does not really work, that the shining city on the hill is actually grimy and dilapidated, and that equality cannot be mandated by law. These wrenching discoveries shatter the false facade of unity and reveal undeniable differences.

John F. Kennedy stated an obvious fact: Life is unfair. Such an acknowledgment of reality is preferable to the continued repetition of truisms as to equality. Recognition of reality is a necessary precursor to change and reform. Recognition by the courts of the ineluctable facts of difference is, I believe, an essential first step toward the goal of equal protection of the laws for every person.

This call for an inclusory jurisprudence is not new. For the past few decades countless lawyers and reformers have urged that the law be extended to every segment of society. Recapitulating the legal achievements from 1920 to 1970, Alan Reitman wrote, "Women, military personnel, persons regarded as mentally ill, school children and juveniles, homosexuals and lesbians have all progressed by forcing society and its institutions to recognize them as just as deserving of rights as others."[7]

The failure to achieve that recognition of full rights cannot be charged to lawyers alone. During the past two decades some lawyers have been diligent, resourceful, and determined. But all too often they have not succeeded. Nor can it be laid wholly to the Reagan Court's idiosyncratic reading of the Constitution. As has been pointed out, stalwart defenders of the Bill of Rights have refused to recognize that it should be read to include the others.[8] The principal barrier has been the lack of a philosophical basis for a jurisprudence predicated on difference rather than on assimilating the rights of the others to the monolithic standard of the reasonable man.

Those not imbued with common law doctrines apparently have less difficulty in accommodating concepts of difference with the rule of law. A statement issued in Paris in July 1989 by the Group of Seven (representing the European Community) on the occasion of the fortieth anniversary of the adoption of the Universal Declaration of Human Rights reaffirmed that commitment.[9] Looking to the future, the group stressed respect for the rule of law and plurality of opinion. The incorporation of a number of its specific beliefs into American jurisprudence would go far to eliminating some of the egregious denials of equal protection of the laws noted in this book. The Group of Seven stated: "We hold that the right of each individual to physical integrity and dignity must be guaranteed." Although this statement was made in the context of torture, it certainly comprehends the rights of women, children, and the elderly to have control of their own bodies and to choose or reject medical and surgical procedures and the administration of medical drugs, and to be free from physical beatings and abuse.[10]

The Group of Seven further stated: "We stress that the rights of the child, the disabled and the elderly require special protection." Under such a mandate, children and the elderly would not be denied different treatment under the law both procedurally and substantively in accordance with their needs.

This linkage of rights and needs has little precedent in the common law, but that is not a valid reason to reject it. Like all human institutions, the common law reflects the limitations of the community in which it originated and developed. That was a patriarchal society in which legal rights were restricted to propertied members of the established church. Religious barriers were outlawed in the United States by the First Amendment. Racial barriers were also outlawed by constitutional amendments and are slowly being eliminated by statutes and judicial decisions. Property restrictions have been gradually but not completely eliminated by a long series of legislative acts. The barriers of the common law against women, children, and the elderly as well as others who have been excluded, if acknowledged, can be eliminated within the framework of the American legal system preserving and strengthening the structure of orderly procedure embodied in the phrase "due process of law." Such actions will also promote the belief in the rule of law which has been America's greatest protection against usurpations of power that threaten democracy.

The United States in the twenty-first century will require a broad jurisprudence that encompasses the views, rights, and needs of all members of the community, including the three groups with which this book is concerned. A century ago, in the stability of Victorian England, Benjamin Disraeli commented on the need for a forward-looking polity. "Conservatism," he wrote, "discards Prescription, shrinks from Principle, disavows Progress; having rejected all respect for antiquity, it offers no redress for the present, and makes no preparation for the future."[11]

The label of "conservatism" and the belief in progress may strike the contemporary mind as quaint. However, it is apparent that every society should make redress for the present and preparation for the future. Because the government of the United States is premised on a belief in the rule of law and the centrality of the legal system, both redress for present wrongs and preparation for future needs are to a considerable extent confided in the law. It will not suffice to rely on Tennyson's complacent view that "Freedom slowly broadens down from precedent to precedent." The precedents of the common law as interpreted by the United States Supreme Court give little assurance that the others will be included in either the freedoms or the protections of the law unless it is acknowledged that they have been wrongfully excluded from its doctrines and its procedures.

The development of such a legal system will have to be undertaken by many lawyers, judges, and legislators as well as by concerned citizens. The modest aim of this book is only to reveal the pervasive disregard by the legal system of the different needs of women, children, and the elderly. This is an essential first step toward achieving the goal of an inclusory jurisprudence based on facts, not legal fictions, and dedicated to the rights and needs of every segment of the population.

Notes

PREFACE

1. R. Unger, "The Critical Legal Studies Movement," 96 *Harv. L. Rev.* 563 (1983); D. Cornell, "Towards a Modern/Postmodern Reconstruction of Ethics," 133 *U. of Pa. L. Rev.* 149 (1985).
2. See, e.g., Richard A. Posner, "The Constitution as an Economic Document," 56 *George Washington L. Rev.* 4 (1987); Richard A. Epstein, "In Defense of the Contract at Will," 51 *U. of Chicago L. Rev.* 947 (1984).
3. H. Kelsen, "The Pure Theory of Law and Analytic Jurisprudence," 44 *Harv. L. Rev.* 55 (1951); E. Morgan, *Introduction to the Study of Law* (Chicago: University of Chicago Press, 1926).
4. Abe Fortas, *Concerning Dissent and Civil Disobedience* (New York: World Publishing Co., 1968), p. 13. Cf. J. Rawls, *A Theory of Justice* (Cambridge, Mass.: Harvard University Press, 1971), in which the author recognizes that even under his schema there would be instances of injustice that would have to be rectified.
5. William J. Brennan, "Constitutional Adjudication and the Death Penalty," 100 *Harv. L. Rev.* 313 (1986).

INTRODUCTION

1. "The Common Law of England has been laboriously built about a mythical figure . . . the figure of 'The Reasonable Man' " (A. P. Herbert, *Uncommon Law* [London: Methuen, 1935], p. 1).
2. In a study of the efficacy of sentences of restitution a doctoral student examined 605 consecutive cases of defendants I had sentenced over a ten-year period. He found from presentence reports and psychiatric examinations of these individuals that 25.7 percent were mentally ill or seriously disturbed. At least 10 percent were retarded. See Elmar Georg Weitekamp, "Restitution: A New Paradigm of Criminal Justice or a New Way to Widen the System of Social Control?," a dissertation in criminology for the Graduate Group in Managerial Science and Applied Economics, University of Pennsylvania, 1989. For an analysis of the problems of the mentally handicapped in court, see Lois G. Forer, "Law and the Unreasonable Person: The 1986 Jonas B. Robitscher Memorial Lecture in Law and Psychiatry," 36 *Emory L. Rev.* 181 (1987).
3. *New York Times v. Sullivan,* 376 U.S. 254 (1964).
4. See, e.g., Herbert Wechsler, "Toward Neutral Principles of Constitutional Law," 73 *Harvard Law Review* 1, 19 (1959); Robert Bork, "Neutral Principles and Some First Amendment Problems," 47 *Ind. L. J.* 1 (1971); M. Tushnet, "Following the Rules Laid Down: A Critique of Interpretation and Natural Principles," 96 *Harv. L. Rev.* 781 (1983); O. Fiss, "Objectivity and Interpretation," 34. *Stanford L. Rev.* 739 (1922); M. Perry, *The Constitution, the Courts and Human Rights: An Inquiry into the Legitimacy of Constitutional Policymaking by the Judiciary* (New Haven: Yale University Press, 1982); John H. Ely, *Democracy and Distrust* (Cambridge, Mass.: Harvard University Press, 1980).
5. Ronald Dworkin, *Taking Rights Seriously* (Cambridge, Mass.: Harvard University Press, 1987).

6. F. Schauer, "Easy Cases," 58 *Southern California L. Rev.* 399 (1985).
7. Most judges no longer permit prosecutors to strike all blacks from jury panels when the defendant is black. This practice may be imperiled by a recent Supreme Court decision holding that it is not unconstitutional for a prosecutor to strike all blacks from a jury (*Batson v. Kentucky,* decided January 22, 1990). In metropolitan areas both civil and criminal juries are racially mixed. The increased number of nonwhite trial judges has also had a salutary effect in eliminating many racially prejudiced decisions.
8. Robert Coles, *The Call of Stories* (Boston: Houghton Mifflin, 1988).
9. A study of emotional problems in adults who had histories of childhood abuse was based on 21 patients (Judith Lewis Herman, "Childhood Trauma in Borderline Personality Disorder," (Volume number) 146 *American Journal of Psychiatry* 490 [April 1989]). A study of public attitudes toward sentencing was based on 422 respondents (J. Doble and J. Klein, *Prison Overcrowding and Alternative Sentencing: The Views of the People of Alabama* [New York: The Public Agenda Foundation, 1989]). The monumental study of the American jury conducted at the University of Chicago covered 1,512 cases. Responses to a questionnaire were received from 555 self-selected judges (H. Kalven and H. Zeisel, *The American Jury* [Boston: Little, Brown, 1966]). In neither the public attitude study nor the jury study was the sex or age of the offenders, victims or respondents noted. See also "National Survey of Crime Severity," Center for Studies in Criminology and Criminal Law, University of Pennsylvania, 1978, in which the questionnaire did not note the sex or age of the criminal or victim, nor did it note these facts with regard to the respondents.
10. David Margolick, "At the Bar," *New York Times,* January 6, 1989, p. B9.

1. THE MYTH OF EQUAL PROTECTION

1. Oliver W. Holmes, *The Common Law* (Boston: Little, Brown, 1923).
2. Joseph Alsop, *FDR: A Centenary Remembrance* (New York: Viking Press, 1981).
3. See *Murray v. Giarrantano,* U.S. 57 *Law Week* 4889 (1989), denying death row inmates free counsel in state habeas corpus proceedings.
4. *U.S. v. Kras,* 409 U.S. 434 (1973).
5. See W. W. Holdsworth, *A History of English Law,* 3d ed. (London: Methuen, 1922), vol. II, p. 455 et seq.; Frederic William Maitland and Francis C. Montague, *A Sketch of English Legal History* (New York

and London: G. P. Putnam, 1915), p. 183 et seq.
6. Sir Edward Coke, *Institutes of the Laws of England* (London: 1797), vol. I, p. 130.
7. William Blackstone, *Commentaries on the Laws of England* (London: 1765–69), book I, ch. 15, 16.
8. See *Parham v. J. R.,* 442 U.S. 584 (1979), citing Blackstone.
9. See, e.g., Genesis: 16: ". . . and thy desire shall be to thy husband and he shall rule over there."
10. See, e.g., Plato's *Republic* describing a meritocracy, not a democracy. Book V discusses how women and children, as possessions of men, should be educated. Gunnar Myrdal in his classic study *The American Dilemma* (New York: Harper & Row, 1962) observed that blacks are treated like children.
11. Bernard Schwartz, *The Bill of Rights: A Documentary History* (New York: McGraw-Hill, 1971).
   Note: The Massachusetts Body of Liberties, 1641, provides protections for "children, idiots, distracted persons," prohibits corporal punishment of women by their husbands except in self-defense, and grants married women, children, and idiots the right to convey property with court approval.
   The Pennsylvania Bill of Rights of 1682 provides for right of adverse possession except in the case of "infants, lunatics, married women, or persons beyond the seas. . . ."
12. See *Michael v. Sonoma County,* 450 U.S. 464 (1981); *Watson v. Fort Worth Bank and Trust Co.,* 108 S. Ct. 1777 (1988).
13. *Boddie v. Connecticut,* 401 U.S. 371 (1971).
14. *DeShaney v. Winnebago County Department of Social Services,* 57 Law Week 4218 (1989).
15. *Geduldig v. Aiello,* 417 U.S. 484 (1974).
16. *Kent v. U.S.,* 383 U.S. 541 (1966).
17. H. Maine, *Ancient Law,* 3d ed. (1877), p. 163.
18. See Kenneth Jost, "Mother Versus Child," *American Bar Association Journal* (April 1989), p. 18. A pregnant woman has been criminally prosecuted for child abuse (to the fetus) because of drinking during pregnancy *Wyoming v. Dfannenstal* [unreported], *Philadelphia Inquirer,* January 22, 1990, p. 2). But see *In re A.C.* decided by the District of Columbia Court of Appeals on April 26, 1990, holding that a terminally ill pregnant woman has a right to refuse a caesarian operation that doctors believed was necessary to save the fetus.
19. See *Prince v. Massachusetts,* 321 U.S. 158 (1944), declaring there is a "private realm of family beyond which the state cannot enter."

20. *F. S. Royster Guano Co. v. Virginia,* 253 U.S. 412, 415 (1920).
21. *Tigner v. Texas,* 310 U.S. 141, 147 (1940).

2. DIVORCE AND CUSTODY

1. Joseph Goldstein, Anna Freud, and Albert J. Solnit, *Beyond the Best Interests of the Child* (New York: Free Press, 1973), pp. 37, 38.
2. Ray L. Deaver and Robert G. Williams, "Interstate Child Support Enforcement Isn't Working, but It Could," *Judges' Journal* (Winter 1988), p. 11.
3. See Lenore J. Weitzman, *The Divorce Revolution* (New York: Free Press, 1981). See also Patricia Schroeder, *The Great American Family* (New York: Random House, 1989).
4. Ibid. Most mothers are employed and carry a double burden. See Arlie Hochschild and Anne Machung, *The Second Shift: Inside the Two-Job Marriage* (New York: Penguin, 1989).
5. *Orr v. Orr,* 440 U.S. 268 (1979).
6. In *McCarty, v. McCarty,* 453 U.S. 210 (1981), the Supreme Court held that a military pension is not community property. Thereafter Congress enacted the Uniformed Services Former Spouse's Protection Act, 10 USC 1408 (d) (1). This statute was construed by the Court to permit servicemen to convert part of their pensions into disability pay, thus defeating the purpose of the act (*Mansell v. Mansell,* U.S. 57 Law Week 4567 [1989]). Civil Service Reform Act, 1981, Supp. 11 USC 4606 (B), permitting pensions to be treated as marital property.
7. See Weitzman, op. cit., p. 262.
8. See Thomas M. Mulroy, "No-Fault Divorce: Are Women Losing the Battle?," *American Bar Association Journal* (November 1989), p. 76. For a study of legal issues in marriage and divorce, see H. H. Foster, Jr., and R. L. Brown, *Contemporary Matrimonial Law* (St. Paul: Law and Business, Inc., 1985).

3. GENDER AND THE CRIMINAL LAW

1. See Sara Gauch, "When Mothers Go to Prison," 16 *Human Rights* 33 (1989); April Saul, "Motherhood Behind Bars," *Philadelphia Inquirer Magazine* August 27, 1989, p. 14.
2. The source book *Criminal Justice Statistics Crime in the U.S.* (Washington, D.C.: Government Printing Office, 1980) reports that women commit only 10 percent of violent crime and 15.8 percent of all crime. See also "For Murderers, Time Is Short," *Philadelphia Inquirer,* April 1, 1986, p. 7A.
3. *Dothard v. Rawlinson,* 43 U.S. 321 (1977).

4. "Mother Changed After Her Baby Dies of Cocaine," *New York Times,* May 10, 1989, p. 18; "Cocaine Use in Pregnancy Amounts to Child Abuse a Judge Rules," *New York Times,* May 4, 1989, p. 22. No cases in which men were convicted of abusing their spouses, children, or friends by infecting them with syphilis or AIDS have been reported. It is only women who are prosecuted for transmitting a disease or illness to a fetus.
5. See *Mistretta v. U.S.,* 109 S. Ct. 647 (1989), upholding the federal sentencing guideline statute; Justice Scalia dissented. Neither the majority nor the dissent considered the inherent bias in the guidelines against women and also children and the elderly.
6. Note that *Wigmore on Evidence,* § 402, states that a rape complainant's prior acts of intercourse are admissible to show her willingness and consent without a promise of marriage. But the defendant's former acts of rape or attempted rape of a third party cannot be treated as indicating a passion or desire for the woman in issue. This statement of the law is predicated on two factual errors: first, that intercourse is consensual only on promise of marriage and second, that it is an act of desire for the rape victim rather than an act of hostility.

4. CIVIL LITIGATION AND GENDER

1. Patty Parsons's unreported case was decided on the authority of *Dothard v. Rawlinson,* 433 U.S. 321 (1977).
2. Such treatment of women in traditionally male occupations is apparently common. Philadelphia Police Sergeant Maureen Rush was interviewed with respect to a jury award of $2,440,000 to Detective Carol Keenan and four male officers who supported her claim of sex discrimination in job assignment. Rush reported that she had "spent much of her first three years on the job walking a beat alone [in a notoriously dangerous neighborhood]. In her rookie year she frequently walked this beat from midnight to 8 A.M." (Emilie Lounsberry, "Detective Wins Suit on Sex Bias," *Philadelphia Inquirer,* January 18, 1990, pp. 14).
3. Title IX Education Amendments of 1972, 86 Stat. 373.
4. *Mississippi University for Women v. Hogan,* 458 U.S. 718 (1982). See also *Sweatt v. Painter,* 339 U.S. 629 (1950), holding that preferment of racial minorities to achieve a diversified student body is constitutionally permissible. Cf. *University of California Regents v. Bakke,* 438 U.S. 265 (1978).
5. See *University of California Regents v. Bakke,* loc. cit., and the veritable library of legal literature it has spawned.
6. The Detroit Symphony Orchestra was threatened with the loss of $1,300,000 in

state funds and a boycott unless it waived its stringent artistic requirements and hired black musicians (Isabel Wilkerson, "Discordant Notes in Detroits Music and Affirmative Action," *New York Times,* March 5, 1989, p. 1). Cf. the response by Michael Morgan, a black assistant conductor of the Chicago Symphony Orchestra, who argued that such an approach hurts qualified minority musicians (Michael Morgan, "Orchestrating in Decline in the Arts," *New York Times,* April 11, 1989, p. 16C). No one discussed the effect on the audience.

5. GENDER AND EQUAL PROTECTION OF THE LAWS

1. Virginia Woolf, *Three Guineas* (New York: Harcourt, Brace & World, Inc. 1938), pp. 59, 61, 62.
2. *U.S. v. Kent,* 383 U.S. 541, 556 (1966).
3. See George C. Coulton, *Medieval Panorama: The English Scene from Conquest to Reformation* (Cambridge, England: Cambridge University Press, 1938), for an account of the law with respect to women during this period.
4. For a factual picture of the lives of women during the fourteenth and fifteenth centuries, see François Poullain De la Barre, *The Woman as Good as the Man,* tr. A. L. (Detroit: Wayne State University Press, 1988).
5. See Sophie H. Drinker, "Votes for Women in 18th Century," *New Jersey Proceedings of the New Jersey Historical Society,* LXXX (January 1962).
6. Julia Davis, "Belva Ann Lockwood," *American Bar Association Journal* (June 1979), p. 924. See also *Bradwell v. Illinois,* 83 U.S. 130 (1873), denying Myra Bradwell the right to practice law.
7. As recently as 1984 only 26 percent of the top-level positions in the New York public school system were held by women even though 59 percent of the teachers were women (Joyce Purnick, "No Increase Found in Women in Top School Posts," *New York Times,* January 8, 1984, p. 31).
8. In most of the Muslim world the testimony of a woman is worth only half that of a man.
9. See Andrea Dworkin, *Pornography* (New York: G. P. Putnam, 1981), and Catharine MacKinnon, *Sexual Harassment of Women* (New Haven: Yale University Press, 1979).
10. Opera based on the life of Susan B. Anthony, libretto by Gertrude Stein and music by Virgil Thomson.
11. *Brown v. Board of Education,* 347 U.S. 483 (1954).
12. Alison Leigh Cowan, "Women's Gains on the Job: Not Without a Heavy Toll," *New York Times,* August 21, 1989, pp. A1, 14.
13. Harper's Index, *Harper's Magazine* (June 1984), p. 11.
14. See Sara E. Rix, ed., *The American Women, 1987–88: A Report in Depth* (New York: W.

W. Norton & Co., 1987). These figures are for the year 1985. Undoubtedly in 1990 more women are the sole support of their children.
15. *Legal Intelligencer* (June 30, 1989), p. 9.
16. See, e.g., *Brown v. Board of Education,* loc. cit., *Baker v. Carr,* 369 U.S. 186 (1962), and *University of California Regents v. Bakke,* 438 U.S. 265 (1978). Compare the decision of the Pennsylvania Supreme Court in *League of Women Voters v. Insurance Federation of Pennsylvania,* October 1, 1989, holding that higher insurance rates for young males than for young females are unconstitutional even though male accident rates are considerably higher than those for females. Plaintiff's lawyer, a female, commented that "in those states with unisex rates, rates to women have not increased significantly" (*Legal Intelligencer* [October 6, 1989], pp. 1, 7). But note the disparity of pay based on sex cited in *County of Washington v. Gunther,* 452 U.S. 161 (1981), amounting to approximately $8,000 per year, but because there was no discriminatory intent, the Court found the factual discrimination did not violate the Constitution. Cf. *Griggs v. Duke Power Co.,* 401 U.S. 355 (1971), involving racial discrimination in which the Court held that disparate treatment even without proof of discriminatory intent was unconstitutional. But see *Ward Cove Packing Co., Inc. v Atonio,* 57 Law Week 4583 (1989). See the differences in pay scales in New York City: Kindergarten teachers, a predominantly female occupation, have a starting salary of $14,500, whereas zookeepers, a predominantly male occupation that has no educational requirements, have a starting salary of $19,343 (Seth Mydans, "Imbalances in Pay for Women Examined by City," *New York Times,* February 12, 1984, p. 54). See also *AFSCME v. Washington,* 770F2d1401 (CA 9, 1985).
17. A master could be appointed to hold hearings and make recommendations to the court. This is a far less drastic remedy than appointing a master to operate a school system or to supervise the operations of prisons and other public institutions.
18. Report of the Pennsylvania Attorney General's Family Violence Task Force, "Domestic Violence", 1988. See also "Study of Domestic Violence in Minneapolis by the Police Foundation," *New York Times,* April 5, 1983, p. 4.
19. For a graphic, accurate, but fictional account of the treatment of women by their male obstetricians, see Marilyn French, *The Women's Room* (New York: Summit Books, 1977).
20. *Geduldig v. Aiello,* 417 U.S. 483 (1974); *General Electric v. Gilbert,* 429 U.S. 123 (1976).
21. Pregnancy Discrimination Act, 42 USC § 2000 (e) (k), as amended 1982. See *Mansell*

v. *Mansell,* U.S. 57 Law Week 4567 (1989), construing the Uniformed Services Former Spouse's Protection Act, 10 USC § 1408 (d) (1), to permit servicemen to convert part of their pensions into disability pay, thus defeating the purpose of the act.

22. *Webster v. Reproductive Health Services,* U.S. 57 Law Week 5023 (1989).
23. Elijah Anderson, "Sex Among Poor Black Teenagers Is a Game of Conquests and Dreams," *Philadelphia Inquirer,* May 14, 1989, p. 7C.
24. Laura L. Crites and Winifred L. Hepperle, *Women, the Courts and Equality* (Beverly, Hills: (Volume numeral eleven) 11 Sage Year Books, 1987), p. 36.
25. See Phyllis L. Crocker, "The Meaning of Equality for Battered Women Who Kill Men in Self Defense," *Harv. Women's L. J.,* 8 (1985), p. 121, pointing out that in 1982 males killed 2,511 females; 17 percent of these crimes were within the family, and of these, 60 percent were men who killed their mates, while 40 percent were women who killed their mates.
26. Women lawyers have shown great interest in combating endemic sexism in the treatment of women lawyers and litigants in court. See, e.g., "Report of New Jersey Task Force on Women in the Courts," *New York Times,* December 26, 1983, p. C20. See also numerous articles on the subject in the *American Bar Association Journal,* but these studies do not consider the gender biases in legal doctrines. The American Bar Association Commission on Women in the Profession reported that in 1988 women held 20 percent of the jobs in the legal profession but constituted only 6 percent of partners in law firms. A study of the Harvard Law School class of 1974 reports that of those in private practice, 50 percent of the men became partners in law firms within ten years, but only 23 percent of the women.
27. W. Prosser, *Handbook on the Law of Torts,* 4th ed. (St. Paul: West Publishing Co.: 1971), § 340.
28. Patricia Wald, "Breaking the Glass Ceiling," 16 *Human Rights* 40 (Spring 1989).
29. Felice N. Schwartz, "Management Women and the Facts of Life," 67 *Harv. Business Review* 65 (1989).
30. Jon Gotschall, "Carter's Judicial Appointments: The Influence of Affirmative Action and Merit Selection on Voting in the United States Courts of Appeal," 67 *Judicature* 164 (1983).
31. John Gruhl, Susan Welch, and Cassia Spohn, "Women as Criminal Defendants: A Test for Paternalism," 37 *Western Political Quarterly* 456 (September 1984).
32. *Hishon v. King and Spaulding,* 476 U.S. 69 (1984); *Roberts v. U.S. Jaycees,* 104 S. Ct. 3294 (1984).
33. John Kenneth Galbraith, "From Stupidity to Cupidity," *New York Review of Books* (November 24, 1988), p. 12.

6. THE CHILD AS DEFENDANT

1. *Schall v. Martin,* 467 U.S. 253 (1979). Adults may not be held in preventive detention, but children are routinely held under circumstances in which adults would be released on their own recognizance on nominal bail.
2. *McKiever v. Pennsylvania,* 403 U.S. 528 (1971).
3. A study of one juvenile court in an affluent suburban community disclosed that the mean time from apprehension to disposition was 218 days (Ann Rankin Mahoney, *Juvenile Justice in Court* [Boston: Northeastern University Press, 1987]).
4. See Lawrence Gonzales, "Welcome to Gladiator School," *Notre Dame* (Winter 1988–89), p. 33.
5. Susan Jacoby, *Wild Justice: The Evolution of Revenge* (New York: Harper & Row, 1983).
6. Claude Lévi-Strauss, *Triste Tropiques* (New York: Atheneum, 1974).
7. See *Mistretti v. U.S.,* 1209 S. Ct. 647 (1989), upholding the constitutionality of such laws.
8. In re *Winship,* 397 U.S. 358 (1970).
9. Abandonment of children is a practice of long standing in the Western world. Under the common law parents were rarely punished for abandoning infants, known as foundlings, or for selling their children. See John Boswell, *The Kindness of Strangers* (New York: Pantheon, 1988), detailing the long history of parental transfer of their children to strangers by abandonment, sale, apprenticeship, and other practices.

7. THE BOY WHO DIDN'T KNOW HIS NAME

1. See *Smith v. OFFER* (Organization of Foster Families for Equality and Reform), 431 U.S. 816 (1977), in which the Supreme Court noted that in the 1970s, 60 percent of foster children had more than one placement and 28 percent had three or more placements. In 1990 the situation has considerably worsened. See Karen S. Peterson, "The Foster Care Crisis," *USA Today,* October 3, 1989, p. 1D.
2. Judith S. Wallerstein, "Children After Divorce: Wounds That Don't Heal," *New York Times Magazine,* January 22, 1990.
3. *Parham v. J. R.,* 442 U.S. 584 (1979).
4. See *Smith v. OFFER,* loc. cit. See also *Secretary of Public Welfare v. Institutionalized Juveniles,* 442 U.S. 640 (1979), holding that children have no right to representation.
5. See Dirk Johnson, "Case of Abandoned Boy Brings Look at Adoption," *New York Times,* April 22, 1990, p. 22.
6. See, e.g., Ann Whitt Thompson, *The Suitcases* (Washington, D.C.: Acropolis Books, 1982). Following the publication of Lois G. Forer, "Bring Back the Orphanage," *Wash-*

ington Monthly (April 1988), p. 17, I received scores of letters from adults who had spent time in both foster homes and orphanages and who vastly preferred the latter. See also interview with Vidal Sassoon by Marian Christy in the *Boston Globe,* October 1, 1989.

7. See note, "Wrongful Adoption," *Ind. L. Rev.,* 20 (1987), p. 709.

8. Richard A. Posner, "Adoption and Market Theory," 67 *B. U. L. Rev.,* 59 (1987).

9. *Allen v. Allen,* 330 p2d 151 (Cal., 1958). See also "Annulment of Adoption," 22 *Journal of Family Law* 549 (1984).

10. *Burr v. Board of County Commissioners,* 401 NE2d 1101 (Ohio, 1986). Note that a bill for a federal Antifraudulent Adoption Practices Act was introduced in Congress in 1984 but was not enacted.

11. See *Prince v. Massachusetts,* 321 U.S. 158 (1944), the leading case upholding parental rights. It has been cited innumerable times but not overruled or limited.

8. THE CHILD AS WITNESS

1. *Wigmore on Evidence,* § 505. Note that Dr. Steven Sharfstein, director of the Mental Health Sciences Division of the National Institute of Mental Health, reports that there is increasing evidence that children do not fantasize but have suffered real trauma (Susan Salasin, "Caring for Victims: An Interview with Steven Sharfstein," *Evaluation and Change* Special Issue [1980], p. 18, published by Minneapolis Medical Research Foundation, Inc., with the NIMH).

2. *Wigmore on Evidence,* § 1053.

3. *Coy v. Iowa,* 108 S. Ct. 2798 (1988). But see *Ohio v. Roberts,* 448 U.S. 66 (1980), permitting hearsay evidence if the witness is unavailable (*Bourjaily v. U.S.,* 107 S. Ct. 2775 [1987]) and permitting hearsay statements of a coconspirator as an exception to the hearsay rule even though the defendant cannot confront the witness.

4. *Mattox v. U.S.,* 156 U.S. 237 (1895). See also *Wigmore on Evidence,* § 1395.

5. 58 Law Week 5044.

6. 58 Law Week 5036.

7. 15 Cox Crim. Cas. 1, 3 (Eng. N. Wales Cir.) 1881.

8. See the case of former Police Officer Warren Poole of Lynn, Massachusetts, whose child victim "froze" during trial and recanted (Bella English, "Graphic Testimony," *Boston Globe,* October 4, 1989, p. 29).

9. The 1988 "Child Abuse Report" of the Pennsylvania Department of Public Welfare Office of Children and Youth states that of children who died of abuse, 83.7 percent were abused by a member of the household—mother, father, paramour, sibling, or

foster parent. Only 6.3 percent were abused by strangers.

10. *DeShaney v. Winnebago County Department of Social Services,* 57 Law Week 4218 (1989).

11. More than forty states now have statutory provisions designed to keep child victims out of court, including closed-circuit television, videotaping the child's testimony, and exceptions to the hearsay rule. See Gregory P. Joseph, "Keeping the Child Witness out of Court," 2 *Human Rights* 22 (Summer 1989). How many of these statutes will be upheld after the Supreme Court decision in *Coy v. Iowa,* loc. cit., is problematic.

9. ALL IN THE FAMILY

1. *Ingraham v. Wright,* 430 U.S. 651 (1977). See *Jackson v. Bishop,* 404 F2d 571 (CA 8, 1968).

2. Report of Pennsylvania Attorney General's Family Violence Task Force, "Violence Against Children," January 1987.

3. See statement of the Reverend Sydney Smith "When a man has been proven to have committed a crime, it is expedient that society should make use of that for the diminution of crime," quoted in Leon Radzinowicz and L. W. Cecil Turner, "A Study of Punishment," 20 *Canadian Bar Rev.* 92 (1943), and Johannes Andanaes, "The Morality of Deterrence," 37 *U. of Chicago L. Rev.* 649 (1970), p. 649.

4. *Prince v. Massachusetts,* 321 U.S. 158 (1944). See *In the Interest of Children* (New York: W. H. Freeman & Co., 1985), by Robert H. Mnookin, a widely cited authority who, in defining the difficulties in according children constitutional rights, points out the differences in maturation and declares apodictically that "children are part of families, and our traditions emphasize the primacy of the parental role in child rearing. The rights of children cannot be defined without reference to their parents."

5. Karen S. Peterson, "The Foster Care Crisis," *USA Today,* October 3, 1989, p. 1D. In 1989 approximately 276,000 children were in some forms of placement outside the family. There is a 38 percent turnover in foster parent homes each year. The average allotment foster parents receive is $212 a month to feed, clothe, and house a child. See also *Newsweek*'s special report "A Hidden Epidemic" (May 14, 1984), detailing child molestation. It is estimated that between 100,000 and 500,000 American children are sexually abused each year. See also Anthony DePalma, "7 in Abuse Case are Disciplined by Foster Unit," *New York Times,* March 31, 1989, p. B2.

6. Alan Cooperman, "U.S. Architect to Help Rebuild Armenian City," *Philadelphia Inquirer,* April 30, 1989, p. 4A.

10. CHILDREN AND EQUAL PROTECTION OF THE LAWS

1. See Ivy Pinchbeck and Margaret Hewitt, *Children in English Society* (London: Routledge & Kegan Paul Ltd., 1969).
2. John Boswell, *The Kindness of Strangers* (New York: Pantheon, 1988).
3. For an account of the use of transportation (exile to Australia and Tasmania) as a legal means of ridding Britain of thousands of poor law violators, both children and adults, see Robert Hughes, *The Fatal Shore* (New York: Alfred A. Knopf, 1987).
4. For a discussion of the use of mental institutions to control children, see Lois A. Weithorn, "Mental Hospitalization of Troublesome Youth: An Analysis of Skyrocketing Admission Rates," 40 *Stanford L. Rev.* 773 (1988). See *Parham v. J. R.*, 442 U.S. 584 (1979), denying children the right to a hearing before being committed by their parents.
5. Charles Green, "From Bad to Worse for the Poor," *Philadelphia Inquirer,* April 23, 1989, p. 3-C.
6. "Fatal Neglect," *Minneapolis Star Tribune,* April 2, 1989, p. 36A.
7. Peter Kilborn, "Panel Finds U.S. Lags on School and Health Care," *New York Times,* April 19, 1989, p. A16.

   The Joint Economic Committee of Congress reported in 1989: "Approximately 13% of 17 year old Americans cannot read, write or count." It also reported that the United States ranks twentieth among the twenty-two principal industrial nations in infant mortality and in the bottom third with respect to life expectancy at birth. As early as 1939, 30 percent of American youth were found to be unemployable because of physical defects (Betty and Ernest K. Lindley, *A New Deal for Youth* [New York: Viking Press, 1939]). Note that children do not receive medication for pain because pediatricians believe children do not feel pain as adults do (Warren E. Leary, "Progress in Treating Children's Pain," *New York* Times, November 17, 1988, p. D20).
8. *U.S. v. Darby,* 312 U.S. 100 (1941), overruling *Hammer v. Dagenhart,* 259 U.S. 20 (1918). See also Child Labor Tax Case, 259 U.S. 20 (1922), holding unconstitutional a tax of 10 percent on the profits of plants using child labor.
9. Sir James Fitzjames Stephens, *The History of the Criminal Law of England* (London: Macmillan, 1883).
10. *Weems v. U.S.,* 217 U.S. 349 (1910).
11. Sheldon and Eleanor Glueck, *One Thousand Juvenile Delinquents* (Cambridge, Mass.: Harvard University Press, 1934).
12. *Powell v. Alabama,* 287 U.S. 45 (1932).
13. *Gideon v. Wainwright,* 372 U.S. 335 (1963).
14. *Miranda v. Arizona,* 384 U.S. 436 (1966).

15. *U.S. v. Kent,* 383 U.S. 541 (1966). Legislatures continue to take the lead in protecting children. See, e.g., the Missing Children's Assistance Act of 1984.
16. *In re Gault,* 387 U.S. 28 (1967). Note that rights for children are still not accepted. See Martha Minow, "Constitutional Bicentennial Symposium The Rights Revolution Are Rights for Children?," *American Bar Foundation Research Journal* (1987) p. 203.
17. *Schall v. Martin,* 104 S. Ct. 2403 (1984).
18. *McKiever v. Pennsylvania,* 403 U.S. 528 (1971).
19. *In re Winship,* 397 U.S. 358 (1970).
20. Jane Gross, "Family Court: Stage for Suffering and Crises," *New York Times,* December 15, 1987, pp. B1, 10.
21. President's Commission on Law Enforcement and Administration of Justice, *Juvenile Delinquency and Youth Crime* (Washington, D.C.: Government Printing Office, 1967).
22. *Goss v. Lopez,* 419 U.S. 565 (1975).
23. *Tinker v. Des Moines Independent Community School District,* 393 U.S. 503 (1969).
24. *Hazelwood School District v. Kuhlmeier,* 108 S. Ct. 562 (1988).
25. *Bethel School District No. 903 v. Fraser,* 478 U.S. 675 (1986).
26. *Abington School District v. Schempp,* 374 U.S. 203 (1963).
27. "Accommodation and Neutrality Under the Establishment Clause: The Foster Care Challenge," 98 *Yale L. J.* 617 (1989).
28. *Wisconsin v. Yoder,* 406 U.S. 205 (1972).
29. *DeShaney v. Winnebago County Department of Social Services,* 57 Law Week 4218 (1989).
30. *Robinson v. California,* 370 U.S. 660 (1962); *Estelle v. Gamble,* 429 U.S. 97 (1976).
31. *Youngberg v. Massachusetts General Hospital,* 463 U.S. 239 (1983).
32. *Ingraham v. Wright,* 430 U.S. 651 (1977).
33. *Jackson v. Bishop,* 404 F2d 571 (CA 8, 1968).
34. Hodgson v. Minnesota, 54 Law Week 4957 at p. 4964. See also Ohio v. Akron Center for Reproductive Health 58 Law Week 4970 upholding a statute requiring notice to one of the minor's parents before an abortion can be ordered.
35. *San Antonio Independent School District v. Rodriquez,* 411 U.S. 1 (1973). See also *Kadrmas v. Dickinson Public Schools,* 108 S. Ct. 2481 (1988); *Phyler v. Doe,* 457 U.S. 202 (1982).
36. Note the extreme deference to public opinion given by the majority of the Supreme Court in holding constitutional the death penalty (*Gregg v. Georgia,* 428 U.S. 153 [1976]).
37. For many years a very small number of persons concerned with the problems of the juvenile courts have advocated a Bill of

Rights for children. (See R. E. Burdick, "Legal Rights of Children," *Columbia Human Rights L. Rev.* [1972]). Recently judges, lawyers, nurses, pediatricians, and social workers who deal with the problems of children have proposed a constitutional amendment to guarantee children due process of law. The adoption of a constitutional amendment is a lengthy process fraught with difficulties and frustrations, as the experience with the Equal Rights Amendment discloses. Legislators are more amenable than judges to public sentiment. Legislation to assure children rights and to correct many of the inequities described in this book offers a more practical remedy.

11. THE ELDERLY IN COURT

1. See *Cruzan v Missouri Dept of Health*, 110 S. Ct. 2841 (1990). Whether courts will recognize "living wills" is unclear. Until such cases reach the Supreme Court, the individuals involved often must undergo years of suffering or degrading existence.
2. The suicide rate among elderly Americans increased 25 percent between 1981 and 1986 (*New York Times,* July 2, 1989, p. 14). Although no published studies explain the reasons for this extraordinary increase, it is not unreasonable to attribute it to the sense of lack of control over their own lives experienced by many elderly persons.

12. LAW AND THE ELDERLY

1. E. M. Brody, "The Aging of the Family," 438 *Annals of the American Academy of Political and Social Sciences,* 13 (1978).
2. *New York Times,* Op-Ed, August 2, 1989, p. 23.
3. Phyllis Rubenfeld, "Ageism and Disability-ism: Double Jeopardy," in *Aging and Rehabilitation: Advances in the State of the Art,* ed. S. J. Brody and G. E. Ruff (New York: Springer Publishing Co., 1986), p. 323 at p. 324.
4. 29 USC § 621 to 634, 81 Stat. 602 (1967), as amended. The act has been construed to require the employer to prove that age is a bona fide occupational qualification. See, e.g., *Gathercole v. Global Associates,* 727 F 2d 1484 (9th Cir., 1988), cert. den., 105 S. Ct. 593 (1989), involving mandatory retirement of an airplane pilot. The equal protection clause has been held not to bar mandatory retirement for elected judges. The Supreme Court denied review of several cases brought by state judges for want of a federal question, perhaps another indication that the Court does not view age as a suspect classification like race.

5. See Tamar Lewin, "Too Much Retirement Time? A Move Is Afoot to Change It," *New York Times,* April 22, 1990, p. 1.
6. Private and public social agencies, however, are aware of discrimination against the elderly. See "Discrimination in Federally Funded Programs," U.S. Commission on Civil Rights, 1977.
7. The federally funded pilot program of the National Judicial College to address the problem of guardianship for the elderly deals with only a minor issue and does not address the needs of those who are legally competent but disadvantaged under present legal procedures. *Gavel* (Spring 1990) p. 10.

13. LOOKING AHEAD

1. Alexis de Tocqueville, *Democracy in America* (New York: Colonial Press, 1900), part II, p. 78.
2. Lord Denning, *What Next in the Law* (London: Butterworth, 1982). Under British censorship law this book was withdrawn and the offending passage deleted. Note that *Wigmore on Evidence,* § 516, expresses the same view. He declares without any supporting evidence: "It is no doubt true that certain races are less strongly moved to constant truth speaking than others. . . ."
3. Frank Michelman, "Law's Republic," 97 *Yale L. J.* 1493, 1506 (1988).
4. Symposium, "If Equality Is Inevitable, What Can be Done About It?" *New York Times,* January 3, 1984, p. E5.
5. *Baker v. Carr,* 369 U.S. 186 (1962); *Reynolds v. Sims,* 377 U.S. 533 (1964).
6. Elizabeth Kristol, "False Tolerance, False Unity," *New York Times,* September 25, 1989, p. A19.
7. Alan Reitman, *The Pulse of Freedom: American Liberties 1920–1970* (New York: W. W. Norton and Co., 1975), p. 331.
8. See dissenting opinion of Justice Hugo Black in *Tinker v. Des Moines School District,* 393 U.S. 503 (1969), declaring that children do not have the right of free speech.
9. "The Group of 7 Statement: Concern from East Europe to China," *New York Times,* July 16, 1989, p. 18.
10. Cf. *Union Pacific Railway Co. v. Botsford,* 141 U.S. 250 (1891), in which the Supreme Court held that an injured male plaintiff could not be compelled to submit to a surgical examination, citing *Cooley on Torts,* 29, stating, "The right to one's person may be said to be a right of complete immunity: to be let alone."
11. Benjamin Disraeli, *Coningsby* (New York: AMS Press, 1976; first published 1884) book II, ch. 5.

Table of Cases and Statutes

CASES

STATUTES

Index